MW00778809

the day-by-day method

Japanese with Ease
Volume One

by **Catherine Garnier**
and **Mori Toshiko**

adapted for English-speakers
by **Lucas Klein** and **Kiril Savino**

Illustrated by J.-L. Goussé

B.P. 25
94431 Chennevières-sur-Marne Cedex
FRANCE

ISBN 978-2-7005-0353-1

 **Method**

Other Assimil titles available in handy book format with cassettes and CDs

"With Ease" series
Arabic with Ease
Armenian with Ease*
Chinese with Ease vol. 1
Chinese with Ease vol. 2
Writing Chinese with Ease
Dutch with Ease
German with Ease
Hungarian with Ease
Italian with Ease
Japanese with Ease vol. 1
Japanese with Ease vol. 2
Writing Japanese with Ease
New French with Ease
Spanish with Ease

For travelling
Dutch from the Word Go!
French from the Word Go!
German from the Word Go!

Advanced language skills
Using French
Using Spanish

"Business"
Business French

For children
Sing your way to French!

* Available soon

CONTENTS

Introduction

First things first, don't be daunted by Japanese. Japanese is actually not hard to pronounce at all, and the differences in pronunciation are very small. Most Japanese sounds are a little shorter than they would be in English, sort of as if the vowels were clipped short. The Japanese often say that when speaking English they have to pretend they're chewing on a mouthful of butter to make all the mushy sounds we have, so you can imagine that for us, speaking Japanese just requires that we enunciate a little more, and pronounce our vowels a little shorter. Throughout the first 35 lessons, we will use both the standard romanization and our own pronunciation key, to help you get the hang of it.

There are only a couple points you'll have to pay attention to in the beginning. We will start with the consonants, which are the easiest:

➤ In Japanese there is neither an **r** nor an **l**, but a sound somewhat between the two. Most times we write the sound with an **r**, though some people have been known to use an **l**. However, the light, almost **l** sound in Japanese, while resembling an **r** in Spanish, might almost sound like a 'd' to an English speaker. To practice the Japanese **r**, try making an **r** sound, but just tap the roof of your mouth quickly with your tongue instead of holding it, and you should be pretty close.

➤ In our pronunciation keys, you'll often come across consonants with a little ' before them, like **'t** or **'k** (represented with the double consonant [**tt** or **kk**] in the official romanization). This apostrophe means that you should hold this consonant, and pronounce it harder than you usually would, almost as if you stop just before you pronounce it. Imagine, for the **'t** sound, that you put your tongue against your teeth, as you usually do to make a **t** sound, but hold it for a second, not letting any sound out. For example, pronounce 'hot tomatoes' to yourself. Notice how you pronounce the last **t** in 'hot' and the first **t** in 'tomatoes' as very nearly the same sound, but you pause a little. That's exactly what the Japanese **'t** sounds like. Same thing with the **'k**, as in 'quick car'. Practice with these: **katta** (*kah'tah*), **ikka** (*ee'kah*), **rokka** (*ro'kah*).

And that's it for the consonants. As for the vowels, they are not much more complicated. Here are a few things to watch out for:

➤ Some Japanese words have what we call 'long' vowels, meaning they are pronounced a little bit longer than usual. In English we call sounds like the **a** in 'cape' a 'long vowel', but don't let that confuse you (in English, long vowels aren't even long). We'll use a '-' to tell you that a vowel should be pronounced for two beats, as in *eeko-*, *sayo-nahrah*, and *ko-hee-* (in the official romanization, you will notice that these are spelled differently in different places. As you learn the Japanese writing system, you will see how and why, but there are only a few variations, nothing like 'knot', 'not', 'naught' in English, at least!)

➤ The **u** sound is one of the few in Japanese that ever changes. Most times, the **u** sound is like 'oo' in English, like in 'fool' or 'moon'. Sometimes at the end of words, however, it is almost not pronounced at all. In those cases, we will signify that with an apostrophe, too. For instance, **desu** (*dés'*), just so you know it's there but don't have to pronounce it. Some other times (when it is written **ū** in the official Romanization), the **u** sound is pretty close to the French 'u'.

➤ As we mentioned above, when pronouncing Japanese vowels, try to pronounce them very crisply and cleanly. Most of the time we English speakers pronounce 'o' as if it was written 'ow', rounding our lips at the end of the sound, but the Japanese never do. The same is true for **e** —which in Japanese is pronounced like 'eh'— and **i**, which is pronounced like 'ee'. You will also come across the sound **ei**, written *é-* in the English pronunciation key. Try to pronounce it as the 'ay' in 'say', but barely pronounce the 'y' at the end of it. Note that **a** is pronounced as in 'car' (or 'ah') and not as in 'bath' or 'sad.' Here is a brief table explaining the conventions we chose for the English pronunciation key…

Japanese sound	English sound	as in…
a	*ah*	'car'
e	*é*	'eh'
ei	*é-*	'play' (without pronouncing the 'y' too much)
u	*oo*	'smooth'
ū	*u-*	as the French 'u'[1].
o	*o*	'open'
i	*ee*	'sweet'
ii	*ee-*	'do you see it'
in	*een*	'thirteen'
ai	*ahee* (in Japanese words) *ai* (in Chinese words)	'trying' 'I', 'hi!'
oi	*oee*	'boiled' (try to really insist on the 'i' sound)
ui	*ooee*	'buoy'
en	*en*	'stain'

[1] To make this sound, just put your lips in the position they would be for blowing out a candle while saying 'ee'. Try it! It works!

… and a few examples:

ookii (*o-kee-*) as in 'oh-key' (remember, hold both sounds a little long);

keigo (*ké-go*), try to pronounce it 'ka(y)go';

hai (*hai*) as 'hi!';
kaimasu (*kaheemahsoo*)…

And that's it. We do not need to talk about that anymore. With these few explanations, a minimal amount of attention, some of our exercises, and a bit of listening, you will be ready to pronounce any and all words in Japanese.

While we will not bore you with a long speech about intonation, since you should be able to pick most of it up from the recordings, we will give you one tip. The easiest way to make your intonation sound authentically Japanese is to try speaking without much intonation at all. Just let your sentences be flat, and then drop off a little at the end. The most important thing is to listen closely to the recordings, and let your own speech start to match theirs, and before you know it, you'll be sounding like a native!

One little reminder to keep in the back of your mind and not forget: **pay attention to long vowels!**

Another great thing about Japanese is its **words**. Take **nouns**, for example. In Japanese, unlike English, you do not even have to worry about singular and plural. It may seem strange at first, but there is no need to worry about the difference between 'pencil' and 'pencils' in Japanese. たまご **tamago** can mean *the egg*, *an egg*, *the eggs*, *some eggs*, etc. じどうしゃ **jidōsha** (*jeedo-shah*) can be *the car*, *the cars*, *a car*, etc. When you count, you say 'one pencil, two pencil, three pencil,' and so on. Easy as pie!

Verbs! We wish we could tell you that the verbs were as easy as the nouns, and while they aren't, they're still nothing to get worried over. Don't fret over long lists of conjugations, because Japanese verbs don't change from speaker to speaker. たべます **tabemasu** (*tahbémahs'*) means *I eat*, *you eat*, *s/he eats*, *we eat*, *they eat* and sometimes even *you will eat, they will eat*. Japanese verbs have many forms, for negative, positive, past, present (though no future). As for irregular verbs, there are only three of them of note, and they're so common, you will remember them easily. You will see most of the common Japanese verbs in the first 15 lessons, and you will learn how to use them to express a myriad of ideas. Of course there are difficulties, such as using different verbs to refer to yourself and others, or sticking different suffixes onto verbs, but we'll deal with that in more detail later.

What will seem a little strange at first is that the words corresponding to our **adjectives** are actually more like verbs. That is, they change form depending on whether they're in the present, past, or negative, and that they are also used for all pronouns. 小さい **chiisai** (*chee-sahee*) means *it's small*, and 小さくない **chiisakunai** (*chee-sahkoonahee*) means *it's not small*, and *I'm not small, he's not small, you're not small* as well. All of this we will discuss little by little in the lessons to come.

But where you need to perform a bit of mental gymnastics right away is that the **word order** of Japanese sentences is pretty much completely opposite from our own. Verbs (or adjectives) always come at the end, and all complements (plus the subject, when there is one) come before it. A sentence like "there are bread and coffee on the table in the kitchen" would becoming "kitchen / of / table / on / bread / and / coffee / there are". It's nothing more than a habit, and soon you'll find that it's quite logical and not as complicated as it seems. But, you ask, if everything comes before the verb, then how do I know what the subject is, and what the objects are, or what they're objects for? Well the Japanese have a little system that's really quite ingenious. After each word they have a syllable (or sometimes two) to perform the task of straightening it all out, whether the word before the verb is the subject or whether it's one of its objects.

For example: パン を たべます
pan o tabemasu
(pan o tahbémahs')

That **pan** means *bread*. The **tabemasu** means *to eat*. And the little **o** between them, that means that the **pan** is the object of **tabemasu**. The whole sentence would simply be *I* (or *you*, *he*, *she*, *we*, or *they*) *eat bread*.

And how about   バス で いきます
basu de ikimasu
(bahs' dé eekeemahs')

basu = *bus*, **ikimasu** = *to go*. The **de** in the middle means that **basu** is the method by which you are going (**ikimasu**). The sentence would be *I* (*you*, etc.) *go by bus*.

Since these little words (particles) have no real meaning by themselves, you will be given their function in square brackets, in the word-for-word translation.

パン を たべます   I eat bread
pan o tabemasu   *(bread / [object] / eat)*
(pan o tahbémahs')

バス で いきます   I go by bus
bas(u) de ikimasu   *(bus / [means] / go)*
(bahs' dé eekeemahs')

There are not, in fact, very many of these particles—ten, to be exact—and because we use them so often, you will surprise yourself after being comfortable with them in about twenty lessons. Obviously, there are still loads of words and particles, as well as constructions a bit more challenging, but we have 100 lessons here, so…

Now we will have to come across something that is rather hard. And that, for us, is **the writing**. And it is true—we cannot hide from it—the

Japanese writing system is difficult. Nevertheless, more than a hundred million people live, work, and play in Japanese—just think of how many Japanese products you use—and they communicate by reading and writing Japanese. So there is no reason not to get there yourself. The written language is an undeniable part of Japanese, and it is for this that we teach you to write. All Japanese texts are written with Japanese characters. Not knowing how to write will only condemn you, at an early date, to making no progress in the language.

What gives Japanese writing its complicated nature is that it employs, in fact, two systems at the same time. If you have had the chance to glance at a Japanese text before, and if you are rather observant, you should be able to spot the two systems pretty quickly. If you have not had the chance, take this little quiz right now. Look at the following passage for a couple minutes and find the elements of each system (answers on page XV)

明治の中ごろは、アメリカおよびイギリス、フランス、ド
イツ、ロシアなど、ヨーロッパ諸国ともさかんに貿易をし
ました。さらに、学問、文学、美術、音楽などの面でもい
ろいろなえいきょうを受けました。

You may have already figured it out, but in any case, the answer is apparent: you have on the one hand very simple characters made up of one, two, or three strokes, while on the other hand you have more complex characters that seem rather like islands in an ocean. And so, *voilà*, you can already distinguish between the elements in the two systems.

The first, where the characters are more simple, is a system of syllabics, which means that each character corresponds to one syllable. We call these characters KANA. If we look at the answers to our sample, they are the characters in paragraphs (1) and (2). Just those at the beginning: の = **no**, ご = **go**, ろ= **ro**, お= **o**, よ= **yo**, び = **bi**, な= **na**, ど= **do**, と= **to**, も= **mo**, さ= **sa**, か= **ka**, etc.

But to complicate matters (and which you have probably already noticed), there are two different kinds of KANA. One kind is used in writing words native to Japanese. These are called HIRAGANA. They are found in list (1) of the answers on page XV. These are the more rounded characters.

The others are used to write words of foreign origin, usually proper names of people or places, as well as common names (the vast majority of which come from American English). These are called KATAKANA, group (2) on the answer page.

Both kinds of KANA are made up of a limited number of characters: 46 for each, corresponding to the combination of almost all existent vowels (5) and consonants (9). (You will find pronunciation tables on pages 333 and 334).

Some HIRAGANA come up regularly, especially those at the end of verbs, and of course particles (those little particles that indicate word function, which we spoke about earlier). You will learn these quickly. And by the time the passive learning section of our course is completed, after Lesson 49, you will have no trouble at all remembering and learning how to write them.

The more complex character set is a different matter. This is the hard part for nearly all those who study Japanese. As much as you need to know these characters, you must also know that "slow and steady wins the race", especially the race against despair before even beginning!

This second system is called KANJI 漢字, which means, simply, 'Chinese' (漢) 'characters' (字) that the Japanese borrowed, as the name indicates, from China. These are often called *ideograms*, which means that each character responds to a **meaning**. So the character 人 means *person*. Used by the Chinese, they have one pronunciation, and used by the Japanese, they have another. Used by Koreans, still another. And if we want to amuse ourselves by writing English with these ideograms, we can write 人 and say *person*.

There is, however, a fundamental difference between the KANA and KANJI systems. The Japanese word *fire* is pronounced **hi** (that's more like *hee* than an English 'hi'). We can write it in *hiragana* as ひ, but this can also be used in any word that uses the syllable **hi**, just as the letter 'a' in English can be used in any number of words as well as stand alone. If we want to use *kanji*, however, we write 火 which is also pronounced **hi**, but can mean nothing except *fire*: 火 = *fire*.

All these explanations lead to one central point. To be careful, we will hang on to this for a moment. To repeat: an ideogram corresponds to a **meaning**. Let's take 煙 which means *smoke* (and where there is smoke there is fire, so we can see the character for *fire*, 火, written in the character for *smoke*. That should help, doesn't it?). The Japanese, before writing their language with Chinese characters, certainly had a way to say *smoke*, which was **kemuri**. But what happened when the Japanese borrowed characters from China? They found the character 煙 and, as it meant *smoke*, used it for writing their **kemuri**. And wherever you see that character, you can pronounce it **kemuri**.

But unfortunately for us, the Japanese had another idea, which was to take not only the writing, but also the pronunciation from the Chinese. In China, the character was pronounced something like **en**, and the Japanese kept this pronunciation for use in compound words. For example, the compound word 煙害 meaning *smoke pollution*, pronounced **engai**, sounds nothing like **kemuri**. In other words, each Chinese character in Japanese has at least two pronunciations. One is the original Japanese word, and the other is an adaptation of the ancient Chinese pronunciation. Sometimes certain characters will have even more pronunciations for each category.

Examples to be discussed in our text:

国 *country*; Japanese: **kuni** *(koonee)*; ancient Chinese, **altered by the Japanese**: **koku**.

音 *sound*; Japanese: **oto** or **ne** *(né)*; ancient Chinese: **on** or **in**.

中 *middle*; Japanese: **naka**; ancient Chinese: **chū** or **jū** *(chu-* or *ju-)*.

Ugh! Don't panic. You don't have to worry about all of this right away. Simply use *kanji* characters where they need to be used, as with all Japanese writing. At the beginning—and throughout the passive learning stage—it will be best just to look at these characters and try little by little to learn only the most common. With this advice you'll be fully prepared to attack the first lesson.

The first stage of your studies with *Japanese with Ease* is **passive**. Until Lesson 49, you will listen and **read aloud**, do your exercises, and have fun by trying to learn some *kana* and Chinese characters. If you want to amaze your friends right away, you can learn to write a few *kana* (you'll find the tables you need on pages 333 and 334), but it isn't mandatory. It will be enough at the beginning to understand, allowing yourself to be immersed in the language.

It is not until Lesson 50 that you will enter the **active** phase of your studies, which is to say that in addition to the daily lesson, you will go back to a lesson you have already seen, and which we will alert you to translate from English into Japanese. As you will already be able to understand a good deal of Japanese, with ear and eye already accustomed to the language, you will be able to make sentences naturally, without too much extra effort, just like a child beginning to speak.

The lessons are packed in groups of seven, with the seventh reviewing what you have studied during the week, helping you put things in order. You will be impressed, each time, with the progress you have made.

What is essential is that you study and review regularly. Better a little work often than an overload of work infrequently. The most challenging, keep in mind, are the first three weeks, because you will be "learning the ropes". But it is like walking: if you go too fast you will run out of breath, but if you don't get a good rhythm you will wear yourself out for no reason. So apply yourself from the beginning and pace yourself. And remember, it is with a good attitude and without wasting energy that you will best learn the Japanese language.

ANSWERS
System 1

(1)　の　ご　ろ　お　よ　び　な　ど　と　も
　　　さ　か　ん　に　を　し　ま　た　ら　で
　　　い　え　きょ　う　け

(2)　ア　メ　リ　カ　イ　ギ　リ　ス　フ　ラ
　　　ン　ド　ツ　ロ　シ　ヨ　ー　ロ　パ

System 2

明　治　中　諸　国　貿　易

学　問　文　美　術　音　楽　面　受

The language recordings, on cassette or CD, accompanying this series contain a recording of the dialogue and practice phrases of each lesson. For the first six lessons, the dialogue has been recorded twice. The first time, each sentence is repeated very slowly so that you can distinguish each syllable. The second time the text is read more quickly. Japanese pronunciation, as you have read in the introduction, should pose few problems for you. After Lesson 8, you will find the words in the text with ease; it won't be necessary to repeat the sentences twice!

1 第一課 **da i i k ka** ① *(dai ee'kah)*

1 – 早 く。 ②
はや
ha ya ku.
(hahyahkoo)

2 行きましょう。 ③
い
i ki ma shō.
(eekeemahsho-)

3 – わかりました。
wa ka ri ma shi ta.
(wahkahreemahshtah)

4 どこ へ。
do ko e.
(doko é)

5 – あそこ へ。
a so ko e.
(ahsoko é)

6 – 暑い です ね。
あつ
a tsu i de su ne.
(ahtsooee des' né)

7 – そう です ね。 ④
sō de su ne.
(so- des' né)

□

Notes

① The first **kanji** you see here is a numeral indication, placed before the number, that means something like the English *-th*, as in, "4th, 5th, 6th…" Of course, it also means *-st*, *-nd*, and *-rd*, as in "1st, 2nd, 3rd", but for simplification, we notate it here as *-th*.

② Look closely at the Chinese character used in this sentence. Above it you'll find small **hiragana** characters. It's common for Japanese to indicate character pronunciation this way. Whenever a Chinese character is used in this textbook, it will have two different pronunciation guides, one in little **hiragana** ▶

1 – Hurry!
2   Let's go.
3 – I understand.
4   Where?
         (where / [destination])
5 – Over there.
         (there / [destination])
6 – It's hot, isn't it!
         (hot / it is / [agreement])
7 – It is, isn't it!
         (so / it is / [agreement])

ဢၣဘ၃ဢၣ

▸ above the character, called **furigana**, 早, and one with the official Japanese romanization, **haya**. Little by little, you'll find yourself getting used to not looking at the romanization at all!

③ A small note on writing. Words in the Chinese language don't change form, but Japanese verbs do vary depending on the context. Here we have a verb form **ikimashō** (*eekeemahsho-*), but we can also find **iku, ikanai** (*eekoo, eekahnah'ee*), etc. So for verbs, we keep the Chinese character for the part of the verb that doesn't change, in this example the *i*, and write the rest in **hiragana**: 行きましょう **i ki ma shō** (*eekeemahsho-*).

④ Japanese particularly like short words for the ends of phrases (we call them final particles). They lend a sense of closure to the sentence, and a sense of tone. In English, for instance, our voices rise toward the end of questions, and drop toward the end of statements. In Japanese the tone stays relatively flat, so they need these sentence-enders to indicate whether they're asking a question, stating a fact, or confirming something. Here, this ね **ne** indicates that the speaker is looking for understanding and agreement from the listener. 暑いですね **a tsu i de su ne** (*ahtsooee des'né*) = *it's hot, don't you think?* (or *it's hot, isn't it.*). そうですね **sō de su ne** (*so- des'né*) = *yes (it is, isn't it.)*. We refer as an 'agreement' in the accompanying translation, as the speaker is looking for confirmation, or agreement, from the listener.

1

<ruby>練<rt>れん</rt>習<rt>しゅう</rt></ruby> renshū *(ren shu-)* – **Practice**

Exercise 1

❶ <ruby>早<rt>はや</rt></ruby>く。
hayaku.
(hahyahkoo)

❷ <ruby>行<rt>い</rt></ruby>きましょう。
ikimashō.
(eekeemahsho-)

❸ <ruby>早<rt>はや</rt></ruby>く <ruby>行<rt>い</rt></ruby>きましょう。
hayaku ikimashō.
(hahyahkoo eekeemahsho-)

❹ わかりました。
wakarimashita.
(wahkahreemahshtah)

✳✳✳

Exercise 2

... に <ruby>言葉<rt>ことば</rt></ruby> を <ruby>入<rt>い</rt></ruby>れ なさい
... ni kotoba o i re na sa i
(nee kotobah o eeré nahsai)

Fill in the blanks with the missing words
(. . . / [place] / word / [object] / enter)

❶ Where? There.
doko e? . . . . . e

❷ It's hot!
atsui desu . .

Answers to Exercise 1

❶ Hurry ❷ Let's go. ❸ Let's go quickly. ❹ I understand.

✳✳✳

❸ Let's go.
iki . . . . .

Answers to Exercise 2

❶ – asoko –. ❷ – ne. ❸ – mashō.

第二課 **da i ni ka** *(dai nee kah)*

ピカソ展
pi ka so te n
(peekahso ten)

1 – 見ました か。①
mi ma shi ta ka.
(meemahshtah kah)

2 – 何 を。
na ni o.
(nanee o)

3 – ピカソ 展。②
pi ka so te n.
(peekahso ten)

4 – まだ です。
ma da de su.
(mahdah des')

5 – いい です よ。③
i i de su yo.
(ee- des' yo)

Notes

① We will come across this か **ka** very often. An accurate translation is impossible, but it isn't truly necessary. It is simply an interrogative particle, meaning that the sentence that precedes it, is a question. Any sentence can become a question with this particle, changing nothing of the original word order. ▶

The Picasso Exhibition
(Picasso / exhibition)

1 – Did you see it?
   (have seen / [question])
2 – What?
   (what / [object])
3 – The Picasso exhibition.
   (Picasso – exhibition)
4 – Not yet.
   (not yet / it is)
5 – It's really good!
   (really good / it is / [engagement])

▸ ② The last **hiragana** of this sentence, ん, is the only exception to the syllabic rule. It is not transcribed as a full syllable, but instead as a final **n** to end a separate syllable.

③ よ **yo** is another final particle. In Lesson 1 you learned about ね **ne**. Here, よ **yo** has the opposite meaning. That is, 'what I am saying is my own opinion, and it only has to do with me'. いい です よ **ii desu yo** = *(I personally think) it's good*. We refer to this above as 'engagement', as the speaker is not asking for confirmation or agreement, and is simply stating a fact or opinion.

6 – そう　です　か。④
　　 sō　　de su　　ka.
　　 (so- des' kah)

7　あした　行きます。
　　 a shi ta　　i ki masu.
　　 (ahshtah eekeemahs')

　　　　　　　　　　　　　　　　　□

Notes

④　We already discussed long vowels in the introduction. Here's a
　　 simple example: **sō**. In Japanese, it's written そう. Here we come
　　 across a rare convention of writing that we have to remember: ▶

＊＊＊

れん　しゅう
練習　**renshū** *(ren shu-)*

Exercise 1

❶ 見ました　か。
　 mimashita　　ka.
　 (meemahshtah kah)

❷ まだ　見ません。
　 mada　mimasen.
　 (mahdah meemahsen)

❸ 見ました　か。
　 mimashita　　ka.
　 (meemahshtah kah)

❹ 見ました。
　 mimashita.
　 (meemahshtah)

6 – Really?
   (so / it is / [question])
7   I'll go tomorrow.
   (tomorrow / go)

ಋಚಜಚಋ

▸ two **hiragana**, そ and う, pronounced as *u* when it's alone. But together そう is pronounced like *so-*, which isn't really any more difficult or confusing than any English spelling rules.

✳✳✳

❺ そう です か。
   sō   desu   ka.
   (so- des' kah)

Answers to Exercise 1
❶ Did you see it? ❷ Not yet. ❸ Did you see it? ❹ Yes. ❺ Oh, really?

3   Exercise 2

... に 言葉 を 入れ なさい
... ni kotoba   o   i re   na sa i
(nee kotobah o eeré nahsai)

Fill in the blanks with the missing words
(. . . / [place] / word / [object] / enter)

❶ I saw.
mimashi . .

❷ Did you see [it]?
mimashita . .

---

3   第三課 da i sa n ka *(dai san kah)*

朝食
chō sho ku
(cho- shokoo)

1 – おはよう　ございます。①②
o ha yō　go za i ma su.
(ohahyo- gozaheemahs')

2 – おはよう　ございます。①②
o ha yō　go za i ma su.
(ohahyo- gozaheemahs')

Notes

① There are many ways of saying *hello* in Japanese. This formula is used when you meet someone for the first time of the day, usually in the morning.

❸ That's great! **3**
　　ii desu . .
❹ Is it good?
　　ii desu . .

Answers to Exercise 2
❶ – ta. ❷ – ka. ❸ – yo. ❹ – ka.

Lesson Three *(-th / three / lesson)*　　**3**

Breakfast
(morning meal)

1 –　Good Morning.
2 –　Good Morning.

ಬಂಛಚಿಂಡ

▸ ② よう cf. Lesson 2, note 4. よ= **yo**; う = **u**, but the two together
make よう **yō** (*yo-*), with a long **o**.

3 – パン を 食べます か。
pa n o ta be ma su ka.
(pan o tahbémahs' kah)

4 – 食べ ます。③④
ta be ma su.
(tahbémahs')

5 – コーヒー を 飲みます か。
kō hī o no mi ma su ka.
(ko-hee- o nomeemahs' kah)

6 – 飲みます。
no mi ma su.
(nomeemahs')

7 – ビール を 飲みます か。
bī ru o no mi ma su ka.
(bee-roo o nomeemahs' kah)

8 – 飲みません。
no mi ma se n.
(nomeemahsen)

9 – りんご を 食べます か。
ri n go o ta be ma su ka.
(ringo o tahbémahs' kah)

10 – 食べません。
ta be ma se n.
(tahbémahsen)

Notes

③ What we have just said in note 1 is only applicable in **hiragana**. For *katakana* we have a different system, marking long vowels with a line: コ = **ko**, コー = **kō**, ヒ = **hi**, ヒー = **hī**, ビ = **bi**, ビー = **bī**. ▶

3 – Would you like some bread?
(bread / [object] / eat / [question])

4 – Yes.
(eat)

5 – Would you like some coffee?
(coffee / [object] / drink / [question])

6 – Yes.
(drink)

7 – Would you like some beer?
(beer / [object] / drink / [question])

8 – No.
(not drink)

9 – Would you like an apple?
(apple / [object] / eat / [question])

10 – No.
(not eat)

▸ ④ In Japanese, the usual way of saying *yes* is to repeat the main
verb of the sentence. To say *no*, simply negate the main verb of
the sentence.

3

11 – それでは 卵 を 食べます か。

   so re de wa　ta ma go　o　ta be ma su　ka.

   (sorédéwah tahmahgo o tahbémahs' kah)

12 – 食べます。

   ta be ma su.

   (tahbémahs')

□

Don't forget, you don't have to try to memorize the kana or the Chinese characters right now, just focus on identifying them and 'how they work'. The habit of seeing them will help you remember them. And this will come earlier than you imagine.

＊＊＊

練習　renshū *(ren shu-)*

Exercise 1

❶ コーヒー を 飲みます か。

   kōhī o nomimasu ka.

   (ko-hee- o nomeemahs' kah)

❷ 飲みます。

   nomimasu.

   (nomeemahs')

❸ コーヒー を 飲みます。

   kōhī o nomimasu.

   (ko-hee- o nomeemahs')

11 – Well then would you like some eggs? **3**
(so / egg / [object] / eat / [question])
12 – Yes.
(eat)

***

④ ビール を 飲^のみます か。
bīru o nomimasu ka.
(bee-roo o nomeemahs' kah)

⑤ 飲^のみません。
nomimasen.
(nomeemahsen)

Answers to Exercise 1
❶ Do you want coffee? ❷ Yes. ❸ I'll drink coffee. ❹ Do you drink beer? ❺ No.

4   **Exercise 2**

... に 言葉 を 入れ なさい
... ni kotoba o i re na sa i
(nee kotobah o eeré nahsai)

Fill in the blanks with the missing words
(. . . / [place] / word / [object] / enter)

❶ I eat eggs.
   tamago . tabemasu

❷ Do you want bread?
   pan o tabemasu . .

---

4   第四課 **da i yo n ka** *(dai yon kah)*

税関
ze i ka n
(zeikan)

1 – カメラ を 持って います か。 ①
ka me ra o mo t te i ma su ka.
(kahmérah o mo'té eemahs' kah)

2 – はい、 持って います。
ha i, mo t te i ma su.
(hai mo'té eemahs')

3 – どこ に あります か。
do ko ni a ri ma su ka.
(doko nee ahreemahs' kah)

❸ Yes .

tabe . . . .

❹ Do you drink coffee?

kō hī o nomi . . . . ka

❺ No.

nomi . . . . .

Answers to Exercise 2

❶ – o –. **❷** – ka. **❸** – masu. **❹** – masu –. **❺** – masen.

Lesson Four *(-th / four / lesson)*   **4**

At Customs
(customs)

1 – Do you have a camera ?
(camera / [object] / possess / [question])
2 – Yes, I do.
(yes / possess)
3 – Where is it?
(where / [place] / exist / [question])

ဆၣလ၁ဆၣလ၁

Notes

① Take a good look at the word 持 って **motte** (*mo'té*). This is
where we find the double **tt** sound. In written Japanese, this
doubling is represented by the little sign つ. It's the same sign used
to point out the double **kk** in the title of Lesson 1: だい いっか
dai ikka (*dai ee'kah*). And look at item 11: けっこう **kekkō**
(*ke'ko-*). And now . . . cheat a little and sneak a peak at Lesson 6!

4

4 – トランク の 中 に あります。
to ra n ku no na ka ni a ri masu.
(torankoo no nahkah nee ahreemahs')

5 – トランク の 中 に 何 が
to ra n ku no na ka ni na ni ga
(torankoo no nahkah nee nanee gah

あります か。
a ri ma su ka.
ahreemahs' kah)

6 – 洋服 と 本 が あります。
yō fu ku to ho n ga a ri ma su.
(yo- fookoo to hon gah ahreemahs')

7 – それ だけ です か。
so re da ke de su ka.
(soré dahké dés' kah)

8 – はい、そうです。
ha i, sō de su.
(hai so- dés')

9 – お 酒 ?
o sa ke?
(o sahké)

10 – ありません。
a ri ma se n.
(ahreemahsen)

11 – はい、けっこう です。
ha i, ke k kō de su.
(hai ke'ko- dés')

4 – It's in my suitcase (trunk).   **4**
(suitcase / [relation] / inside / [place] / exist)

5 – What is in your suitcase (trunk)?
(suitcase / [relation] / inside / [place] / what / [subject] / exist / [question])

6 – There are clothes and books.
(clothes / and / books / [subject] / exist)

7 – That's all?
(that / only / it is / [question])

8 – Yes, that's all.
(yes / so / it is)

9 – Any alcohol?
([familiarity]-alcohol)

10 – I don't have any.
(not exist)

11 – Okay, great.
(yes / perfect / it is)

৺৩৪৫৩

4

練習 **renshū** (ren shu-)

Exercise 1

❶ 洋服 を 持って います か。
yōfuku o motte imasu ka.
(yo-fookoo o mo'té eemahs' kah)

❷ はい、 持って います。
hai, motte imasu.
(hai mo'té eemahs')

❸ どこ に あります か。
doko ni arimasu ka.
(doko nee ahreemahs' kah)

***

Exercise 2

... に 言葉 を 入れ なさい
... ni kotoba o i re na sa i
(nee kotobah o eeré nahsai)

Fill in the blanks with the missing words
(. . . / [place] / word / [object] / enter)

❶ Do you have any books?
hon o motte imasu . .

❷ I have a suitcase.
toranku . motte imasu

❸ Where is it?
. . . . ni arimasu ka

19 • jū kyū

④ あそこ に あります。 **4**
asoko ni arimasu.
(ahsoko nee ahreemahs')

Answers to Exercise 1

❶ Do you have any clothes? ❷ Yes, I do. ❸ Where are they?
❹ They are over there.

✳✳✳

④ It's over there.
asoko ni ari . . . .

⑤ Do you have a camera?
kamera . motte imasu ka

⑥ No.
motte ima . . .

Answers to Exercise 2

❶ – ka. ❷ – o –. ❸ doko –. ❹ – masu. ❺ – o –. ❻ – sen.

5 第五課 **da i go ka** *(dai go kah)*

買物
かい もの

ka i mo no
(kaheemono)

1 – どこ へ 行きます か。
do ko e i ki ma su ka.
(doko é eekeemahs' kah)

2 – デパート へ 行きます。①
de pā to e i ki ma su.
(dépah-to é eekeemahs')

3 – 一緒 に 行きます。②
i s sho ni i ki ma su.
(ee'sho- nee eekeemahs')

4 何 を 買います か。
na ni o ka i ma su ka.
(nanee o kaheemahs' kah)

5 – 靴 下 を 買 い ま す。
ku tsu shi ta o ka i ma su.
(kootsooshtah o kaheemahs')

6 – 着きました。
tsu ki ma shi ta.
(tsookeemahshtah)

Notes

① パー **pā** (*pa-*). Remember (Lesson 3, note 3), the dash is there
simply because the **a** is long, and the word is in **katakana**. ▶

Shopping
(shopping)

1 – Where are you going?
(where / [destination] / go / [question])

2 – I'm going to the department store.
(department store / [destination] / go)

3 – I'll go with you.
(together / [adverbial] / go)

4 What are you buying?
(what / [object] / buy / [question])

5 – I'm buying socks.
(socks / [object] / buy)

6 – Here we are!
(be arrived)

ഇവങ്ങവ

▸ ② Again we meet the little つ, this time not to indicate a **tt** or **kk**, but for the **shsh**: いっしょ **issho** (*ee'sho-*). Notice, too, that the last **hiragana** is written smaller, too: ょ. We saw this before, in lesson 2, but in normal size: よ = **yo**. There was no way to write the syllables beginning with **sh** out of the 46 **kana**, except for **shi**. So the Japanese developed a writing convention of following **shi** (し) with a small **yo** (ょ) and getting しょ **sho**.

5

7　入りましょう。③
ha i ri ma　shō.
(haheereemahsho-)

8 – ここ に 靴下 が あります。
ko ko　ni ku tsu shi ta ga　a ri masu.
(koko nee kootsooshtah gah ahreemahs')

9 – でも 高い です ね。
de mo　ta ka i　de su　ne.
(démo tahkai dès' né)

10 – そう です ね。
sō　de su　ne.
(so- dés' né)

11　やめます。
ya me ma su.
(yahmémahs')

□

***

練習　**renshū** *(ren shu-)*

Exercise 1

❶ あそこ に 靴下 が あります。
asoko ni kutsushita ga arimasu.
(ahsoko nee kootsooshtah gah ahreemahs')

❷ ここ に トランク が あります。
koko ni toranku ga arimasu.
(koko nee torankoo gah ahreemahs')

❸ どこ へ 行きます か。
doko e ikimasu ka.
(doko é eekeemahs' kah)

7 Let's go in.
8 – Here are the socks.
(here / [place] / socks / [subject] / exist)
9 – But they're expensive.
(but / be expensive / it is / [agreement])
10 – Yes, they are.
(so / it is / [agreement])
11 I'll pass!
(quit)

Notes

③ 入(はい)りましょう **hairimashō** (*haireemahsho-*). Remind you of something? Look back to Lesson 1: 行(い)きましょう **ikimashō** (*eekeemahsho-*). Look at the end of these words: しょう. Here we have a **shi** (し), followed by a small **yo** (ょ), and then an **u** (う). Coming after the note above, we know that しょ, **shi** plus **yo**, equals **sho**. If we add the う **u**, it's only because the **o** in **shō** is long: しょう = **shō**.

***

❹ 洋服(ようふく) を 買(か)います。
yōfuku o kaimasu.
(yo-fookoo o kaheemahs')

❺ どこ に あります か。
doko ni arimasu ka.
(doko nee ahreemahs' kah)

Answers to Exercise 1

❶ There are the socks. ❷ Here are the suitcases. ❸ Where are you going? ❹ I'm buying clothes. ❺ Where are they?

5   Exercise 2

...に 言葉 を 入れ なさい
... ni kotoba o i re na sa i
(nee kotobah o eeré nahsai)

Fill in the blanks with the missing words
(. . . / [place] / word / [object] / enter)

❶ What are you buying?
nani . kaimasu ka

❷ What are you eating?
. . . . o tabemasu ka

---

6   第六課 da i ro k ka *(dai ro'kah)*

東京 タワー
tō kyō ta wā
(to- kyo- tah wah)

1 – 東京 タワーを 知って
tō kyō ta wā o shi t te
(to-kyo- tahwah o shee'té

い ます か。①
i ma su ka.
eemahs' kah)

2 – はい、知って います。
ha i, shi t te   i ma su.
(hai shee'té eemahs')

③ Where are you going?
doko . ikimasu . .

④ I'm going over there.
. . . . ikimasu

⑤ That's expensive!
takai desu . .

Answers to Exercise 2
❶ – o –. **❷** nani –. **❸** – e – ka. **❹** asoko e –. **❺** – ne.

Lesson Six *(-th / six / lesson)* 6

The Tower of Tōkyō
(Tōkyō tower)

1 – Do you know the Tower of Tōkyō?
(Tōkyō Tower / [object] / know / [question])
2 – Yes, I know it.
(yes / know)

৪০঩৪০঩

Notes

① The Tower of Tōkyō is a lot like the Eiffel Tower. While it's
taller by a few meters, it's also newer (constructed in 1958).
Flocks of tourists, both Japanese and foreign, squeeze in to
admire the panoramic view from the top.

6

3 – ここ から どう 行きます か。
ko ko ka ra dō i ki ma su ka.
(koko kahrah do- eekeemahs' kah)

4 – まず 目黒 駅 まで 歩きます。②
ma zu me gu ro e ki ma de a ru ki ma su.
(mahzoo mégooro ékee mahdé ahrookeemahs')

5 近い です。
chi ka i de su.
(cheekai dés')

6 そこから 渋谷 駅 まで
so ko ka ra shi bu ya e ki ma de
(soko kahrah sheebooya ékee mahdé

電車 で 行きます。②③
den sha de i ki ma su.
denshah dé eekeemahs')

7 それから 渋谷 駅 から タワー
so re ka ra shi bu ya e ki ka ra ta wā
(sorékahrah sheebooyah ékee kahrah tahwah

まで バスで 行きます。
ma de ba su de i ki ma su.
mahdé bahs' dé eekeemahs')

8 タワー に 水族館 が あります。
ta wā ni su i zo ku ka n ga a ri ma su.
(tahwah nee sooeezokookoon gah ahreemahs')

Notes

② Meguro and Shibuya are the names of two train stations in downtown Tōkyō. Located a few minutes from each other on one of the main lines, they are at the centers of two of Tōkyō's principal neighborhoods. ▶

3 – How do you get there from here?
(here / from / how / go / [question])

4 – First, we walk to the Meguro station.
(first / Meguro-station / until / walk)

5 That's very close
(be close / it is)

6 From there, we go by train until the Shibuya station.
(there / from / Shibuya-station / until / train / [means] / go)

7 Then we take the bus from the Shibuya station to the Tower.
(then / Shibuya-station / from / Tower / until / bus / [means] / go)

8 In the Tower there's an aquarium.
(Tower / [place] / aquarium / [subject] / exist)

ॐ☘ॐ

▶ ③ 電車 **densha** (*denshah*). In Lesson 5, we saw (in notes 2 and 3) how to write **sho**. **sha** is written with the same principle: し **shi** + a little や **ya** = しゃ. For the syllables with **sh**, we now know how to write **shi** し, **sho** しょ, and **sha** しゃ.

6

9 おもしろい　です。

o mo shi ro i　de su.

(omosheeroee dés')

10 おみやげ　の　店　も　たくさん

o mi ya ge　no　mi se　mo　ta ku sa n

(omeeyahgé no meesé mo tahkoosan

あります。

a ri ma su.

(ahreemahs')

□

✳✳✳

れん　しゅう

練習　**renshū** *(ren shu-)*

Exercise 1

❶ タワー　へ　行きます。

tawā e ikimasu.

(tahwah é eekeemahs')

❷ 着きました。

tsukimashita.

(tsookeemash'tah)

❸ 入りました。

hairimashita.

(haeereemahsh'tah)

29 • ni jū kyū

9 That's interesting. **6**
   (interesting / it is)

10 There are also many souvenir shops.
   (gift / [relation] / shop / also / many / exist)

***

④ タワー まで 歩^{ある}きました。
tawā made arukimashita
(tahwah mahdé ahrookeemash'tah)

⑤ タワー に 店^{みせ} が たくさん あります。
tawā ni mise ga takusan arimasu
(tahwah nee meesé gah tahkoosan ahreemahs')

Answers to Exercise 1
❶ I'm going to the Tower. ❷ I arrived. ❸ I entered. ❹ I walked to the Tower. ❺ There are many stores at the Tower.

... に 言葉 を 入れ なさい
... ni kotoba   o   i re   na sa i
(nee kotobah o eeré nahsai)

Fill in the blanks with the missing words
(. . . / [place] / word / [object] / enter)

❶ I'm going to Meguro
meguro . ikimasu

❷ I went to Meguro
meguro e iki . . . .

❸ I went from Meguro to Shibuya
meguro . . . . shibuya made ikimashita

---

7   第七課 da i na na ka *(dai nanah kah)*

まとめ
matome
(mahtomé)

Revision and Notes

Let's take a break after six lessons and look at what we've learned.
You'll be surprised.

1. Verbs. No doubt you've already remarked on the similarities.
Let's recapitulate:

Lessons 2, 5, 6   行きます **ikimasu** *(eekeemahs')*

Lesson 3   食べます **tabemasu** *(tahbémahs')*

❹ I went from Shibuya to the Tower of Tōkyō
shibuya kara tōkyō-tawā .... iki ......

❺ I went there by bus.
basu .. ikimasu

❻ Let's go by bus.
basu de iki .....

Answers to Exercise 2
❶ – e –. ❷ – mashita. ❸ – kara –. ❹ – made – mashita. ❺ – de –.
❻ – mashō.

Lesson Seven *(-th / seven / lesson)*   **7**

Lesson 3	飲みます **nomimasu** *(nomeemahs')*
Lessons 4, 5, 6	あります **arimasu** *(ahreemahs')*
Lesson 5	買います **kaimasu** *(kaheemahs')*
Lesson 6	歩きます **arukimasu** *(ahrookeemahs')*

The suffix ます **masu** *(mahs')* is the most common form for ALL verbs for ALL PERSONS in the PRESENT TENSE, and very often for the future tense, too (see Lesson 2, item 7). For certain forms, we've also seen the negative equivalent: all you have to do is replace ます **masu** *(mahs')* with ません **masen** *(mahsen)*:

食べます   **tabemasu** (*tahbémahs'*) *to eat* (I eat, you eat, s/he eats, they eat...)

食べません   **tabemasen** (*tahbemahsen*) *not to eat* (I/you don't eat, he doesn't eat...)

飲みます   **nomimasu** (*nomeemahs'*) *to drink*

飲みません   **nomimasen** (*nomeemahsen*) *not to drink*

買います   **kaimasu** (*kaheemahs'*) *to buy*

買いません   **kaimasen** (*kaheemahsen*) *not to buy*

And you will soon see for yourself how to make the negative forms for other verbs.

And we have also seen another series of similarities: 見ました **mimashita** (*meemahshtah*), Lesson 2, item 1; わかりました **wakarimashita** (*wahkahreemahshtah*), Lesson 1, item 3; 着きました **tsukimashita** (*tsookeemahshtah*), Lesson 5, item 6. Here, to express the past tense, we replace ます **masu** (*mahs'*) with ました **mashita** (*mahshtah*).

And don't forget Lesson 1, item 2: 行きましょう **ikimashō** (*eekeemahsho-*), or lesson 5, item 7, 入りましょう **hairimashō** (*haheereemahsho-*).

Here, it's ましょう **mashō** (*mahsho-*) that replaces ます **masu** (*mahs'*). This is the form you use to express a command to yourself and, eventually, to those with you: "Let's go!" or "Let's enter". So we already have, after just six lessons, four fundamental forms you can use, if you like, to construct sentences with all the verbs we've seen. Not too shabby, eh?

2. Pay special attention to あります **arimasu** (*ahreemahs'*) from Lessons 5 and 6. This verb is a little bit odd, because it corresponds to our *there is* or *there are*, but it actually means "to be found, to exist (in a certain place), are located", and it's only used for inanimate objects (for living beings, we use another verb). So remember this construction: *There are stores*: 店 が あります **mise ga**

arimasu (*meesé gah ahreemahs'*), where 店 **mise** (*meesé*) is the subject of あります **arimasu** (*ahreemahs'*). "Stores exist (here) / There is a store (here)".

3. Since we're talking about the subject, have you noticed that in addition to just あります **arimasu** (*ahreemahs'*), no other sentences have a grammatical subject? Where in English we have to say "I, you, etc.", in Japanese they don't say anything. Corresponding words do, of course, exist, but this is one of the keys to Japanese: **As long as it's not essential to comprehension, the Japanese language does not require a subject.**

If someone looks at you and asks: ビール を 飲みます か **bīru o nomimasu ka** (*bee-roo o nomeemahs' kah*), and gives no other indication, then it's pretty obvious the question is directed at you. So there's no reason to be so precise about it. This automatically means "Would **you** like some beer?". If the person asking the question would like to address the question to someone else, then he or she could use the person's name in the place of subject. In your answer, the same thing can happen: if you're replying about yourself, then it's obvious that there's an implied "I ...". And 飲みます **nomimasu** (*nomeemahs'*) is all you need to say *I drink*.

4. To respond with a "yes", you should know that we almost never use the word that simply means "yes" (or, for that matter, "no"), but we repeat the verb in its affirmative form (for "no", of course, we use the negative form). To give more force to the answer, we can add to the verb the word はい **hai**, which means *yes*, as in Lesson 4, item 2: はい、 持って います **hai, motte imasu** (*hai mo'té eemahs'*), *Yes, I have one*, and Lesson 6, item 2: はい、 知って います **hai, shitte imasu** (*hai shi'té eemahs'*), *Yes, I know*. But the はい **hai** is never obligatory.

5. In the introduction, we spoke about the 10 grammatical particles, those little syllables that indicate the function of the preceding word. And so, without even noticing, we have already come across and used 7 of these particles, and used them many times:

を   **o** (Lessons 2, 3, 4, 5, 6) for the object complement;

が   **ga** (Lessons 4, 5, 6) for the subject;

に   **ni** (Lessons 4, 5, 6) to indicate where something **is located**; *in*; *at*;

へ   **e** (Lessons 1, 5) to indicate the place where one is going; *to*;

で   **de** (Lesson 6) for the complement of means; *by*;

から **kara** (Lesson 6) which always expresses the point of departure; *from*;

まで **made** (Lesson 6) which balances **kara** and expresses destination; *until*.

Of course you haven't memorized them all yet, but don't worry, we haven't seen the last of them!

6. In the notes to each lesson, we've already discussed a lot about the writing of Japanese. But in the first six lessons, we've already come across the most delicate orthographical points. And we'll be seeing them all over and over again, so you just need to pay a bit of attention. To go over it one more time:

***

➢ The **hiragana** ん is transcribed as **n** all on its own at the end of a syllable (Lesson 2, note 2).

➢ The う **u** that shows up in **hiragana** to tell us that the preceding syllable is long (Lesson 2, note 4): そう **sō** (*so-*).

➢ In **katakana**, the dash that indicates that the following vowel is long (Lesson 3, note 3).

➢ The little つ that tells us that the preceding consonant is doubled, or given extra stress: いっか **ikka** (*ee'kah*), もって **motte** (*mo'té*), いっしょ **issho** (*ee'sho*) (Lesson 4, note 1; Lesson 5, note 2).

➢ The way of writing **sh** before a vowel other than *i*: し **shi** (*shee*), しょ **sho** (*sho*), and しゃ **sha** (*shah*) (Lesson 5, note 2; Lesson 6, note 3).

We've spoken a lot about writing in the notes and in the revision lesson, but calm down, it won't be that hard! In these 7 Lessons, we have already covered just about everything irregular that can come up with the kana. *At any rate, for the moment there's no need to have everything memorized by heart, but only to understand, so that you can read the following lessons with ease. You'll see, when you get to the next revision chapter, that how to write will seem obvious, and at the following review, you won't even be thinking about it at all! Just remember, pay attention to the pronunciation, especially to the long vowels!*

✳✳✳

8　第八課 ① dai hak ka *(dai ha'kah)*

映画
ei ga
(é- gah)

きのう　　なに
1 – 昨日　何　を　しました　　か。
　　　kinō　　nani　o　shi ma shi ta　　ka.
　　　(keeno- nanee o sheemahshtah kah)

とも　だち　　　き
2 – 友　達　が　来ました。
　　　tomo dachi ga　　ki ma shi ta.
　　　(tomodahchee gah keemahshtah)

いっしょ　　　えい　が　　い
3 　一緒 に 映画 に 行きました。②③④
　　　is sho ni ei ga ni i ki ma shi ta.
　　　(ee'sho- nee é-gah nee eekeemahshtah)

なん　　　えい　が　　み
4 – 何 の 映画 を見ました か。⑤
　　　nan no　ei ga　o mi ma shi ta　ka.
　　　(nan no é-gah o meemahshtah kah)

Notes

① Again this little つ (a *hiragana* normally pronounced **tsu** in its normal size), to indicate that we have a double **kk** (cf. Lesson 7, par. 6).

② Of all the particles (cf. Lesson 7, par. 5), it's the に **ni** that will be the most challenging. But... it is relative. From now to the next revision chapter, we will have just about completed it. Here, with the word 一緒 **issho** (*ee'sho-*), it is part of an expression that works just like an English adverb: 一緒 に ▶

37 • san jū shichi *or* san jū nana

Lesson Eight *(-th / eight / lesson)* **8**

The Cinema
(cinema)

1 – What did you do yesterday?
(yesterday / what / [object] / did / [question])

2 – A friend came.
(friend / [subject] / came)

3 We went to the movies together.
(together / [adverbial] / movie / [goal] / went)

4 – What movie did you see?
(what / [relation] / movie / [object] / watched / [question])

☙❧☙❧

▸ **issho ni** (*ee'sho- nee*): *together*. The **ni** makes 'together' an adverb in this case. Consider how in "we are together", it is an adjective, while in "we went to the movie together", it's an adverb. In Japanese, the latter requires a **ni**.

③ 映画 **eiga** (*é-gah*). In Japanese **eiga** means both *a movie* and *the movies*, so it can be used in the sentence 'We watched an American movie', and 'We went to the movies'.

④ Still the same に **ni**, but this time, it follows a noun which expresses an activity 映画 **eiga** (*é-gah*), *the movies*, and is followed by a verb that indicates movement 行きました **ikimashita** (*eekeemahshtah*), *went*. In this case, に **ni** means that this activity is the goal of the movement. The same **ni**, after a destination, means *to*. Even though a movie is not a place per se, it is the same as the English "going *to* the movies," where "the movies" really stands for "the movie theater".

⑤ The word 何 *what*, has two forms: なに **nani** (cf. item 1), but also, as in here in item 4, なん **nan** *(nan)* when it comes before a の **no**.

5 – アメリカの 映画 を 見 ました。
 a me ri ka no ei ga o mi ma shi ta.
 (ahméreekah no é-gah o meemahshtah)

6 チャップリン の 「モダン・
 cha p pu ri n no mo da n
 (chah'p'reen no modahn

 タイムズ」 を 見 ました。⑥
 ta i mu zu o mi ma shi ta.
 taimz' o meemahshtah)

7 – おもしろかった です か。
 o mo shi ro ka t ta desu ka.
 (omosheerokah'tah des' kah)

8 – わかりません。
 wa ka ri ma se n.
 (wahkahreemahsen)

9 眼鏡 を 忘れました。
 me gane o wasu re ma shi ta.
 (mégahné o wahsoorémahshtah)

10 よく 見えません でした。⑦
 yo ku mi e ma se n de shi ta.
 (yokoo meeémahsen deshtah)

□

Notes

⑥ These brackets serve the same purpose as quotes in English, surrounding the titles of books, movies, magazines, and some brand names, or bits of dialogue in books.

⑦ A new form of verb! Simply the negative version of ました **mashita** (*mahshtah*) (the past tense). よく 見えました **yoku** ▸

5 – We saw an American movie.   **8**
(America / [relation] / movie / [object] / watched)

6   We saw Chaplin's *Modern Times*.
(Chaplin / [relation] / Modern Times / [object] / watched)

7 – Was it good?
(was interesting / it is / [question])

8 – I don't know

9   I forgot my glasses
(glasses / [object] / forgot)

10   I couldn't see very well.
(well / could not see)

෨෬ඐ෬ඐ

▸ **miemashita** (*yokoo meeémahshtah*), *I could see well*, is in the negative, よく 見えません でした **yoku miemasen deshita** (*yokoo meeémahsen deshtah*), *I couldn't see well*. Now you know how to make the past tense negative!

練習 renshū
れん しゅう

Exercise 1

❶ 友達 と 一緒 に 買物 に 行きました。
とも だち　　いっしょ　　　かい もの　　い

tomodachi to issho ni kaimono ni ikimashita.
(tomodahchee to ee'sho- nee kaheemono ni eekeemahshtah)

❷ 何 を 買いました か。
なに　　　か

nani o kaimashita ka.
(nanee o kaheemashtah kah)

❸ 映画 の 本 を 買いました。
えい が　　　ほん　　か

eiga no hon o kaimashita.
(é-gah no hon o kaheemahshtah)

***

Exercise 2

... に 言葉 を 入れ なさい
こと ば　　　い

❶ Have you seen Chaplin's movies?

chappurin .. .... o mimashita ka

❷ Could you see well?

.... mie .... ka

❸ What books did you buy?

.. ... hon o kaimashita ka

❹ A friend came.

tomodachi .. ... mashita

8

④ 眼鏡 を 買いました か。
megane o kaimashita ka.
(mégané o kaheemahshtah kah)

⑤ 買いません でした。
kaimasen deshita.
(kaheemahsen deshtah)

Answers to Exercise 1

❶ I went shopping with a friend. ❷ What did you buy? ❸ I bought a book about movies. ❹ Did you buy glasses? ❺ No.

✳✳✳

❺ I didn't go.
iki . . . .

Answers to Exercise 2

❶ – no eiga –. ❷ yoku – mashita –. ❸ nan no –. ❹ – ga ki –.
❺ – masen deshita.

第九課 ① dai kyū ka *(dai kyu- kah)*

だい きゅう か

中華 料理 ①
ちゅう か　りょう り

chū ka　ryō ri

(chu-kah ryo-ree)

1 – 今晩　中華　料理　を
こん ばん　ちゅうか　りょうり

kon ban　chū ka　ryō ri　　o

(konban chu-kah ryo-ree o

食べましょう　か。②
た

ta be ma　shō　　ka.

tahbémahsho- kah)

2 – ああ、　いい　です　ね。

a a,　　i i　de su　ne.

(ah- ee- dés' né)

3 中華　料理　が　大好き　です。
ちゅうか　りょうり　　　　だい す

chū ka　　ryō ri　ga　dai su ki　de su.

(chu-kah ryo-ree gah dais'kee dés')

4 – 私　も。
わたくし

watakushi　mo.

(wahtahkooshee mo)

Notes

① Here we meet the final difficulty of spelling in Japanese. There are
many syllables with what we call a "semivowel". A semivowel is,
for example, the *y* sound in words like "few", "hue", or "barbecue".
In our lesson here, it is the *y* in **kyū** and **ryō**. We can write **yu**
or **yo** with *kana* (the syllabic system) as **yu** ゆ and **yo** よ, but we
can't write the **k** or **r** on their own! So the Japanese have devised a
convention of fiddling with the size of characters. Take the kana for ▶

In a Chinese Restaurant

(Chinese cuisine)

1 – Shall we go to a Chinese restaurant tonight?
(tonight / Chinese cuisine / [object] / let's eat / [question])

2 – Oh! What a great idea!
(oh / good / it is / [agreement])

3   I love Chinese cuisine.
(Chinese cuisine / [subject] / favorite / it is)

4 – Me, too.
(me / also)

ഓ ൫ഀ ൚ ൞

▸ **ki** or **ri** – き or り – and follow it with a shrunken **yu** ゆ or **yo** よ. So we get **kyu**, きゆ; **kyo**, きよ; **ryu**, りゆ; and **ryo**, りよ. And because in this case (**kyū** and **ryō**) we are dealing with long vowels, we add the う (**u**) kana (cf. Lesson 2, note 4), which indicates a long vowel, leaving us with **kyū**, きゆう and **ryō**, りよう. For **chū** (*chu-*), we have a problem writing **ch** before a vowel other than **i**. Does this remind you of anything? Take a look at Lesson 5, where we had the same problem with **sh**. And we have the same solution: a big **chi** ち, followed by a small **yu** ゆ, **yo** よ, or **ya** や: **chu** ちゆ, **cho** ちよ, and **cha** ちや. And if the vowel is long: **chū** ちゆう and **chō** ちよう.

② 料理 **ryōri** (*ryo-ree*) is a word that means *cooking*, as in, 'the manner of preparing food', but Japanese will also use this word in the way English will use 'restaurant', with the name of such and such a country: 中華 料理 **chūka ryōri** (*chu-kah ryo-ree*), *Chinese cooking* or *Chinese restaurant*, 日本 料理 **nihon ryōri** (*neehon ryo-ree*), *Japanese cuisine*, *Japanese restaurant*.

9

5 スープ と 肉 と 魚 を
sū pu to niku to sakana o
(su-poo to neekoo to sahkanah o

とりましょう。③
to ri ma shō.
toreemahsho-)

6 – そう です ね。
sō de su ne.
(so- des né)

7 – お 箸 で 食べます か。④
o hashi de ta be ma su ka.
(o hahshee dé tahbémahs' kah)

8 – いいえ、フォーク で 食べます。③
i i e, fō ku de ta be ma su.
(ee-é fo-koo dé tahbémahs')

9 – おねがい します。 フォーク
o ne ga i shi ma su. fō ku
(onégahee sheemahs') (fo-koo

を 下さい。
o kuda sa i.
o koodahsai)

Notes

③ Remember? This little dash is used to indicate a long vowel in *katakana*, used for foreign words.

④ 箸 **hashi** (*hahshee*) on its own means *chopsticks*. So then why お 箸 **o hashi** (*oh hahshee*)? Very often, words that express objects in daily life are preceded by this little お **o**, like a notation of familiarity.

5 Let's have soup, meat and fish. **9**
(soup / and / meat / and / fish / [object] / let's take)

6 – Yes.
(so / it is / [agreement])

7 – Do you eat with chopsticks?
([familiarity]-chopsticks / [means] / eat / [question])

8 – No, I eat with a fork.
(no / fork / [means] / eat)

9 – Excuse me! A fork, please!
(please) (fork / [object] / give me)

中華料理 が 大好き です。

私も。

Don't be overwhelmed by this influx of notes. It won't last long! But while on the one hand we still have a few points to settle in terms of writing, on the other hand we are dealing with more and more difficult sentences! But we promise, the next review chapter will be the last time we talk about issues of spelling and writing. After that, all you will have to do is remember them.

9

10 – はい、どうぞ。
   ha i, dō zo.
   (hai do-zo)

11 – ありがとう。
    a ri ga tō.
    (ahreegahto-)

12 おいしい です か。
    o i shi i de su ka.
    (oeeshee- des' kah)

13 – とても おいしい です。
    to te mo o i shi i de su.
    (totémo oeeshee- des')

14 – また 来ましょう。
          き
    ma ta ki ma shō.
    (mahtah keemahsho-)

□

***

練習 **renshū**
れん しゅう

Exercise 1

❶ テレビ が 大好き です。
          だい す
   terebi ga daisuki desu.
   (térébee gah dais'kee dés')

❷ とても 暑い です ね。
          あつ
   totemo atsui desu ne.
   (totémo ahtsooee dés'né)

❸ 昨日 スープ と 魚 を
   きのう   さかな
   kinō sūpu to sakana o
   (keeno- su-poo to sahkanah o

10 – Yes, here you are.
11 – Thank you.
12 Is it good?
      (be good / it is / [question])
13 – It's delicious.
      (very / be good / it is)
14 – Let's come again.
      (again / let's come)

***

食べました。
tabemashita.
tahbémash'tah)

❹ フォーク で 食べません。
fōku de tabemasen.
(fo-koo dé tahbémahsen)

❺ お 箸 を 下さい。
o hashi o kudasai.
(o hahshee o koodahsai)

Answers to Exercise 1
❶ I love television. ❷ It's very hot! ❸ Yesterday I had (ate) soup and fish. ❹ I don't eat with a fork. ❺ Chopsticks, please.

Exercise 2

... に 言葉 を 入れ なさい
<small>ことば　　い</small>

❶ I love meat.
niku .. daisuki desu

❷ We eat fish with a fork.
sakana . fōku .. tabe ....

❸ It's very good.
...... oishii desu

❹ Bread, please.
pan o ....

---

10 第十課 <small>だい じゅっ か</small> ① **dai juk ka** *(dai ju'kah)*

テレビ
te re bi
(térébee)

1 – お 相撲 を 見ました か。②
<small>す もう　　　　　み</small>
　　o　su mō　o　mi ma shi ta　ka.
(o soomo- o meemahshtah kah)

2 – はい、 テレビ で 見ました。
<small>　　　　　　　　　　　　　　み</small>
　　ha i,　te re bi　de　mi ma shi ta.
(hai térébee dé meemahshtah)

Notes

① じゅ **ju** (*ju*). As with **shu** (*shu*) and **chu** (*chu*), a large じ **ji** and a small ゅ **yu** gives us じゅ **ju**. And then, remember, the little っ ＋ か for **kka**.

⑤ Tomorrow I'm going to a Chinese restaurant.   **10**
ashita chūka ryōri . . . .

⑥ Great idea!
.. desu ..

Answers to Exercise 2
❶ – ga –. ❷ – o – de – masu. ❸ totemo –. ❹ – kudasai. ❺ – ni
ikimasu. ❻ ii – ne.

Lesson Ten *(-th / ten / lesson)*   **10**

Television
(television)

ಇಲ ಉ ಜಿ ಇ ಉ

1 – Did you see the sumō wrestling?
   ([familiarity]-sumō / [object] / watched / [question])
2 – Yes, I saw it on television.
   (yes / television / [means] watched)

ಇಲ ಉ ಜಿ ಇ ಉ

▸ ② Sumō wrestling is a sport –or more like a spectacle– very popular
in Japan. Don't try this at home. The first rule of the sport is to be as
absolutely obese as possible, and the competitors truly are mammoth.
It's a far cry from the short and skinny stature of most Japanese... more
like 150+ kilos of wrestling mass. The battle takes place in a circle
of strict dimensions, with only two fighters, face to face. The goal is
to push your opponent out of the ring. Matches are often broadcast
on Japanese television, and the champions are real stars in Japan.
In the phrase お相撲 **o sumō**, we once again find the お **o** of
familiarity (cf. Lesson 9, note 4).

3 – また　お　相撲　の　シーズン
ma ta　　o　su mō　no　shī zu n
(mahtah o soomo- no shee-zoon

です　ね。
de su　　ne.
dés' né)

4 – そう　です　ね。
sō　　de su　　ne.
(so- dés' né)

5 – よく　テレビ　を　見ます　か。
yo ku　te re bi　　o　mi ma su　ka.
(yokoo térébee o meemahs' kah)

6 – 時々　　　見ます。③
toki doki　　mi ma su.
(tokeedokee meemahs')

7 – テレビ　で　何　を　見ます　か。
te re bi　de nani　o　mi ma su　ka.
(térébee dé nanee o meemahs' kah)

8 – ニュース　と　ホーム・ドラマ　を
nyū　su　to　hō mu・do ra ma　o
(nyu-soo to ho-moo dorahmah o

見ます。④
mi ma su.
meemahs')

Notes

③ We use the little sign 々 to avoid writing the same *kanji* (Chinese character) twice. Here, it would be the same as writing **tokidoki**. 時時

3 – It's the new sumō season.
(anew / [familiarity]-sumō / [relation] / season / it is / [agreement])

4 – That's right!
(so / it is / [agreement])

5 – Do you often watch television?
(often / television / [object] / watch / [question])

6 – Sometimes.
(sometimes / watch)

7 – What do you watch on television?
(television / [means] / what / [object] / watch / [question])

8 – I watch the news and the television dramas
(news / and / home dramas / [object] / watch)

കൗഗ്ലൗഗ

▶ ④ ホーム・ドラマ *home-drama*: a few actors, a few props, lots of sentimentality, and a whole lot of *tears*: this is home-drama, television dramas of fifteen minutes (or sometimes even a whole hour), broadcast on television in the middle of the day, relaying family dramas such as problems between a couple, between parents and children, etc.

10

9 – どちら が 好き です か。⑤
do chi ra　　ga　　su ki　　de su　　ka.
(docheerah gah s'kee dés' kah)

10 – どちら も 好き です。
do chi ra　　mo　　su ki　　de su.
(docheerah mo s'kee dés')

☐

Notes

⑤ どちら **dochira** (*docheerah*), literally, "which of the two options". The word is used with an adjective, as in the example above, to ask a question comparing the merits of two objects. ▶

***

練習 **renshū**

Exercise 1

❶ どちら が 高い です か。
dochira ga takai desu ka.
(docheerah gah tahkai dés' kah)

❷ よく テレビ を 見ます。
yoku terebi o mimasu.
(yokoo térébee o meemahs')

❸ テレビ で 映画 を 見ました。
terebi de eiga o mimashita.
(térébee dé é-gah o meemahshtah)

❹ テレビ が 大好き です。
terebi ga daisuki desu.
(térébee gah daisookee dés')

53 • go jū san

9 – Which do you prefer?
   (which / [subject] / be liked / it is / [question])

10

10 – I like both.
   (both / be liked / it is)

ഇൻജൻ

▸ We don't even need, as you see, to use a word meaning "more", as you would in English. Thus, "Which do you like?", rather than "Which do you like more?"

***

❺ テレビ の ニュース が 好き です。
 terebi no nyūsu ga suki desu.
 (térébee no nyu-soo gah s'kee dés')

Answers to Exercise 1

❶ Which one of these two is more expensive? ❷ I often watch television. ❸ I saw a movie on television. ❹ I love television. ❺ I like the news on television.

11 Exercise 2

...に 言葉 を 入れ なさい

❶ Do you often watch sumō?

o sumō . . . . ka

❷ I watch the news and movies.

. . . . eiga o mimasu

❸ Which of the two is closer?

. . . . chikai desu ka

---

11 第十一課 dai jū ik ka *(dai ju- ee'kah)*

朝
asa
(ahsah)

1 – 朝　何　時　に　起きます　か。①
asa　nan　ji　ni　o ki ma su　ka.
(ahsah nan jee nee okeemahs' kah)

2 – 十　一　時　に　起きます。①
jū　ichi　ji　ni　o ki ma su.
(ju- eechee jee nee okeemahs')

3 – 遅い　です　ね。
oso i　de su　ne.
(osoee dés' né)

4 夜　何　時　に　寝ます　か。
yoru　nan　ji　ni　ne ma su　ka.
(yoroo nan jee nee némahs' kah)

❹ I saw it on television.   **11**
.... mimashita

❺ Oh really?
... desu ka

Lesson Eleven *(-th / ten-one / lesson)* **11**

The Morning
(morning)

1 – What time do you wake up in the morning?
(morning / what-o'clock / [time] / wake up / [question])

2 – I wake up at eleven o'clock.
(ten-one-o'clock / [time] / wake up)

3 – That's late!
(be late / it is / [agreement])

4 What time do you go to sleep at night?
(night / what-o'clock / [time] / sleep / [question])

തോൽ

Notes

① Oh, yes, there's also this に **ni**. This time, it's used with time
words. It lets us know at what moment the action happens:
何時に **nan ji ni** (*nan jee nee*), *at what time*; 十一時に **jū
ichi ji ni** (*ju- eechee jee nee*), *at 11 o'clock*; 三時に **san ji ni**
(*san jee nee*), *at 3 o'clock*.

5 – 夜中 の 三 時 に 寝ます。
yo naka no san ji ni ne ma su.
(yonahkah no san jee nee némahs')

6 でも 今日 は 十 時 に
de mo kyō wa jū ji ni
(démo kyo- wah ju- jee nee

起きました。
o ki ma shi ta.
okeemahshtah)

7 – それでも 遅い です ね。
so re de mo oso i de su ne.
(sorédémo osoee dés' né)

8 – 午後 から 夜中 まで バー
go go ka ra yonaka ma de bā
(gogo kahrah yonahkah mahdé bah-

で 働いて います。②③
de hatara i te i ma su.
dé hahtahraheeté eemahs')

9 – それなら わかります。
so re na ra wa ka ri ma su.
(sorénahrah wahkahreemahs')

10 大変 です ね。
taihen de su ne.
(taihén dés'né)

□

***

5 – I go to bed at three in the morning. **11**
(middle night / [relation] / three-o'clock / [time] / sleep)

6 But today I got up at ten o'clock.
(but / today / [emphasis] / ten-o'clock / [time] / get up)

7 – That's still late!
(all the same / be late / it is / [agreement])

8 – I work in a bar from the afternoon until late at night.
(afternoon / since / middle night / until / bar / [place] / be working)

9 – In that case, I understand.
(in that case / be understandable)

10 That's terrible!
(terrible / it is / [agreement])

Notes

② 働いて います **hataraite imasu** (*hahtahraheeté'eemahs'*). For the first time, we have here an example of the other grand series of Japanese verbs. Until now it was the model …ます …**masu** (*mahs'*) and its variations (cf. Lesson 7, par. 1). For our second model, we have …て います …**te imasu** (*té eemahs'*) and variations. This lets us know that the action the verb describes is in fact happening at the moment of speech. バ ー で 働いて います **bā de hataraite imasu** (*bah-déhah-tahraeeté'eemahs'*), *I work*, in the sense of "I am employed in such a place": "Currently, I am employed (at a bar)". This is a lot like -ing in English, though we use it for more than just things happening right at this moment.

③ We have seen で **de** (*dé*) used to indicate means (cf. Lesson 6, item 7). Here we have another use for で **de**, where it shows us the place an action takes place.

✳✳✳

11

<ruby>練<rt>れん</rt>習<rt>しゅう</rt></ruby> **renshū**

Exercise 1

❶ <ruby>夜<rt>よる</rt></ruby> <ruby>早<rt>はや</rt></ruby>く <ruby>寝<rt>ね</rt></ruby>ます。

yoru hayaku nemasu.

(yoroo hahyahkoo némahs')

❷ <ruby>昨日<rt>きのう</rt></ruby> <ruby>早<rt>はや</rt></ruby>く <ruby>起<rt>お</rt></ruby>きません でした。

kinō hayaku okimasen deshita.

(keeno- hahyahkoo okeemahsen déshtah)

❸ <ruby>八<rt>はち</rt></ruby> <ruby>時<rt>じ</rt></ruby> に <ruby>起<rt>お</rt></ruby>きます。

hachi ji ni okimasu.

(hahchee jee nee okeemahs')

✳✳✳

Exercise 2

...に <ruby>言葉<rt>ことば</rt></ruby> を <ruby>入<rt>い</rt></ruby>れ なさい

❶ I work in a store.

mise .. hataraite imasu

❷ What time do you wake up?

. . . . okimasu ..

❸ Do you go to bed early?

. . . . . . nemasu ka

❹ My friend is coming at 1 o'clock.

tomodachi ga . . . . kimasu

❺ What do you do at night?

. . . . shimasu ka

❹ どこ で 働いて います か。

doko de hataraite imasu ka.
(doko dé hahtahraheeté eemahs' kah)

❺ 何 時 に 買物 に 行きます か。

nan ji ni kaimono ni ikimasu ka.
(nan jee nee kaheemono nee eekeemahs' kah)

❻ テレビ を 見ません か。

terebi o mimasen ka.
(térébee o meemahsen kah)

Answers to Exercise 1

❶ At night I go to bed early. ❷ Yesterday I did not get up early. ❸ I get up at 8 o'clock. ❹ Where do you work? ❺ What time do (will) you go shopping? ❻ You don't watch television?

***

夜 何時 に 寝ます か。

HOUHOUHOU...

Answers to Exercise 2

❶ – de –. ❷ nan ji ni – ka. ❸ hayaku –. ❹ – ichi ji ni –. ❺ yoru nani o –.

だい じゅう に か
第十二課 dai jū ni ka *(dai ju- nee kah)*

喫茶店

きっ さ てん

kis sa ten

(kee'sahten)

1 – こんにち は。①
ko n ni chi wa.
(konneechee wah)

2 – こんにち は。
ko n ni chi wa.
(konneechee wah)

3 – あそこ の 喫茶店 へ

きっ さ てん

a so ko no kis sa ten e
(ahsoko no kee'sahten é

い
行きましょう。
i ki ma shō.
eekeemahsho-)

4 – いらっしゃいませ。②
i ra s sha i ma se.
(eerah'shaheemahsé)

5 – 山田 さん は 何 に しますか。③④

やま だ　　　　　　　　　なに

yama da sa n wa nani ni shi ma su ka.
(yahmahdah san wah nanee nee sheemahs' kah)

Lesson Twelve *(-th / ten-two / lesson)*   **12**

In the Café
(café)

1 – Hello!
2 – Hello!
3 – Let's go in that café.
(over there / [relation] / café / [destination] / let's go)
4 – Welcome!
5 – What will you have Mrs Yamada?
(Yamada-Mrs. / [announce] / what / [goal] / do)

ೋೃಞೕಞ

Notes

① Here is another way to greet someone. We have seen おはよう ございます **ohayō gozaimasu** *(ohahyo- gozaheemahs')* (cf. Lesson 3, note 1), but こんにち は **konnichi wa** *(konnee-chee wah)* is reserved for meeting someone during the day, roughly the same as *good day* or *hello*.

② This is the ritual greeting reserved for waiters in a café or restaurant, or salespersons in shops, when welcoming clients and customers. Literally, it means: "Please come in".

③ The word さん **san** *(san)* has to follow the proper name of the person to whom you are speaking, but never your own. To speak of yourself, you just need to say your own name. In general, outside the family, Japanese speakers rarely use the word that means "you", but will address others by name, plus さん **san**.

④ Once again with に **ni** *(nee)*. Here we take the expression as a whole: …に します **...ni shimasu** *(nee sheemahs')*: *to decide on (something), to choose (something)*.

6 – 私　　は　　　コーヒー。⑤
watashi　wa　　kō　hī.
(wahtahshee wah ko-hee-)

7 – じゃあ、コーヒー　と　ビール
jaa,　　kō　hī　to　bī　ru
(jah- ko-hee- to bee-roo

を　下さい。
o　kuda sa i.
o koodahsai)

8 お菓子を食べ　ま　しょう　か。
o ka shi o ta be ma shō　　ka.
(o kahshee o tahbémahsho- kah)

9 – いいえ、　けっこう　です。⑥
i i e,　ke k kō　　de su.
(ee-é ké'ko- dés')

10 – 本当　です　か。
hon tō　de su　ka.
(honto- dés' kah)

11 – ええ、本当　に　けっこう　です。
e e,　hon tō　ni　ke k kō　　de su.
(é- honto- nee ké'ko- dés'

今　ダイエット　を　して　います。⑦
ima　da i e t to　　o　shi te　i ma su.
eemah daié'to o sheeté ee mahs')

Notes

⑤ 私 We have already seen the pronunciation **watakushi** (*wah-tahkooshee*) (Lesson 9, item 4), which is most common. But here, **watashi** (*wahtahshee*) is more familiar, and used most often by women. Of course, it still means *I, me*.

6 – I'll have a coffee.
(me / [announce] / coffee)

7 – Good, a coffee and a beer, please.
(good / coffee / and / beer / [object] / give)

8 Should we have some cake?
([familiarity]-snack / [object] / let's eat / [question])

9 – No, not for me, thanks.
(no / fine / it is)

10 – Really?
(true / it is / [question])

11 – Yes, really. Right now I'm on a diet.
(yes / true / [adverbial] / fine / it is) (now / diet / [object] / be doing)

ഇൽ ﻭﺯﻭﺯ

▸ ⑥ This is the usual expression to refuse something. Literally, it means "It's perfect the way it is, I don't need anything else."

⑦ しています **shite imasu** *(sheeté eemahs')* (cf. lesson 11, note 2), *right now, I'm doing...; currently, I'm doing...*

12

12 – ああ、そう です か。いつ
a a, sō de su ka. i tsu
(ah- so- dés' kah) (eetsoo

から。
ka ra.
kahrah)

13 – 昨日 から。
きのう
kinō ka ra.
(kino- kahrah)

□

***

Exercise 1

❶ お 菓子 も 食べます。
か し   た
o kashi mo tabemasu.
(o kahshee mo tahbémahs')

❷ コーヒー が 好き です か。
す
kōhī ga suki desu ka.
(ko-hee- gah s'kee dés' kah)

❸ 大好き です。
だい す
daisuki desu.
(dais'kee dés')

❹ あそこ の 店 で カメラ を 買いました。
みせ   か
asoko no mise de kamera o kaheemashita.
(ahsoko no meesé dé kahmérah o kaheemahshtah)

12 – Oh really? Since when?   **12**
(oh / so / it is / [question]) (when / since)

13 – Since yesterday.
(yesterday / since)

✳✳✳

❺ いつ から 働<ruby>働<rt>はたら</rt></ruby>いて います か。
itsu kara hataraite imasu ka.
(eetsoo kahrah hahtahraheeté eemahs' kah)

❻ わかりません。
wakarimasen.
(wahkahreemahsen)

Answers to Exercise 1

❶ I'll have the cakes, too. ❷ Do you like coffee? ❸ I love it. ❹ I bought a camera in the store over there. ❺ Since when have you been working. ❻ I don't know.

13 Exercise 2

...に 言葉 を 入れ なさい
こ と ば　い

Fill in the blanks with the missing words

❶ Hello.

. . . .

❷ Shall we buy apples, too?

ringo . . kai . . . . . ka

❸ I'm going to the store over there.

. . . . mise e ikimasu

---

13 第十三課 dai jū san ka *(dai ju- san kah)*
だい じゅう さん か

約束
やく そく
yaku soku
(yahkoosokoo)

1 – 今朝　フランス　人　の　友達
　　けさ　　　　　じん　　ともだち
　　kesa　　fu ra n su　jin　no tomo dachi
(késah fooransoojeen no tomodahchee

を　デパート　の　前　で　一
　　　　　　　　　まえ　　　いち
o　de pā to　no mae de　ichi
o dépah-to no mahé dé eechee

時間　待ちました。①②
じ かん　ま
ji kan　machi ma shi ta.
jeekan mahcheemahshtah)

④ Until when are you on a diet?

.... made daietto o shimasu ka

⑤ When did he come?

.... kima ..... ka

⑥ Do you like the movies?

eiga .... ka

Answers to Exercise 2

❶ konnichi wa. ❷ – mo – mashō –. ❸ asoko no –. ❹ itsu –.
❺ itsu – shita –. ❻ – ga suki desu –.

Lesson Thirteen *(-th / ten-three / lesson)* **13**

The Date
(date)

1 – This morning I waited for my French friend for
an hour in front of the department store.
*(this morning / France-person / [relation] / friend / [object] /
department store / [relation] / before / [place] / one-hour / waited)*

૭૦૦૩૪૦૦૩

Notes

① Without a doubt, after に **ni**, the particle that appears the
most is の **no**. This particle also has many different usages
and meanings. In this sentence, it indicates apposition: フラ
ンス人 の 友達 **furansujin no tomodachi** *(fooransoojeen
no tomodahchee)*: *French friend*, or, literally "friend *who is* a
French Person".

② A reminder: we use で **de** *(dé)* to indicate the place where an
action happens (cf. Lesson 11, note 3).

13

2 – 随分　待ちました　ね。
zuibun machimashita ne.
(zooeeboon mahcheemahshtah né)

3 – はい。
hai.
(hai)

4 – 来ました　か。
kimashita ka.
(keemahshtah kah)

5 – いいえ、来ません　でした。③
iie, kimasen deshita.
(ee-é keemahsen déshtah)

6 – どう　した　の　でしょう。
dō shita no de shō.
(do- shtah no désho-)

7 – わかりません。
wakarimasen.
(wahkahreemahsen)

8 – こまりました　ね。
komarimashita ne.
(komahreemahshtah né)

9 – ええ、買物　が　できません
ee, kaimono ga dekimasen
(é- kaheemono gah dékeemahsen

でした。
deshita.
déshtah)

10　今晩　友達　に　電話　を　します。④
konban tomodachi ni denwa o shimasu.
(konban tomodahchee nee denwah o sheemahs')　□

2 – You waited a long time!   **13**
(much / waited / [agreement])

3 – Yes

4 – Has he come?
(came / [question])

5 – No, he hasn't come.
(no / hasn't come)

6 – How can that be?
(how / did / that could be)

7 – I don't know.

8 – That's irritating.
(was annoyed / [agreement])

9 – Yes, I couldn't do my shopping.
(yes / shopping / [subject] / not have been possible)

10 I'll call him tonight.
(tonight / friend / [attribution] / telephone / [object] / do)

෨෬෫෬

Notes

③ cf. Lesson 8, note 7.

④ In English we have a slew of personal pronouns – he, him, she, her, they, them – to keep us from repeating the same name over and over again. Japanese doesn't bother with them... just repeat the name, and that's it. Also note in this passage yet another usage for に **ni**, for the person who is the recipient of the action.

練習 renshū

Exercise 1

❶ 買物 が できました か。
かい もの

kaimono ga dekimashita ka.
(kaheemono gah dékeemahshtah kah)

❷ アメリカ人 の 友達 が 来ました。
じん　　　とも だち　　き

amerikajin no tomodachi ga kimashita.
(ahméreekahjeen no tomodahchee gah keemahshtah)

❸ デパート の 中 で 待ちました。
なか　　ま

depāto no naka de machimashita.
(dépah-to no nahkah dé mahcheemahshtah)

***

Exercise 2

...に 言葉 を 入れ なさい
こと ば　　い

❶ I waited in front of the store.
mise .. .. machimashita

❷ Do you know how to make Chinese food?
chūka ryōri . . . . ka

❸ Did your American friend come?
amerika . . . . . tomodachi ga kimashita ka

❹ Tonight I'm going by bus to the movies.
. . . . . . basu .. eiga .. ikimasu

❺ I didn't wait.
machi . . . .

❹ 何 時間 待ちました か。
なん じ かん ま

nan jikan machimashita ka.
(nan jeekan mahcheemahshtah kah)

❺ わかりません。

wakarimasen.
(wahkahreemahsen)

❻ デパート に 行きません でした。
い

depāto ni ikimasen deshita.
(dépah-to nee eekeemahsen déshtah)

Answers to Exercise 1

❶ Did you do your shopping? ❷ My American friend has come.
❸ I waited in the department store. ❹ How many hours did you
wait? ❺ I don't know. ❻ I didn't go to the department store.

✳✳✳

❻ I waited for two hours.
　 ni ..... machimashita

Answers to Exercise 2

❶ – no mae de –. ❷ – ga dekimasu –. ❸. – jin no –. ❹ konban
– de – ni –. ❺ – masen deshita. ❻ – jikan –.

*Don't forget to read the Japanese phrases out loud. You're learning
how to speak, not how to mumble!*

まとめ
ma to me
(mahtomé)

Revision and Notes

Already Lesson 14! You see, we are making progress. And a little pause should do you well.

1. You will profit by having taken some time to go through all the orthographical rules rather thoroughly. In the preceding lessons, we've come across a few complicated syllables, such as **kyō**, **ryō**, **kyū**, **chū**, **jū**, and so on. In fact, these syllables are not of actual Japanese origin, but from when Japanese borrowed and adapted many Chinese words (we discussed this in the introduction, on page XII). There are two cases:

➤ Syllables with **sh** + **a**, **o**, **u**, and **ch** + **a**, **o**, **u**. In *kana*, there is only **shi** し and **chi** ち, but there is no **sha**, **sho**, **shu**, or **cha**, **cho**, **chu**. So we use **shi** し and **chi** ち followed by a small **ya** や, **yo**, よ, or **yu** ゆ:

sha しゃ	**sho** しょ	**shu** しゅ
cha ちゃ	**cho** ちょ	**chu** ちゅ

and if the **o** or **u** is long, then: **shō** しょう, **shū** しゅう, **chō** ちょう, and **chū** ちゅう.

➤ Syllables such as **kyō**, **kyū**; **ryō**, **ryū**. That is, a consonant + **y** + **o** or **u** (**a** is very rare). Here we take the *kana* representing the sound of the syllable followed by **i**: **ki** き, **ri** り, and add a small **yo** よ or **yu** ゆ. For instance:

kyo きょ	**kyu** きゅ	**ryo** りょ	**ryu** りゅ

and when the vowel is long, then:

kyō きょう   **kyū** きゅう   **ryō** りょう   **ryū** りゅう

In fact, it doesn't even matter which consonant the syllable begins with: **hyō** ひょう, **nyū** にゅう.

2. And now a little test to see if you're curious:

Let's take another look at item 9 of Lesson 10:

どちら が 好き です か **dochira ga suki desu ka** (*docheerah gah s'kee dés' kah*) and look at the two underlined *hiragana*. The first one is GA, the second one KA. Seem a bit familiar? The shape is identical, only there are a couple 'extra' dots on the GA. We find these little dots on the *hiragana* underlined with a dash: ど **do** and で **de** (*dé*). And if you look closely, you'll find these little dots all over the place on *hiragana*. Have you noticed? It's one of the ways the Japanese devised to enlarge the 46 signs that make up *katakana* and *hiragana* (cf. introduction, page IX). Here are the *kana* for syllables where the consonant is non-voiced: **ka**, **ta**, **shi**, **ho**: か、た、し、ほ in *hiragana*; and カ、タ、シ、ホ in *katakana*. And we just add two little dots to indicate when the syllable begins with a voiced consonant: が ガ **ga**, だ ダ **da**, じ ジ **ji**, ぼ ボ **bo**. And look again at Lesson 8, item 6, the title of the Chaplin film, *Modern Times*: モダン・タイムズ **mo***da***n-***tai***muzu**

To indicate that a syllable begins with a *p*, we use the *kana* for transcribing the consonant *h* and add a small circle. So the same symbol can be used three times –how's that for economical!

ha は ハ	**ba** ば バ	**pa** ぱ パ
hi ひ ヒ	**bi** び ビ	**pi** ぴ ピ

You'll find a complete table of the *kana* on pages 333 and 334.

14

3. Let's go back one more time to the particles, to reiterate the usages we have already learned for に **ni** and で **de** (*dé*). Two usages for で **de** (*dé*): to indicate means (cf. Lesson 13, item 6) バス で 来ました **basu de kimashita** (*bahs' dé keemahshtah*): *He came by [means of] bus*; and also to indicate the place where an action happens (Lesson 13, item 1):

デパート の 前 で 待ちました。

depāto no mae de machimashita
(dépah-to no mahé dé mahcheemahshtah)

I waited in front of the department store. The action is "to wait", and the place is "in front of the department store".

We have *five* usages for に **ni**!

➢ The place where something exists (cf. Lesson 6, item 8).
➢ To form an adverb, such as 一緒 に **issho ni**, *together*.
➢ An activity that represents the goal of motion (cf. Lesson 8, item 3):

映画 に 行きました

eiga ni ikimashita
(é-gah nee eekeemahshtah)

We went to the movies where "movies" does not mean "the movie theatre", but rather "the movies" as an activity.

➢ The person who is the recipient of an action (cf. Lesson 13, item 10):

友達 に 電話 を します。

tomodachi ni denwa o shimasu
(tomodahchee nee denwah o sheemahs')

I telephoned my friend.

➢ To indicate the time (cf. Lesson 11, items 1, 2, 4, 5, 6)

Over all, everything that marks something having to do with a specific point in time or in space (in, at), and as an adverbial suffix.

4. Without a doubt there is a sentence you have memorized –maybe without even knowing it –because it comes up so frequently. That is: そう です か **sō desu ka** (*so- dés' kah*). In the word-for-word translation, you have seen that it means そう "so" です "it is" か "[question]". In fact, it has become an expression the Japanese use endlessly simply to demonstrate that the listener is still paying attention to what the speaker is saying. It is kind of like our "Oh, really?" or "Oh, yeah?". And sometimes it changes a little bit: そう です ね **sō desu ne** (*so- dés' né*), which is stronger, as it demonstrates agreement and the listener actually taking part in the conversation (cf. Lesson 1, note 4). If you're listening to a speaker with whom you're familiar, you can abbreviate it to そう か **sō ka** (*so- kah*) or そう ね **sō ne** (*so- né*), but that's not advised with those you don't know well, or with those who might not take kindly to such an abbreviation! It's inevitable though that in dialogue in Japanese you will often come across this expression.

You are now about to begin the third series of lessons. That means you are well on your way to learning Japanese, and you surely have many questions. That is exactly the way it is going to continue. Don't worry right now about retention: above all, understand. Observe how the sentences are formed, take in each word with help from the translation and parenthetical explanation, and take in as much as possible. Your main task for the moment is to figure out "how it works". Of course, the sentences are almost the complete inverse of ours, and they can be a little difficult to follow, but the system has its own inscrutable logic. Just about always, it is a word, then a particle to indicate its function. And that is what you have got to take in.

And for the moment, don't worry about the writing; just continue to read and try to absorb the kana, *which* kana *corresponds to which syllable, and let your eyes do the work by getting used to it bit by bit. If you hesitate from time to time, then you can look at the table on pages 333 and 334 for your reference.*

But don't try to force yourself to retain anything. Look, absorb, understand, and in the process you will find that, before you know it, you have learned a lot of Japanese.

ೞഌൠ

15 第十五課 dai jū go ka *(dai ju- go kah)*

紹介
shō kai
(sho-kai)

1 – 小林　道子　と　申します。
ko bayashi michi ko　to　mō shimasu.
(kobahyahshee meecheeko to mo-sheemahs')

2 東京　に　住んで　います。
tō kyō　ni　su n de　i ma su.
(to-kyo- nee soondé eemahs')

3 三　年　前　に　結婚　しました。
san nen mae　ni　kek kon shi mashi ta.
(san nén mahé nee ke'kon sheemahshtah)

4 子供　が　二人　います。
ko domo　ga　futari　i ma su.
(kodomo gah f'tahree eemahs')

5 女　の　子　と　男　の　子　です。
onna no ko　to otoko no　ko　de su.
(o'nah no ko to otoko no ko dés')

6 – お嬢さん　は　いくつ　です　か ①②
o jō sa n　wa　i kutsu　de su　ka.
(ojo-san wah eekootsoo dés' kah)

Notes

① お嬢さん **o jō san** *(ojo-san)*. This word can only be used to talk about someone else's child, and never for a child of your own. It designates a daughter and can be used even with a girl ▶

Lesson Fifteen *(-th / ten-five / lesson)* **15**

Introduction

1 – My name is Michiko Kobayashi.
   (Kobayashi / Michiko / [quotation] / called)

2 I live in Tōkyō.
   (Tōkyō / [place] / live)

3 I have been married for three years.
   (three-years-before / [time] / marry-did)

4 I have two children.
   (child / [subject] / two people / exist)

5 One boy and one girl.
   (girl / and / boy / it is)

6 – How old is your daughter?
   (your daughter / [announce] / how much / it is / [question])

৪৩৪৩

▶ as old as 20. There are many cases in Japanese where there is one word to talk about something close to one's self, and another for talking about the same thing related to another person. The Japanese value politeness, which is both treating yourself humbly and treating others with respect, and this often shows up in these small differences in vocabulary.

② Now it is time to talk about the particle は **wa** (*wah*) that we have already seen here and there. It will likely cause a couple of problems, because it is unlike anything we use when speaking English.

To begin, we should note that it is pronounced **wa**, even though it's written with the *hiragana* は, which is usually pronounced **ha**. It is one of two *hiragana* with dual pronunciations (the other one is へ, pronounced **he** (*hé*) except when the particle indicates destination, when it's pronounced **e** (*é*)). This particle は **wa** has two usages. The first (Lesson 12, items 5 and 6), where it follows a name or a pronoun at the beginning of a sentence, serves to introduce the person or thing being spoken

7 – 今 十 五 歳 です。
ima jū go sai de su.
(eemah ju- go sai dés')

8 – え？
e?
(é)

9 – はい。 実 は 三 年 前 に
ha i. jitsu wa san nen mae ni
(hai jeetsoo wah san nen mahé nee

再婚 し ま した。 ②
sai kon shi ma shi ta.
saikon sheemahshtah)

10 – お坊ちゃん は いくつ です か。③
o bot cha n wa i ku tsu de su ka.
(obo'chan wah eekootsoo dés' kah)

11 – まだ 一 歳 です。
ma da is sai de su.
(mahdah ee'sai dés')

□

Notes

② of, as a new subject of conversation. Literally, お嬢さ
ん は いくつ です か **o jōsan wa ikutsu desu ka** (*ojo-
san wah eekootsoo dés' kah*) could be: "**Speaking of** your
daughter, how old is she?" And 私 は コーヒー **watashi
wa kōhī** (*wahtahshee wah ko-hee-*) would be "**As for me**,
coffee" (Lesson 12, item 6). In this book, we transcribe it as
"[announce]".

The second usage, following an adverb, is to strengthen the
sense of the adverb. We call this usage "[emphasis]". This is the
usage we come across in item 9 of this lesson. ▶

7 – Now she is 15 years old.
(now / ten-five-years old / it is)

8 – Huh?

9 – Yes. Actually, I remarried three years ago.
(yes) (really / [emphasis] / three-years-before / [time] / remarry-did)

10 – And how old is your little son?
(your little son / [announce] / how much / it is / [question])

11 – He's only one year old.
(yet / one-year old / it is)

ഇ൦൬ഽൟ

▶ And there, it's finished. The explanation might seem a little long, but this particle は **wa** (*wah*) is one of the keys of Japanese. Understand well what it means and you have already made a great leap. And you'll see, you're on the right track.

③ お坊ちゃん **obotchan** (*o bo'chahn*). cf. Note (1). Here is another word that specifically indicates someone else's child. It means *son*, but we use it only to talk of younger boys, under the age of 13 or 14.

練習 <ruby>れん<rt></rt></ruby><ruby>しゅう<rt></rt></ruby> renshū

Exercise 1

❶ 女 の 子 が います。
onna no ko ga imasu.
(o'nah no ko gah eemahs')

❷ いくつ です か。
ikutsu desu ka.
(eekootsoo dés' kah)

❸ 六 歳 です。
roku sai desu.
(rokoo sai dés')

❹ 今 どこ に 住んで います か。
ima doko ni sunde imasu ka.
(eemah doko nee soondé eemahs' kah)

✳✳✳

Exercise 2

... に 言葉 を 入れ なさい

❶ How old is your son?
obotchan wa . . . . ka

❷ Fifteen years old.
jū go . . . .

❸ I live in Tōkyō.
tōkyō . . . . imasu

15

❺ 二年前 に この カメラ を
ni nen mae ni kono kamera o
(nee nen mahé nee kono kahmérah o

買いました。
kaimashita.
kaheemahshtah)

Answers to Exercise 1
❶ I have a daughter. ❷ How old is she? ❸ Six years old.
❹ Where do you live now? ❺ I bought this camera two years ago.

✳✳✳

❹ I have two daughters.
onna no ko . . . . imasu

❺ I bought these glasses five years ago.
kono megane . . . . kaimashita

Answers to Exercise 2
❶ – ikutsu desu –. ❷ – sai desu. ❸ – ni sunde –. ❹ –ga futari –.
❺ – o go nen mae ni –.

16 第十六課 dai jū rok ka *(dai ju- ro'kah)*

日曜日
nichi yō bi
(neecheeyo-bee)

1 – 今日 は 日曜日 です。 ①
kyō wa nichi yō bi de su.
(kyo- wah neecheeyo-bee dés')

2 お 天気 が いい です ね。
o ten ki ga i i de su ne.
(o tenkee gah ee- dés' né)

3 ピクニック に 行きましょう か。
pi ku ni k ku ni i ki ma shō ka.
(peekoonee'koo nee eekeemahsho kah)

4 – いい です ね。
i i de su ne.
(ee- dés' né)

5 田中 さん と 山本 さん を
ta naka sa n to yama moto sa n o
(tanahkah san to yahmahmoto san o

誘いましょう。 ②
saso i ma shō.
sahsoeemahsho-)

Sunday

1 – Today is Sunday.
(today / [announce] / Sunday / it is)

2 The weather is nice.
([familiarity]-weather / [subject] / be good / it is / [agreement])

3 What if we had a picnic!
(picnic / [goal] / let's go / [question])

4 – Oh, that sounds good.
(good / it is / [agreement])

5 We could invite Mr. Tanaka and Miss Yamamoto!
(Tanaka-Mr. / and / Yamamoto-Miss / [object] / let's invite)

ഔഓഃഔ

ピクニック に 行きましょう か。

Notes

① cf. Lesson 15, note 2.

② The word さん **san** (*san*) must always follow the name of the person you are talking about, regardless of age or gender. But you **never** use it for yourself (see Lesson 15, item 1).

6 – ああ それ は いい 考え
a a　so re　wa　i i　kanga e
(ah- soré wah ee- kangahé

です ね。
de su　ne.
dés' né)

7 – どこ へ 行きましょう か。
do ko　e　i ki ma shō　ka.
(doko é eekeemahsho- kah)

8 – 江ノ島 は いかが です か。③
e no shima wa　i ka ga　de su　ka.
(énosheemah wah eekahgah dés' kah)

9 何 を 持って 行きましょう か。
nani o　mo tte　i ki ma shō　ka.
(nanee o mo'té eekeemahsho- kah)

10 – サンド・ウイッチ に お 寿司
sa n do　u i t chi　ni　o　su shi
(sando wee'chee nee o sooshee

に みかん に お 菓子。④⑤
ni　mi ka n　ni　o　ka shi.
nee meekan nee o kahshee)

11 子供 の ため に ジュース も
ko domo no ta me　ni　jū　su mo
(kodomo no tahme nee ju-su mo

持って 行きましょう。⑥
mo tte　i ki ma shō.
mo'té eekeemahsho-)

6 – Oh, that's a great idea!
(oh / that / [announce] / good / idea / it is / [agreement])

7 – Where shall we go?
(where / [destination] / let's go / [question])

8 – How about Enoshima?
(Enoshima / [announce] / how / it is / [question])

9 What should we bring?
(what / [object] / bring / go / [question])

10 – Sandwiches, sushi, tangerines, and cakes.
(sandwich / [addition] / [familiarity]-sushi / [addition] / tangerine / [addition] / [familiarity]-cakes)

11 Let's also bring juice for the children.
(children / [relation] / for / [adverbial] / juice / also / bring / let's go)

ৎ০৩৪৩৫

Notes

③ Enoshima is a little island (**shima** means *island*), roughly 4 kilometers (2 miles) around, located in Sagami Bay to the south of Tōkyō, close to Kamakura, a very popular spot for day trips for Tōkyō-ites.

④ This に **ni** (*nee*) just won't leave us alone. Here we have to look at it again, in yet another usage. Here, it serves to link many elements in a list, without a verb at the end. It is this に **ni**, for instance, that we use when we are ordering in a restaurant, as if we were adding things up.

⑤ 寿司 **sushi**. Sushi is one of the most typical Japanese dishes. Japanese eat those thin strips of raw fish on riceballs. A good sushi can cost you a lot since it is getting more and more difficult to find good quality fresh fish in Japan.

⑥ お願い します **onegai shimasu** (*onégahee sheemahs'*) is a very important and common expression in Japanese. It is used both as a general *please*, as in バターお願い します **bata-onegai shimasu** (*bahtah- onégahee sheemahs'*), *please pass the butter*, and this more ritualized 'please' as in 'Would you like some tea?' 'Yes, please'.

12 – 田中　さん　と　山本　さん　に
ta naka　sa n　to yamamoto　sa n　ni
(tanahkah san to yahmahmoto san nee

すぐ　電話　を　かけましょう。
su gu　den wa　o　ka ke ma　shō.
soogoo denwah o kahkemahsho-)

13 – はい。　おねがい　します。⑥
ha i.　o ne ga i　shi ma su.
(hai) (onégahee sheemahs')

□

***

練習　renshū

Exercise 1

❶ 今日 は お 天気 が いい です ね。
kyō wa o tenki ga ii desu ne.
(kyo- wah o tenkee gah ee- dés' né)

❷ サンド・ウイッチ を 持って
sando-uitchi o motte
(sando wee'chee o mo'té

行きましょう。
ikimashō.
eekeemahsho-)

❸ 山本 さん の 友達 を 誘いましょう。
yamamoto san no tomodachi o sasoimashō.
(yahmahmoto san no tomodahchee o sahsoeemahsho-)

12 – I'll call Mr. Tanaka and Miss Yamamoto right   **16**
away.
(Tanaka-Mr. / and / Yamamoto-Miss / [object] / right away /
telephone / [object] / use)

13 – Yes. Please.

***

④ 小林 さん の ため に 買いました。
kobayashi san no tame ni kaimashita.
(kobahyahshee san no tahme nee kaheemahshtah)

⑤ すぐ 行きましょう。
sugu ikimashō.
(soogoo eekeemahsho-)

Answers to Exercise 1
❶ The weather is nice today. **❷** I'll bring sandwiches. **❸** Let's invite Mr. Yamamoto's friend. **❹** I bought it for Mrs. Kobayashi. **❺** Let's go right away.

17 Exercise 2

…に 言葉 を 入れ なさい

❶ I telephoned Mr. Yamada.
yamada . . . . kakemashita

❷ Today is Sunday.
kyō . . . . desu

❸ I'm bringing books for my friend.
tomodachi . . . . hon o . . . . . ikimasu

---

17 第十七課
dai jū nana ka *(dai ju- nahnah kah)*

のみ の 市
no mi   no   ichi
(nomee no eechee)

1 – その 箱 の 右 の 茶碗 は
so no hako no migi no cha wan wa
(sono hahko no meegee no chahwan wah

いくら です か。
i ku ra   de su   ka.
eekoorah dés' kah)

2 – これ です か。
ko re   de su   ka.
(koré dés' kah)

3 – いいえ、その 左 の 茶碗 です。
i i e,   so no hidari no cha wan de su.
(ee-é sono heedahree no chahwan dés')

89 • hachi jū kyū

❹ I'll telephone right away.
.... denwa o ....

❺ Yes, please.
hai ....

Answers to Exercise 2
❶ – san ni denwa o –. ❷ – wa nichiyōbi –. ❸ – no tame ni – motte –.
❹ sugu – kakemasu. ❺ – onegai shimasu.

Lesson Seventeen *(-th / ten-seven / lesson)* **17**

The Flea Market
(flea / [relation] / market)

1 – How much is that teacup to the right of the box?
(that / box / [relation] / right / [relation] / teacup / [announce] / how much / it is / [question])

2 – This one?
(this one / it is / [question])

3 – No, the teacup, on the left.
(no / that one / left / [relation] / teacup / it is)

4 – ええ と・・・ これ は 三万円
e e to... ko re wa san man en
(é- to koré wah san man én

です。①
de su.
dés')

5 – 三万円 です か。 高い です
san man en de su ka. taka i de su
(san man én dés' kah) (tahkahee dés'

ね。
ne.
né)

6 – あ、 ごめん なさい。 三千円
a, go me n na sa i. san zen en
(ah gomen nahsai) (san zen en

です。
de su.
dés')

7 – ちょっと 見せて 下さい。
cho t to mi se te kuda sa i.
(cho'to meesété koodahsai)

8 – はい、 どうぞ。
ha i, dō zo.
(hai do-zo)

9 – 古い もの です か。
furu i mo no de su ka.
(foorooee mono dés' kah)

4 – Uhh... it's 30,000 yen.
  (uhh) (that / [announce] / three-10,000-yen / it is)

5 – 30,000 yen! That's expensive!
  (three-10,000-yen / it is / [question]) (be expensive / it is / [agreement])

6 – Oh, sorry! It's 3,000 yen.
  (oh / sorry) (three-1,000-yen / it is)

7 – Show it to me for a bit.
  (a bit / please show)

8 – Yes. Here.

9 – Is it old?
  (be ancient/ thing / it is / [question])

ೞೱೞೲ

Notes

① A 万 **man** (*man*) is a unit with four zeros: 1,0000 (= 10,000) that the Japanese employ on a daily basis, for example to indicate price. While the western counting system is based on thousand, the Asian system is based on ten-thousand. That is, while we say "ten, hundred, thousand, ten thousand, hundred thousand", the Japanese say *ten,* 十 **jū**; *hundred,* 百 **hyaku**; *thousand,* 千 **sen**; *ten-thousand,* 万 **man**; *ten ten-thousand,* 十万 **jū man**. While it takes a bit of getting used to, the Japanese method is just as simple as the Western style; you might want to imagine placing the comma after four zeros, instead of just after three, to help you visualize it better.

10 – そう　です　よ。　江戸　時代
　　　sō　　de su　yo.　　e do　ji dai
(so- dés' yo) (édo jeedai

の　もの　です。②③
no　mo no　de su.
no mono dés')

11 – では　これ　を　下さい。　はい
　　de wa　　ko re　　o　kuda sa i.　　ha i
(déwah koré o koodahsai) (hai

三　千　円。
san zen en.
san zen en)

12 – どうも　ありがとう　ございます。
　　　dō mo　a ri ga tō　　go za i ma su.
(do-mo ahreegahto- gozaheemahs')

13 – あれ。　茶碗　の　裏　に「Made
　　a re.　　cha wan　no　ura　ni　"Made
(ahre) (chahwan no oora nee "Made

In Hong Kong」と　書いて　ある。
In Hong Kong"　to　ka i te　a ru.
In Hong Kong" to kaheeté ahroo)

やられた。④
ya ra re ta.
(yahrahrétah)

10 – Oh, yes! It's from the Edo era.
(so / it is / [engagement]) (Edo-era / [relation] / thing / it is)

11 – Well, then I'll take it. Here's 3,000 yen.
(well / this / [object] / give) (yes / three-1,000-yen)

12 – Thank you very much.

13 – (alone) What?! On the bottom of teacup it says "Made In Hong Kong"! I've been had!
(what?!) (teacup / [relation] / bottom / [place] / "Made In Hong Kong" / [quotation] / be written) (have been done)

සටෙ⬭ටಣ

Notes

② cf. Lesson 14, revision and notes, paragraph 4.

③ In Japan, historical time is counted by historical epoch or period. The Edo era ran from 1603 to 1867. It was a period of peace, where Japan closed communication with the outside world. They created a modern society under a new economic and technological plan, and in the already very populous cities, developed all forms of art. Edo is also the ancient name for Tōkyō when the capitol of the country was in Kyōto.

④ Up until now, we have always seen the verb form that ends in ます **masu** (*mahs'*) and its derivatives. ある **aru** (*ahroo*) is the exact equivalent of あります **arimasu** (*ahreemahs'*), which we have seen so often. Similarly, the following やられた **yarareta** (*yahrahrétah*) is the equivalent of やられました **yararemashita** (*yahrahrémahshtah*), which is much more familiar to us. Why these differences? We will get to that in the revision chapter. For the moment, it is enough just to recognize them.

Don't forget: the key, for the moment, is understanding. From time to time, certain expressions will appear difficult. Don't let it worry you. They will be explained in greater detail later on... Everything will be covered! As they say in Japan: "You can't make flowers grow by pulling on them!" Be patient!

練習　renshū

Exercise 1

❶ この 魚 は 高い です ね。
kono sakana wa takai desu ne.
(kono sahkanah wah tahkai dés' né)

❷ ちょっと 待って 下さい。
chotto matte kudasai.
(cho'to mah'te koodahsai)

❸ 喫茶店 は すぐ 左 に あります。
kissaten wa sugu hidari ni arimasu.
(kee'sahten wah soogoo heedahree nee ahreemahs')

***

Exercise 2

... に 言葉 を 入れ なさい

❶ How much is it?
. . . .

❷ It's 20,000 yen.
. . . . . en desu

❸ It's on the right.
. . . . ni arimasu

❹ 右 の 本 を 見せて 下さい。
migi no hon o misete kudasai.
(meegee no hon o meesété koodahsai)

❺ カメラ屋 は デパート の 裏 に
kameraya wa depāto no ura ni
(kahmérahyah wah dépah-to no oorah nee

あります。
arimasu.
ahreemahs')

Answers to Exercise 1
❶ This fish is expensive! ❷ Wait just a moment, please. ❸ The café is immediately to your left. ❹ Show me the book on the right, please. ❺ The camera shop is located behind the department store.

✳✳✳

❹ It's on the left.
. . . . arimasu

❺ The teacup on the right, please.
. . . . . . chawan . . . .

Answers to Exercise 2
❶ ikura desu ka. ❷ ni man –. ❸ migi –. ❹ hidari ni –. ❺ migi no
– o kudasai.

第十八課
だい じゅう はっ か

dai jū hak ka *(dai ju- hah'kah)*

ほん や
本屋

hon ya
(hon yah)

1 – いらっしゃいませ。①
  i ra s sha i ma se.
  (eerah'shaheemahsé)

2 – トルストイ　の　「戦争　と
せん そう
  to ru su to i no sen sō to
  (toroosootoee no senso- to

へい わ
平和」　は　あります　か。
  hei wa wa a ri ma su ka.
  hé-wah wah ahreemahs' kah)

3 – 「戦争　と　平和」　です　か。
せん そう　　　へい わ
  sen sō to hei wa de su ka.
  (senso- to hé-wah dés' kah)

4 はい、　あります。
  ha i, a ri ma su.
  (hai ahreemahs')

5 しょうしょう　お　待ち　下さい。
ま　　　　くだ
  shō shō o ma chi kuda sa i.
  (sho-sho- o mahchee koodahsai)

Notes

① cf. Lesson 12, note 2. The method for greeting a customer.

At the bookstore
(bookstore)

1 – Greetings!
(enter)

2 – Do you have Tolstoy's *War and Peace*?
(Tolstoy / [relation] / war / and / peace / [announce] / exist / [question])

3 – *War and Peace*?
(war / and / peace / it is / [question])

4 Yes, I have it.
(yes / exist)

5 Please wait a moment.
(a bit / please wait)

ଽୠଔଽୠଔ

実 は 今 家内 が 留守 です。

6 – それから 料理 の 本 を
so re ka ra ryō ri no hon o
(sorékahrah ryo-ree no hon o

見せて 下さい。
mi se te kuda sa i.
meesété koodahsai)

7 – 日本 料理 です か、フランス
ni hon ryō ri de su ka, fu ra n su
(neehon ryo-ree dés' kah fooransoo

料理 です か、中華 料理
ryō ri de su ka, chū ka ryō ri
ryo-ree dés'kah chu-kah ryo-ree

です か。②③
de su ka.
dés' kah)

8 – 実 は 今 家内 が 留守 です。④
jitsu wa ima ka nai ga ru su de su.
(jeetsoo wah eemah kanai gah roosoo dés')

9 自分 で 料理 を しなければ
ji bun de ryō ri o shi na ke re ba
(jeeboon dé ryo-ree o sheenahkérébah

なりません。
na ri ma se n.
nahreemahsen)

10 – それでは この 本 を おすすめ
so re de wa ko no hon o o su su me
(sorédéwah kono hon o osoosoomé

します。
shi ma su.
sheemahs')

6 – And then, could you show me a cookbook? **18**
(and then / cooking / [relation] / book / [object] / please show)

7 – Japanese cuisine, French cuisine, Chinese cuisine?
(Japan-cooking / it is / [question] / France-cooking / it is / [question] / Chinese-cooking / it is / [question])

8 – It's just that my wife is away.
(actually / [emphasis] / now / my wife / [subject] / absence / it is)

9 I have to do the cooking myself.
(oneself / [means] / cooking / [object] / I must do)

10 – In that case, I recommend this book.
(in that case / this / book / [object] / [polite]-recommendation-do)

ഔരുജ്ഞ

Notes

② In 日本料理 **nihon ryōri** (*neehon ryo-ree*) and フランス料理 **furansu ryōri** (*fooransoo ryo-ree*), 日本 **nihon** (*neehohn*) and フランス **furansu** (*fooransoo*) are indeed the names for Japan and France, respectively. But for 中華料理 **chūka ryōri** (*chu-kah ryo-ree*), the 中華 **chūka** (*chu-kah*) cannot be used separately. To refer to the country China, we use another word: 中国 **chūgoku** (*chu-gokoo*).

③ In English we can say "Is it this **or** that?", "Is it like this **or** like that?". In Japanese, we have to repeat the entire phrase, adding です か **desu ka** (*dés' kah*) each time. It's like saying "Is it like this or is it like that?".

④ 家内 **kanai** (*kanai*): *my wife*. This term cannot be used to speak of anyone else's wife. It's the same situation as in Lesson 15 (cf. Lesson 15, notes 1 and 3).

11 実 は 私 も これ で
jitsu wa watakushi mo ko re de
(jeetsoo wah wahtahkooshee mo koré dé

作ります。
tsuku ri ma su.
tsookooreemahs')

12 簡単 に できます。
kan tan ni de ki ma su.
(kantan nee dékeemahs')

13 – それでは これ に します。
so re dewa ko re ni shi ma su.
(sorédéwah koré nee sheemahs')

14 – 毎度 ありがとう ございます。⑤
mai do a ri ga tō go za i ma su.
(maido ahreegahto- gozaheemahs') □

***

練習 renshū

Exercise 1

❶ 家内 です。
kanai desu.
(kanai dés')

❷ 今 山田 さん は 留守 です。
ima yamada san wa rusu desu.
(eemah yahmahdah san wah roosoo dés')

❸ これ は 魚 です か、肉 です か。
kore wa sakana desu ka, niku desu ka.
(koré wah sahkanah dés' kah neekoo dés' kah)

11   In fact, I use this myself.
       (in fact / [emphasis] / me / also / this / [means] / make)
12   It's really very easy.
       (easy / [adverbial] / be possible)
13 – Well then I'll take it.
       (well / this / [goal] / do)
14 – Thank you very much.

ೞഝ

Notes

⑤ When we have a scene that takes place in a store, we will find
   phrases usually employed by salespeople, generally reserved for
   their use only. ありがとう ございます **arigatō gozaimasu**
   (*ahreegahto- gozaheemahs'*) is one of the ways to say *thank
   you*. But 毎度 ありがとう ございます **maido arigatō
   gozaimasu** (*maido ahreegahto- gozaheemahs'*) literally
   means: "For every time (that you come here), thank you", and
   is a phrase exclusively used by salespeople. It is not for you,
   unless you work in a store in Japan!

✳✳✳

❹ お 菓子 を 自分 で 作ります。
   o kashi o jibun de tsukurimasu.
   (o kahshee o jeeboon dé tsookooreemahs')

❺ 映画 の 本 を 見せて 下さい。
   eiga no hon o misete kudasai.
   (é-gah no hon o meesété koodahsai)

Answers to Exercise 1

❶ This is my wife. ❷ Mr. Yamada is away right now. ❸ Is this fish
or meat? ❹ I make my own cakes myself. ❺ Please show me a book
on the movies.

19 **Exercise 2**

...に 言葉 を 入れ なさい

❶ Is that a boy or a girl?

otoko no ko . . . . . . onna no ko . . . . . .

❷ I'll take this book.

. . . . hon . . . .

❸ Me too, my wife is also away.

watakushi . . . . ga rusu desu

---

19 第十九課
dai jū kyū ka *(dai ju- kyu- kah)*

コンサート
ko n sā to
(kon sah- to)

1 – この　　うつくしい　人　は　　だれ
ko no　　u tsu ku shi i　hito　wa　　da re
(kono ootsookooshee- h'to wah dahré

です　　か。
de su　　ka.
dés' kah)

2 – この　写真　の　人　　です　　か。
ko no　sha shin　no　hito　de su　　ka.
(kono shahsheen no h'to dés' kah)

④ Have you got *War and Peace*?   **19**
「sensō to heiwa」 . . . . ka

⑤ Is this *War and Peace*?
「sensō to heiwa」 . . . . ka

Answers to Exercise 2

① – desu ka – desu ka. ② kono – ni shimasu. ③ – mo kanai –. ④ – wa arimasu –. ⑤ – desu –.

Lesson Nineteen *(-th / ten-nine / lesson)*   **19**

The Concert
(concert)

1 – Who is this beautiful person?
(this / be beautiful / person / [announce] / who / it is / [question])

2 – The young woman in the photo?
(this / photo / [relation] / person / it is / [question])

ざんねん です ね。

19

3 – はい、そう です。
ha i, sō de su.
(hai so- dés')

4 – 山口 文子 です。 ①
yama guchi fumi ko de su.
(yahmahgoochee foomeeko dés')

5 – 女優 です か。
jo yū de su ka.
(joyu- dés' kah)

6 – いいえ、女優 では ありません。
i i e, jo yū de wa a ri ma se n.
(ee-é joyu- dé wah ahreemahsen)

歌手 です。 ②
ka shu de su.
(kahshoo dés')

7 – どんな 歌 を 歌います か。
do n na uta o uta i ma su ka.
(do'nah ootah o ootah ee mahs' kah)

8 – ジャズ です。
ja zu de su.
(jazoo dés')

9 こんど の 土曜日 に サン・
ko n do no do yō bi ni sa n
(kondo no doyo-bee nee san

プラザ で コンサート が あります。
pu ra za de ko n sā to ga a ri ma su.
p'rahzah dé konsah-to gah ahreemahs')

一緒 に いかが です か。 ③
is sho ni i ka ga de su ka.
(ee'sho- nee eekahgah dés' kah)

3 – Yes, that's right.   **19**

4 – That's Yamaguchi Fumiko.
(Yamaguchi / Fumiko / it is)

5 – Is she an actress?
(actress / it is / [question])

6 – No, she's not an actress. She's a singer.
(no / actress / isn't) (singer / it is)

7 – What kind of music does she sing?
(what kind of / song / [object] / sing / [question])

8 – Jazz.
(jazz / it is)

9 Next Saturday she's having a concert at San
Plazza. Shall we go together?
*(next time / [relation] / Saturday / [time] / San Plazza /
[place] / concert / [subject] / exist) (together / [adverbial] /
how / it is / [question])*

ஐஂ௸௸ஂ௸

Notes

① The only instant the name of a person is not followed by さん
san (*san*) is when it is the name of a celebrity or well-known
person. Just as in English we would never say "Mister William
Shakespeare", in Japanese you don't need the さん **san**. And
remember, the last name **always** goes first in Japanese, given
name second.

② で は ありません **de wa arimasen** (*dé wah ahreemahsen*).
It's a bit long, but it's nothing more than the negative equivalent
of です **desu** (*dés'*). です **desu**: *it is*; で は ありません
de wa arimaen: *it isn't*.

③ サン・プラザ **san puraza** (*san p'rah zah*), *San Plazza*, a
popular concert hall, is located in Nakano, one of the western
districts of Tōkyō.

19

10 – とても　ざんねん　です　が、
to te mo　za n ne n　de su　ga,
(totémo za'nen dés' gah

都合　が　わるい　です。
tsu gō　ga　wa ru i　de su.
tsoogo- gah wahrooee dés')

11 – ざんねん　です　ね。　写真　より
za n ne n　de su　ne.　sha shin yo ri
(za'nen dés' né) (shahsheen yoree

もっと　うつくしい　人　です　よ。
mo t to　u tsu ku shi i　hito　de su　yo.
mo'to ootsookooshee- h'to dés' yo)

12 – ほんとう？約束　を　やめよう
ho n tō?　yaku soku　o　ya me yō
(honto-) (yahkoosokoo o yahméyo-

か　な。　でも　それ　は　むり
ka na.　demo　so re　wa　mu ri
kah nah) (démo soré wah mooree

だ　なあ。④⑤
da　na a.
dah nah-)

13 – それでは　また　この　次　の
so re de wa　ma ta　ko no　tsugi　no
(sorédéwah mahtah kono tsoogee no

機会　に　お　誘い　しましょう。
ki kai　ni　o　saso i　shi ma shō.
keekai nee o sahsoee sheemahsho-)

14 – ぜひ　おねがい　します。
ze hi　o ne ga i　shi ma su.
(zéhee onégahee sheemahs')

10 –   It's really too bad, but I can't go.   **19**
    (very / too bad / it is / but / convenience / [subject] / be bad /
    it is)

11 –   That's too bad. She's more beautiful in person
    than in the photo!
    (too bad / it is / [agreement]) (photo / more than / much
    more / be ravishing / person / it is / [engagement])

12 –   Really? I wonder if I should cancel my plans…
    But no, I guess I can't.
    (really) (promise / [object] / let's quit / [question] / [reflection])
    (but / that / [announce] / impossible / it is / [reflection])

13 –   Well, then I'll just take you next time.
    (well / anew / this / next / [relation] / occasion / [time] /
    [polite]-invite-do)

14 –   Oh, yes, please!
    (absolutely / please)

ॐ ಚಿ ಚಿ ॐ

Notes

④ やめよう **yameyō** (*yahméyo-*). Until now, all verbs translated
as "let's go" or "let's eat", etc., have ended in ましょう **mashō**
(*mahsho-*). Here is another form to say the same thing. Likewise
だ **da** (*dah*) is another way of saying です **desu**, and means exactly
the same thing. We'll soon get to a full explanation of these forms…
just a bit of suspense, until paragraph 4 of Lesson 21.

⑤ Remember those little words we find at the end of sentences,
those final particles that give a certain nuance to what has just
been said? We have seen ね **ne** (*né*) (Lesson 1, note 4), and
then we saw よ **yo** (*yo*), (Lesson 2, note 3). And now, here is
な **na** (*nah*), which you will use very often when speaking to
yourself, or when you are thinking out loud. In the word-for-
word translation, we note it with a [reflection].

練習 <ruby>練<rt>れん</rt></ruby><ruby>習<rt>しゅう</rt></ruby> **renshū**

Exercise 1

❶ ビール は いかが です か。
bīru wa ikaga desu ka.
(bee-roo wah eekahgah dés' kah)

❷ <ruby>今<rt>こん</rt></ruby><ruby>度<rt>ど</rt></ruby> の <ruby>日<rt>にち</rt></ruby><ruby>曜<rt>よう</rt></ruby><ruby>日<rt>び</rt></ruby> に どこ へ <ruby>行<rt>い</rt></ruby>きます か。
kondo no nichiyōbi ni doko e ikimasu ka.
(kondo no neecheeyo-bee nee doko é eekeemahs' kah)

❸ どんな <ruby>映<rt>えい</rt></ruby><ruby>画<rt>が</rt></ruby> が <ruby>好<rt>す</rt></ruby>き です か。
donna eiga ga suki desu ka.
(do'nah é-gah gah sookee dés' kah)

***

Exercise 2

... に <ruby>言<rt>こと</rt></ruby><ruby>葉<rt>ば</rt></ruby> を <ruby>入<rt>い</rt></ruby>れ なさい

❶ Is today Saturday or Sunday?
... wa . . . . . . desu ka, ... desu ka

❷ What kind of person is that?
. . . . desu ka

❸ Who is this person?
kono . . . . wa . . . . desu ka

❹ That's not a café, that's a bookstore.
kissaten . . . ., ... desu

❹ 私 は 都合 が いい です。

わたくし — つ ごう

watakushi wa tsugō ga ii desu.

(wahtahkooshee wah tsoogo- gah ee- dés')

❺ 昨日 より 暑い です ね。

き のう — あつ

kinō yori atsui desu ne.

(keeno- yoree ahtsooee dés' né)

Answers to Exercise 1

❶ How would you like a beer? ❷ Where are you going next Sunday?
❸ What sort of movies do you like? ❹ That's a convenient time for
me. ❺ It's hotter than yesterday.

✱✱✱

❺ The soap-operas are more amusing than the news.

hōmu-dorama wa nyūshu . . . .
desu

Answers to Exercise 2

❶ kyō – doyōbi –. nichiyōbi –. ❷ donna hito –. ❸ – hito – dare –.
❹ – de wa arimasen, honya –. ❺ – yori omoshiroi –.

だい に じゅっ か
第二十課
dai ni juk ka *(dai nee ju'kah)*

きん えん
禁煙
kin en
(keenen)

1 – この 辺 に タバコ屋 が
ko no hen ni ta ba ko ya ga
(kono hen nee tahbahkoyah gah

あります か。
a ri ma su ka.
ahreemahs' kah)

2 – あります。
a ri ma su.
(ahreemahs')

とお
3 – 遠い です か。
too i de su ka.
(to-ee dés' kah)

4 – いいえ、そんな に 遠く
i i e, so n na ni too ku
(ee-é sonnah nee to-koo

ありません。①
a ri ma se n.
ahreemahsen)

5 – どこ です か。
do ko de su ka.
(doko dés' kah)

No Smoking

1 – Is there a tobacco shop nearby?
(this / area / [place] / tobacco shop / [subject] / exist / [question])

2 – Yes.
(exist)

3 – Is it far?
(be far / it is / [question])

4 – No, not very.
(no / so / [adverbial] / not be far)

5 – Where is it?
(where / it is / [question])

ありがとう ございます。
たすかりました。

Notes

① 遠い **tooi** *(to-ee)*, *to be far*; 遠く ありません **tooku arimasen** *(to-koo ahreemahs')*, *not to be far*. Yes, you have probably already figured it out. To negate an adjective, you replace the final い **i** *(ee)* with a く **ku** *(ku)* and add ありません **arimasen** *(ahreemahsen)*. Try it with 古い **furui** *(foorooee)*, *old, ancient*, which we have seen in Lesson 17, item 9. *Not old* is... 古く ありません **furuku arimasen** *(foorookoo ahree-mahsen)*. Well done!

6 – 本屋 の 隣 です。
hon ya　no　tonari　de su.
(honyah no tonahree dés')

7 まず この 道 を まっすぐ
ma zu　ko no　michi　o　ma s su gu
(mahzoo kono meechee o mah'soogoo

行きます。②
i ki ma su.
eekeemahs')

8 それから 左 に まがります。
so re ka ra　hidari　ni　ma ga ri ma su.
(sorékahrah heedahree nee mahgahreemahs')

9 右側 に 大きい 本屋 が
migi gawa　ni　oo ki i　hon ya　ga
(meegeegahwah nee o-kee- hohnyah gah

あります。
a ri ma su.
ahreemahs')

10 その 隣 です。
so no tonari de su.
(sono tonahree dés')

11 – ありがとう ございます。
a ri ga tō ' go za i ma su.
(ahreegahto- gozaheemahs')

たすかりました。
ta su ka ri mashi ta.
(tahsookahreemahsheetah)

6 –   Next to the bookstore.
      (bookstore / [relation] / neighbor / it is)

7   First you take this road, straight ahead.
      (first / this / road / [object] / straight ahead / go)

8   Then turn left.
      (then / left / [place] / turn)

9   On the right there is a large bookstore.
      (right side / [place] / be big / bookstore / [subject] / exist)

10   It's right next-door.
      (of this / neighbor / it is)

11 – Thank you. I am saved!

ฬงคงฆ

Notes

② It may seem a bit strange to find that in Japanese, you say "go a
  road" 道 を 行きます **michi o ikimasu** (*meechee o eekeemahs'*), in stead of go 'on' or 'by' a road. It is not that odd,
  however, if you think about how we say "take this road," or
  "walk the plank," where we use the same kind of construction.

12 三日前 から 禁煙 して いました
mik ka mae ka ra kin en shi te i ma shi ta
(mee'kah mahé kahrah keenen sheeté eemahshtah

が、 続きません でした。
ga, tsuzu ki ma se n de shi ta.
gah tsoozookeemahsen déshtah)

13 – つらい です ね。 僕 も 禁煙
tsu ra i de su ne. boku mo kin en
(tsoorai dés' né) (bokoo mo keenen

して います が、 タバコ が
shi te i ma su ga, ta ba ko ga
shté eemahs' gah tahbahko gah

すいたい な。③④
su i ta i na.
sooeetai nah)

14 – それでは 一緒 に タバコ屋 へ
so re de wa is sho ni ta ba ko ya e
(sorédéwah ee'sho nee tahbahkoyah é

行きましょう。
i ki ma shō.
eekeemahsho-)

☐

***

12 I quit smoking three days ago, but I didn't stick to it. **20**
(three days-before / since / quitting smoking-was doing / but / didn't continue)

13 – Yes, it's hard. I quit smoking, too, but... I want a cigarette!
(be painful / it is / [agreement]) (I / too / quitting smoking-be doing / but / cigarette / [subject] / be object of desire of smoking / [reflection])

14 – Well then let's go to the tobacco shop together!
(then / together / [adverbial] / tobacco shop / [destination] / let's go)

ಬಂಛಲಾಡಚ

Notes

③ In English, when we speak of ourselves, we have "I / me / myself" and that's it. In Japanese, as you have no doubt noticed, these words are not used very often. Moreover, there are more ways of saying "I / me". We have already seen, for instance, 私 **watakushi** (*wahtahkooshee*) (Lesson 9, item 4; Lesson 12, item 6; Lesson 18, item 11). 私 **watakushi** can be used by both men and women, but 僕 **boku** (*bokoo*), which we have here, can **only be used by men**. It's also quite informal, usually used among men, in a casual situation.

④ タバコ **tabako** (*tahbahko*) obviously comes from our word "tobacco", but be careful, because タバコ **tabako** (*tahbahko*) actually means *cigarette*.

✳✳✳

20

<ruby>練<rt>れん</rt></ruby><ruby>習<rt>しゅう</rt></ruby> **renshū**

Exercise 1

❶ <ruby>今<rt>いま</rt></ruby> <ruby>何<rt>なに</rt></ruby> を して います か。
ima nani o shite imasu ka.
(eemah nanee o sheeté eemahs' kah)

❷ <ruby>二<rt>に</rt></ruby> <ruby>十<rt>じゅう</rt></ruby> <ruby>年<rt>ねん</rt></ruby><ruby>前<rt>まえ</rt></ruby> から <ruby>東京<rt>とうきょう</rt></ruby> に <ruby>住<rt>す</rt></ruby>んで います。
ni jū nen mae kara tōkyō ni sunde imasu.
(nee ju- nen mahé kahrah to-kyo- nee soondé eemahs')

❸ <ruby>田中<rt>たなか</rt></ruby> さん を <ruby>待<rt>ま</rt></ruby>って います が、<ruby>来<rt>き</rt></ruby>ません。
tanaka san o matte imasu ga, kimasen.
(tanahkah san o mah'te eemahs' gah keemahsen)

***

Exercise 2

... に <ruby>言葉<rt>ことば</rt></ruby> を <ruby>入<rt>い</rt></ruby>れ なさい

❶ That's not fun.
omoshiro . . . .

❷ I'm having my breakfast.
chōshoku o tabe . . . .

❸ It's a big bookstore.
. . . .

❹ I've worked in this store for 8 years.
. . . . kono mise de hataraite
imasu

❹ 本屋 は 喫茶店 の 隣 に あります。
<small>ほん や　　　　きっ さ てん　　　　となり</small>

honya wa kissaten no tonari ni arimasu.

(honyah wah kee'sahten no tonahree nee ahreemahs')

❺ この トランク は そんな に 高く ありません。
<small>たか</small>

kono toranku wa sonna ni takaku arimasen.

(kono torankoo wah so'nah nee tahkahkoo ahreemahsen)

Answers to Exercise 1

❶ What are you doing right now? ❷ I've lived in Tōkyō for 20 years. ❸ I'm waiting for Mr. Tanaka, but he doesn't come. ❹ The bookstore is next to the café. ❺ This trunk is not really expensive.

✳✳✳

❺ Is it the street on the right or on the left?

.... no michi desu ka, ... desu ka

Answers to Exercise 2

❶ – ku arimasen. ❷ – te imasu. ❸ ookii honya desu. ❹ hachi nen mae kara –. ❺ migi – hidari no michi –.

21 第二十一課
dai ni jū ikka *(dai nee ju- ee'kah)*

まとめ
matome

Revision and Notes

A little break will always do us good! As we all know, the difficult thing is not to begin, but to continue. And to continue, we have to be certain we have a strong foundation. These revision and notes chapters are here for that purpose, so read them carefully and attentively. It is probably a good idea to take a little time and go back to some of the notes and sentence patterns we mentioned in the revision chapters. That is how you can be sure of your pursuit of excellence in Japanese.

1. By now you should already be pretty familiar with the syllabic writing system, at least for the *hiragana*. So we will begin this lesson with a bit of discussion on the Chinese characters, which in Japanese we call *kanji*, which is literally: 漢 **kan** = *Chinese* and 字 **ji** = *character*. You were warned, at the beginning, that these would be a little tough, and by now you can tell you haven't been tricked! But little by little we will take apart all the mystery.

What are not complicated are the nouns. Of course, for each noun, there is one (or often two) different *kanji* (the most common first). Let's take a look at the first nouns we met in Lesson 17:

➤ *Box*, pronounced **hako**, is written 箱; inversely, the character 箱 means *box* and is pronounced, in Japanese, **hako**.

➤ *Right* is pronounced **migi** (*meegee*) and written 右; or we could say that 右 means *right* and is pronounced **migi**.

Lesson Twenty-One (-th / two-ten-one / lesson) **21**

There, those are the most simple: one character for one word. But now take the words that show up in Lesson 18. We will find a lot of compound words in *kanji*, but the principle is the same:

➤ *War* is pronounced **sensō** (*senso-*) and written 戦争; the first character is pronounced **sen** (*sen*), the second, **sō** (*so-*).

➤ *Peace* is pronounced **heiwa** (*hé-wah*) and written 平和; the first character is pronounced **hei** (*he-*), the second, **wa** (*wah*).

Take a look at some of the other nouns from Lesson 18: the title, 本屋 **honya** and 料理 **ryōri** (item 6), 家内 **kanai** and 留守 **rusu** (item 8), and 自分 **jibun** (item 9). They are all composed in the same fashion. And that is the most frequent usage: two characters for one word, though sometimes even more... We have already seen one word written with three *kanji*: 喫茶店 **kissaten**. The first *kanji*, 喫 means *to drink*, the second 茶 *tea*, and the third 店 *store*. So 喫茶店 **kissaten** is a *café*. But look at the last character, 店. Here, in a compound word, it's pronounced **ten** (*ten*). Now look back at Lesson 6, item 10, and you will find the same character. But it is pronounced **mise** (*meesé*). You will remember what we discussed in the introduction, that it is a given for Japanese that most characters have more than one pronunciation. In general, the pronunciation of a character will only change depending on whether it is used alone or as a part of a compound word. The character 店 is pronounced **ten** when part of a compound word, but **mise** when standing alone. But don't panic! It is much more simple than it seems. And never forget, what is most important right now is just **to understand**. And if you are attentive, you will always notice when the same character is pronounced differently. And now you have the explanation.

2. Adjectives. Now that we are beginning to be introduced to longer sentences, we are finding words that are very much like our adjectives, but not exactly. These words can take different forms –for instance the negative form (cf. lesson 20, note 1). You can negate an adjective easily by dropping the final *i* and adding く　ありません **ku arimasen** (*koo ahreemahsen*). The only adjective you have to pay special attention to is いい **ii**, *to be good*. It has a twin, よい **yoi** (*yoee*), which means the same thing, but it is on this twin that we make the negative: よく　ありません **yoku arimasen** (*yokoo ahreemahsen*). Fortunately, Japanese is like English in that the adjective always comes before the noun:

> An *ancient thing*: 古い もの **furui mono** (*foorooee mono*)
> **furui** = *be ancient*; **mono** = *thing* (cf. Lesson 17, item 9)

> A *large bookstore*: 大きい 本屋 **ookii honya** (*o-kee- honyah*)
> **ookii** = *large*; **honya** = *bookstore*

> A *beautiful woman*: うつくしい 人 **utsukushii hito** (*ootsoo-kooshee- h'to*)
> **utstukushi** = *beautiful*; **hito** = *person* (cf. Lesson 19, item 1 and Lesson 16, item 6)

3. Particles. In the last cycle of chapters we have come across two new particles: は **wa** (*wah*) and より **yori** (*yoree*). And guess what? They are the last two!

より **yori** is used only when one is making a comparison such as "more… than" (cf. Lesson 19, item 11). As for は **wa**, it is one of the keystones of the Japanese sentence, and we will see it often. Best thing to do is go back every once in a while and re-read the explanation in Lesson 15, note 2.

4. Verbs. Let's go back for a moment to the verb forms used in Lesson 17, item 13, and in Lesson 19, item 12. They are different from those we have seen earlier, or which end in ます **masu**, ません **masen**, ました **mashita**, or ましょう **mashō** (cf. Lesson 7, paragraph 1). You have surely seen by now that Japanese verbs change based on the position of the speaker, in three degrees of 'politeness', low, middle and high.

The middle degree is what we have been studying up until now, as it is the most common: a conversation with someone you know rather well, but with whom you have never been particularly close or intimate, or else with someone you are meeting for the first time, but who is, so to speak, "your equal". The middle degree is characterized by です **desu** to say *it is* and by verb forms ending in ます **masu**, ません **masen**, ました **mashita**, and ましょう **mashō**.

We will discuss the high degree in lessons to come. We use it in cases where you need to show your high respect, or even deference.

Low degree is what we came across in Lesson 17, item 3, and in Lesson 19, item 12. It is how we show that we are speaking with someone familiar: an old friend, a member of the family... and of course, we use it when talking to ourselves. For the low degree, instead of です **desu** we say だ **da** to mean *it is*. In place of the ending ます **masu**, we use the most neutral form of the verb, the one you will find in Japanese dictionaries. For instance, here for あります **arimasu**, which we know well, it would be ある **aru** (*ahroo*). For the past, when in place of the ending ました **mashita**, it only needs to be た **ta**.

Examples:
Middle Degree: やられました **yararemashita**
Low Degree: やられた **yarareta**
With exactly the same meaning: "I've been had" or "I've been taken". Where in the middle degree we find ましょう **mashō**, such as やめましょう **yamemashō**, *let's give up*, we find here for low degree やめよう **yameyō**.

This system might seem a little bit strange! It is indeed very different from what happens with our verbs in English! But don't worry about it. Don't forget: for the moment, just worry about UNDERSTANDING, and recognizing the differences, seeing "how it works". We will discover easily enough how all verbs fit with their given situations. Just remember to pay attention to the notes where we indicate change of degree (whether higher or lower) and all will go well!

第二十二課
だい に じゅう に か

dai ni jū ni ka *(dai nee ju- nee kah)*

郵便局
ゆう びん きょく

yū bin kyoku
(yu- been kyo ku)

1 – 郵便局 は どこ に あります か。
ゆう びんきょく

yū bin kyoku wa do ko ni a ri ma su ka.
(yu-beenkyokoo wah doko nee ahreemahs' kah)

2 – すぐ 後ろ に あります。
うし

su gu ushi ro ni a ri ma su.
(soogoo usheero nee ahreemahs')

3 – あ。 これは、 どうも ありがとう。

a. ko re wa, dō mo a ri ga tō.
(ah) (koré wah do-mo ahreegahto-)

4 ギリシャ へ の 航空 郵便 葉書
こう くう ゆう びん は がき

gi ri sha e no kō kū yū bin ha gaki
(geereeshah é no ko-ku- yu-been hahgahkee

の 料金 は いくら です か。
りょうきん

no ryō kin wa i ku ra de su ka.
no ryo-keen wah eekoorah dés' kah)

5 – イギリス まで です か。

i gi ri su ma de de su ka.
(eegeereesoo mahdé dés' kah)

At the Post-Office
(Post Office)

1 – Where can I find the post-office?
(post-office / [announce] / where / [place] / exist / [question])

2 – Just behind you.
(just / behind / [place] / exist)

3 – Oh! Thank you very much.
(oh) (this / [announce] / thank you very much)

4 What is the price for one air-mail letter to Greece?
(Greece / [destination] / [relation] / air-mail-postcard / [relation] / price / [announce] / how much / it is / [question])

5 – To England?
(England / until / it is / [question])

ဢဢဢဢ

ちょっと　お　待ち　下さい。
今　調べます　から。

6 – いいえ。イギリス まで で は
i i e   i gi ri su   ma de   de   wa
(ee-é) (eegeereesoo mahdé dé wah

ありません。①
a ri ma se n.
ahreemahsen)

7 ギリシャ まで です。
gi ri sha   ma de   de su.
(geereeshah mahdé dés')

8 – ああ。ギリシャ です か。
a a.   gi ri sha   de su   ka.
(ah-) (geereeshah dés' kah)

ちょっと お 待ち 下さい。
cho t to   o   ma chi   kuda sa i.
(cho'to o mahchee koodahsai)

9 今 調べます から。②
ima   shira be ma su   ka ra.
(eemah sheerahbémahs' kahrah)

10 はい、ありました。ギリシャ
ha i,   a ri ma shi ta.   gi ri sha
(hai ahreemahshtah geereeshah

まで は、葉書 一 枚、
ma de   wa,   ha gaki ichi   mai,
mahdé wah hahgahkee eechee mai

百 十 円 です。③
hyaku jū en   de su.
hyahkoo ju- en dés')

6 – No. Not to England.
(no) (England / until / it is not)

7 To Greece.
(Greece / until / it is)

8 – Oh. To Greece? Wait just a minute, please.
(oh) (Greece / it is / [question]) (a little / [polite]-please wait)

9 Let me take a look.
(now / look up / because)

10 Ah, here it is. One postcard, to Greece, that's 110 yen.
(yes / exist) (Greece / until / [emphasis] / postcard / one-sheet / 100-10-yen / it is)

૭౧ୠஔ

Notes

① で は ありません **de wa arimasen** (*dé wah ahreemah-sen*) is the negative form of です **desu** (*dés'*) in middle degree. Thus, it means: *it isn't.*

② Literally: "Because I'm looking for it right now."

③ As you have already seen, in Japanese we don't differentiate between singular and plural. Sometimes, though, we need to know how many objects there are. In this case, we use numbers, but we go further than that, too: we add a specific word, called a *measure word*, that specifies the kind of object we are talking about. Here 枚 **mai** (*mai*) lets us know that we are talking about objects that are thin (that is, like a sheet of paper). For other types of objects (books, round objects, etc.), we use other words. In English we do this some of the time, with "5 sheets of paper", "2 slices of pie", "one cup of milk".

11 十 枚 で 千 百 円 に
<ruby>十<rt>じゅう</rt></ruby> <ruby>枚<rt>まい</rt></ruby> <ruby>千<rt>せん</rt></ruby> <ruby>百<rt>ひゃく</rt></ruby> <ruby>円<rt>えん</rt></ruby>
jū mai de sen hyaku en ni
(ju- mai dé sen hyahku en nee

なります。③
na ri ma su.
nahreemahs')

12 – はい。千 百 円 です。
ha i. sen hyaku en de su.
(hai) (sen hyahku en dés')

13 – ありがとう ございます。
a ri ga tō go za i ma su.
(ahreegahto- gozaheemahs')

✳✳✳

<ruby>練習<rt>れん しゅう</rt></ruby> **renshū**

Exercise 1

❶ いいえ。郵便局 では ありません。
iie. yūbinkyoku de wa arimasen.
(ee-é) (yu-beenkyokoo dé wah ahreemahsen)

❷ 目黒 駅 の 隣 の デパート の
meguro eki no tonari no depāto no
(mégooro ékee no tonahree no dépah-to no

後ろ に 住んで います。
ushiro ni sunde imasu.
oosheero nee soondé eemahs')

❸ 葉書 を 二 十 枚 買いました。
hagaki o ni jū mai kaimashita.
(hahgahkee o nee ju- mai kaheemahshtah)

11 For ten, that's 1,100 yen. **22**
(ten-sheets / [means] / 1000-100-yen / [goal] / become)

12 – Here you are. One thousand one hundred yen.
(yes) (1000-100-yen / it is)

13 – Thank you very much.

∗∗∗

❹ ギリシャ 料理 は 駅 の 後ろ の
girisha ryōri wa eki no ushiro no
(geereeshah ryo-ree wah ékee no oosheero no

タバコ屋 の 左 に あります。
tabakoya no hidari ni arimasu.
tahbahkoyah no heedahree nee ahreemahs')

❺ ちょっと 見せて 下さい。
chotto misete kudasai.
(cho'to meesété koodahsai)

Answers to Exercise 1
❶ No, this is not the post-office. ❷ I live behind the department store beside the Meguro Station. ❸ I bought 20 postcards. ❹ The Greek restaurant is to the left of the tobacco shop behind the train station. ❺ Show it to me for a bit.

...に 言葉 を 入れ なさい

❶ What is the price for a postcard to the United States?

amerika made .. hagaki .. ryōkin wa .....

.... ..

❷ Where is the library?

hon ya .. doko .. ..

❸ Give me five postcards.

hagaki o .. ..

---

23 第二十三課

dai ni jū san ka *(dai nee ju- san kah)*

仕事

shi goto

(sheegoto)

1 – 上 の 息子 さん は お

ue no musu ko sa n wa o

(ooé no moosooko san wah o

元気 です か。①

gen ki de su ka.

genkee dés' kah)

2 – 今年 大学 を 卒業 しました。

kotoshi dai gaku o sotsu gyō shi ma shi ta.

(kotoshee daigahkoo o sotsoogyo- sheemahshtah)

④ That'll be 1,000 yen.

. . . . . . ni . . . .

⑤ It's just on the right.

. . . .

Answers to Exercise 2

❶ – no – no – ikura desu ka. ❷ – wa – ni arimasu ka. ❸ – go mai kudasai. ❹ sen en – narimasu. ❺ sugu migi ni arimasu.

Lesson Twenty-Three   23

Work
(work)

1 – How is your older son?
(above / [relation] / son / [announce] / [polite]-good health / it is / [question])
2 – This year he finished university.
(this year / university / [object] / graduation-did)

Notes

① 息子 さん **musuko san** (*moosooko san*) is only used to refer to someone else's son (cf. Lesson 15, notes 1 and 3). お 元気 **o genki** (*o genkee*) is only used in speaking of another person. To talk about yourself (or about someone in your immediate family), we say 元気 **genki** (*genkee*). Likewise, in item 6, we have お 勤め **o tsutome** (*otsootomé*). 勤め **tsutome** (*tsutomé*) on its own means *a job*. The preceding お **o** is often used to make a word more polite when referring to someone who is not close to you.

3 – 東大 でした ね。②③
とう だい
tō dai　de shi ta　ne.
(to-dai déshtah né)

4 – はい、そう です。
ha i,　sō　de su.
(hai so- dés')

5 – それ は おめでとう ございます。④
so re wa o me de tō　go za i ma su.
(soré wah omédéto-gozaheemahs')

6　どこ に お 勤め です か。①
と
do ko　ni　o tsuto me　de su　ka.
(doko nee o tsootomé dés' kah)

7 – 四月 から 自動車 関係 の
し がつ　じ どう しゃ　かん けい
shi gatsu　ka ra　ji dō sha　kan kei　no
(sheegahtsoo kahrah jeedo-shah kanké- no

会社 に 勤めて います。
かい しゃ　と
kai sha　ni　tsuto me te　i ma su.
kaishah nee tsootomété eemahs')

8 – それ は よろしい です ね。⑤
so re　wa　yo ro shi i　de su　ne.
(sore wah yoroshee- dés' né)

9 – でも 今 入院 して います。
いま にゅう いん
de mo ima nyū in　shi te　i ma su.
(démo eemah nyu-een sheeté eemahs')

10　五月 に 交通 事故 に
ご がつ　こう つう　じ こ
go gatsu　ni　kō tsū　ji ko　ni
(go gahtsoo nee ko-tsu- jeeko nee

あいました。
a i ma shi ta.
aimahshtah)

3 – University of Tōkyō, right?
(University of Tōkyō / it was / [agreement])

4 – Yes, that's right.

5 – All my congratulations.

6 Where does he work?
(where / [place] / [polite]-work / it is / [question])

7 – Since April he's been working at an automobile company.
(April / since / car-connection / [relation] / company / [place] / be working)

8 – That's really great!
(that / [announce] / [polite]-good / it is / [agreement])

9 – But he's in the hospital at the moment.
(but / now / enter hospital-be doing)

10 In May he was in an automobile accident.
(May / [time] / traffic-accident / [goal] / have met)

₠₡₢₣

Notes

② 東大 **tōdai** (*to-dai*) is the abbreviation of 東京大学 **Tōkyō daigaku** (*to-kyo- daigahkoo*). It is very common for Japanese to form abbreviations out of Chinese character words (*kanji*) by using one of the characters per word in a compound word. It is kind of like abbreviations in English, where we use the first letter of each word to create an acronym.
The National University of Tōkyō is the highest ranked university in Japan. Many of Japan's civil servants and administrators are recruited from the university each year.

③ でした **deshita** (*déshtah*) is the past-tense form of です **desu**. It means *it was*.

④ This is the general formula for congratulations after a happy event. It is also used to wish happy new year.

⑤ よろしい **yoroshi** (*yoroshee-*). This is a conversation where the two speakers obey a certain etiquette. In a conversation such as this, いい **ii** (*ee-*), which we have often seen, is not possible. It is replaced, instead, by よろしい **yoroshii**. We can see that いいです **ii desu** (*ee- dés'*) is middle-degree, and that よろしいです **yoroshii desu** (*yoroshee- dés'*) is in high degree.

11 – それ は お気の毒 に。⑥
so re wa o ki no doku ni.
(soré wah okeenodokoo nee)

12 その後 いかが です か。
so no go i ka ga de su ka.
(sonogo eekahgah dés' kah)

13 – おかげさまで、よくなりました。
o ka ge sa ma de, yo ku na ri ma shi ta.
(okahgésahmah dé yokoo nahreemahshtah

来週 退院 します。⑦
rai shū tai in shi ma su.
raishu- taieen sheemahs')

14 – 安心 しました。
an shin shi ma shi ta.
(ansheen sheemahshtah)

***

練習 renshū

Exercise 1

❶ 昨日 の 朝 でした。
kinō no asa deshita.
(keeno- no ahsah déshtah)

❷ 来週 から 禁煙 します。
raishū kara kin.en shimasu.
(raishu- kahrah keen.én sheemahs')

❸ 自動車 は 四月 に 買いました。
jidōsha wa shigatsu ni kaimashita.
(jeedo-shah wah sheegahtsoo nee kaheemahshtah)

11 – That's really too bad!
24

12   How's he been since then?
(since then / how / it is / [question])

13 – Very well, thank you. He gets out next week.
(thanks to you / well / became) (next week / leave hospital-do)

14 – I'm relieved!
(calmness-did)

ಬಂಡಿಬಂಡಿ

Notes

⑥ Literally, "That's an unpleasant thing."

⑦ おかげさま で **okagesama de** *(okahgésahmah dé)*. Literally, it means, "Thanks to you." In fact, it is the usual way when thanking someone for asking about the condition of you or those close to you.

✻✻✻

❹ いつ 大学 を 卒業 しました か。
itsu daigaku o sotsugyō shimashita ka.
(eetsoo daigahkoo o sotsoogyo- sheemahshtah kah)

❺ ―お坊ちゃん は お 元気 です か。
–obotchan wa o genki desu ka.
(obo'chan wah o genkee dés' kah)

―おかげさま で、元気 です。
–okagesama de, genki desu.
(okahgésahmah dé genkee dés')

Answers to Exercise 1

❶ That was yesterday morning. ❷ I'm going to quit smoking next week. ❸ I bought my car in April. ❹ When did he graduate? ❺ –How is your little boy? –Very well, thank you.

... に 言葉 を 入れ なさい

❶ Where does your older son work?

ue no musuko .... .. doko ni . tsutome desu ka

❷ I am living in Tōkyō this year.

.... tōkyō ni sunde .....

❸ It was a car company.

...... kankei .. ..

❹ I'll go in April or May.

shi .... ka ...... ni ikimasu

❺ I'll wait until next Sunday.

raishū .. .. machimasu

---

24 第二十四課
dai ni jū yon ka *(dai nee ju- yon kah)*

アパート
a pā to
(ahpah-to)

1 – やっと いい アパート が
ya t to i i a pā to ga
(yah'to ee- ahpah-to gah

みつかりました。
mi tsu ka ri ma shi ta.
meetsookahreemahshtah)

2 とても 狭い です。
to te mo sema i de su.
(totémo sémai dés')

135 • hyaku san jū go

❶ – san wa – o –. ❷ kotoshi kara – imasu. ❸ jidōsha – no kaisha deshita. ❹ – gatsu – gogatsu –. ❺ – no nichiyōbi made –.

Lesson Twenty-Four   24

The Apartment
(apartment)

1 – I've finally found a good apartment.
(finally / be good / apartment / [subject] / has been found)

2 It's very small.
(very / be narrow / it is)

24

3 けれども 駅 から 歩いて
ke re do mo eki ka ra aru i te
(kérédomo ékee kahrah ahrooeeté

五 分 です。
go fun de su.
go foon dés')

4 – それ は 便利 です ね。
so re wa ben ri de su ne.
(soré wah benree dés' né)

5 – でも うるさく ありません か。
de mo u ru sa ku a ri ma se n ka.
(démo ooroosahkoo ahreemahsen kah)

6 – 電車 の 音 は 全然 聞こえません
den sha no oto wa zen zen ki ko e ma se n
(denshah no oto wah zenzen keekoémahsen

が、 隣 の 幼稚園 の 子供 が
ga, tonari no yō chi en no kodomo ga
gah tonahree no yo-cheeen no kodomo gah

うるさい です。①
u ru sa i de su.
ooroosai dés')

7 – 何 階 です か。
nan kai de su ka.
(nan kai dés' kah)

8 – 四 階 です。
yon kai de su.
(yon kai dés')

9 – 眺 め は いかが です か。
naga me wa i ka ga de su ka.
(nahgahmé wah eekahgah dés' kah)

3 However, it's a five minute walk from the train **24**
station.
(but / train station / from / walking / five-minutes / it is)

4 – That's convenient!
(that / [announce] / convenient / it is / [agreement])

5 But isn't it noisy?
(but / not be noisy [question])

6 – I can't hear the trains at all, but the children in
the kindergarten next door are noisy.
*(train / [relation] / noise / [announce] / at all / cannot be
heard / but // neighbor / [relation] / kindergarten / [rela-
tion] / children / [subject] / be noisy / it is)*

7 – What floor is it on?
(what-floor / it is / question)

8 – The fourth floor.
(four-floor / it is)

9 – How is the view?
(view / [announce] / how / it is / [question])

ಬಿ೮ಽಬಿಂಞ

Notes

① In the accompanying word-for-word translation, we have added
a new sign: the double-slash // means that in the Japanese sentence there is a separation between two propositions. That
means we're making progress! And we are going to be coming
across some longer sentences, too.

10 – それ が… ちょうど 向かいに 二
so re ga...　　chō do mu ka i ni ni
(soré gah) (cho-do mookahee nee nee

十 階 の ビル が 立って います
juk kai no bi ru ga ta t te i ma su
ju'kai no beeroo gah tah'té eemahs'

から、 何も 見えません。
ka ra,　nani mo mi e ma se n.
kahrah naneemo meeémahsen)

11 家賃 だけ が 気 に 入って
ya chin da ke ga ki ni i t te
(yahcheen dahké gah kee nee ee'té

います。
i ma su.
eemahs')

12 それほど 高く ありません。
so re ho do taka ku　a ri ma se n.
(soréhodo tahkahkoo ahreemahsen)　　　□

練習　renshū

Exercise 1

❶ 私 の アパート は 十二 階 に
watakushi no apāto wa jū ni kai ni
(wahtahkooshee no ahpah-to wah ju-nee kai nee

あります。
arimasu.
ahreemahs')

10 – Oh, that... Because of the 20-storey building across the street, I can't see anything. **24**
(that / [subject]) (exactly / opposite side / [place] / two-ten-story / [relation] / building / [subject] / be standing / because // anything / can't be seen)

11 The rent is the only thing I like about the place
(rent / only / [subject] / spirit / [place] / enter)

12 It isn't too expensive!
(that much / not be expensive)

૭૦૦૩૭૦૦૩

❷ 電車　の　音　は　聞こえません　が
densha no oto wa kikoemasen ga
(dénshah no oto wah keekoémahsen gah

自動車　の　音　は　聞こえます。
jidōsha no oto wa kikoemasu.
jeedo-shah no oto wah keekoémahs')

❸ 眼鏡　を　忘れました　から、何も
megane o wasuremashita kara, nanimo
(mégahné o wahsoorémahshtah kahrah naneemo

見えません。
miemasen.
meeémahsen)

❹ デパート　まで　バス　で　七　分　です
depāto made basu de nana fun desu
(dépah-to mahdé bahsoo dé nanah foon dés'

から、便利　です。
kara, benri desu.
kahrah benree dés')

❺ ―うるさく ありません か。
–urusaku arimasen ka.
(ooroosahkoo ahreemahsen kah)

―<ruby>全然<rt>ぜんぜん</rt></ruby> うるさく ありません。
–zenzen urusaku arimasen.
(zenzen ooroosahkoo ahreemahsen)

***

Exercise 2

... に <ruby>言葉<rt>こと ば</rt></ruby> を <ruby>入れ<rt>い</rt></ruby> なさい

❶ I'm not buying anything.

. . . .

❷ I hear the noise from the kindergarten.
yōchien . . . .

❸ Because it's far, I'm going by bus.
tooi desu . . . . , ...

❹ It's not very far.

. . . .

---

25 <ruby>第二十五課<rt>だい に じゅう ご か</rt></ruby>
dai ni jū go ka *(dai nee ju- go kah)*

<ruby>小説<rt>しょうせつ</rt></ruby>

shō setsu
(sho-sétsoo)

1 – <ruby>今<rt>いま</rt></ruby> <ruby>小説<rt>しょうせつ</rt></ruby> を <ruby>書<rt>か</rt></ruby>いて います。
ima shō setsu o ka i te i ma su.
(eemah sho-sétsoo o kaheeté eemahs')

❶ My apartment is on the twelfth floor. ❷ I don't hear any noise from the train, only from the cars. ❸ I forgot my glasses, so I can't see anything. ❹ It's seven minutes by bus to the department store, so it's convenient. ❺ –It isn't noisy? –Not at all.

✳✳✳

❺ I can only see the building on the right.

. . . . ga miemasu

Answers to Exercise 2

❶ nanimo kaimasen. ❷ – no oto ga kikoemasu. ❸ – kara, basu de ikimasu. ❹ sorehodo tooku arimasen. ❺ migi no biru dake –.

Lesson Twenty-Five   25

The Novel
(novel)

1 – I'm writing a novel right now.
   (now / novel / [object] / be writing)

2 – へえ、どんな 小説 です か。
he e, do n na shō setsu de su ka.
(hé- do'nah sho-sétsoo dés' kah)

3 – 推理 小説 です。
sui ri shō setsu de su.
(sooeeree sho-sétsoo dés')

4 – 出版 する つもり です か。
shup pan su ru tsu mo ri de su ka.
(shu'pan sooroo tsoomoree dés' kah)

5 – まだ わかりません。
ma da wa ka ri ma se n.
(mahdah wahkahreemahsen)

6 – どんな 話 です か。
do n na hanashi de su ka.
(donnah hanahshee dés' kah)

7 – 主人公 は ファッション・モデル
shu jin kō wa fa s sho n mo de ru
(shujeenko- wah fah'shon modéroo

です。
de su.
dés')

8 知らないで スパイ と 結婚
shi ra na i de su pa i to kek kon
(sheerahnaidé s'pai to ké'kon

します。
shi ma su.
sheemahs')

9 – おもしろそう です ね。①
 o mo shi ro sō de su ne.
(omosheeroso- dés' né)

2 – Oh! What kind of novel?
(oh / what kind / novel / it is / [question])

3 – A detective novel.
(detective novel / it is)

4 – Do you intend to publish it?
(publish-do / intention / it is / [question])

5 – I don't know yet.
(not yet / not know)

6 – What is it about?
(what kind / story / it is / [question])

7 – The main character is a model.
(main character / [announce] / fashion model / it is)

8 Without knowing it, she marries a spy.
(not knowing / spy / [partnership] / marriage-do)

9 – Sounds interesting!
(seem interesting / it is / [agreement])

ಓ಴ಌ಴ಌಌ

Notes

① おもしろそう **omoshirosō** (*omosheeroso-*). We already know おもしろい **omoshiroi** (*omosheeroee*), *interesting*. If we replace the い **i** of the adjective with そう **sō** (*so-*), then we get おもしろそう **omoshirosō** (*omosheeroso-*), which means *to seem interesting*.

10 何 ページ ぐらい に なります か。
nan pē ji gu ra i ni na ri ma su ka.
(nan pé-jee goorai nee nahreemahs' kah)

11 – 五 百 ページ ぐらい に
go hyaku pē ji gu ra i ni
(go hyahkoo pé-jee goorai nee

なる と 思います。
na ru to omo i ma su.
nahroo to omoeemahs')

12 – へえ。長い です ね。
he e. naga i de su ne.
(hé-) (nahgai dés' né)

13 もう どのぐらい 書きました か。
mō do no gu ra i ka ki mashi ta ka.
(mo- dono goorai kahkeemahshtah kah)

14 – まだ 五 ページ です。
ma da go pē ji de su.
(mahdah go pé-jee dés')

□

練習 renshū

Exercise 1

❶ 駅 まで どのぐらい です か。
eki made donogurai desu ka.
(ékee mahdé donogoorai dés' kah)

10   About how many pages will it be?
(what-page / about / [goal] / become / [question])

11 – I think it will be about 500 pages.
(five-hundred-page / about / [goal] / become / [quotation] / think)

12 – Wow! That's long!
(wow) (be long / it is / [agreement])

13   How much have you written?
(already / how much about / wrote / [question])

14 – Only five.
(up to now / five-page / it is)

ജഗ്ഞോ

❷ この お 菓子 は おいしそう です ね。
かし
kono o kashi wa oishisō desu ne.
(kono o kahshee wah oeesheeso- dés' né)

❸ どんな 本 を 買いました か。
ほん　か
donna hon o kaimashita ka.
(do'nah hon o kaheemahshtah kah)

❹ 再婚 する つもり です。
さい こん
saikon suru tsumori desu.
(saikon sooroo tsoomoree dés')

❺ 来週 退院 する と 思います。
らいしゅう　たいいん　　　　　おも
raishū tai.in suru to omoimasu.
(raishu- tai.een sooroo to omoeemahs')

Answers to Exercise 1
❶ About how far is it to the train station? ❷ This snack looks delicious! ❸ What kind of book did you buy? ❹ I plan on remarrying. ❺ I think he will leave the hospital next week.

... に 言葉 を 入れ なさい

❶ I think I will publish it.

shuppan .... .. omoimasu

❷ I have the intention of becoming a singer.

kashu .. .... tsumori desu

❸ What kind of person is she?

....

だい に じゅう ろっ か
26 第二十六課
dai ni jū rok ka *(dai nee ju- ro'kah)*

ちゅう ごく　　　　　　　い
中国　　へ　行く
chū goku e　　i ku
(chu-gokoo é eekoo)

らい ねん　　　　　はる　　　　ちゅうごく
1 – 来年　の　春　に　中国　へ
rai nen　no　haru　ni　chū goku　e
(rainen no hahroo nee chu-gokoo é

い
行く　つもり　でした。
i ku　tsu mo ri　de shi ta.
eekoo tsoomoree déshtah)

ちゅうごく ご
2 – 中国語　は　できます　か。①
chū goku go　wa　de ki ma su　ka.
(chu-gokoogo wah dékeemahs' kah)

わたくし
3 – 私　　は　できません。
watakushi　wa　de ki ma se n.
(wahtahkooshee wah dékeemahsen)

❹ I am writing a postcard.
   hagaki o . . . .

❺ These forks seem expensive.
   kono fōku wa . . . . . . desu

Answers to Exercise 2
❶ – suru to –. ❷ – ni naru –. ❸ donna hito desu ka. ❹ – kaite imasu.
❺ – takasō –.

Lesson Twenty-Six   26

Voyage to China
(China / [destination] / to go)

1 – I was planning on going to China next spring.
     *(next year / [relation] / spring / [time] / China / [destina-
     tion] / go / intention / it was)*
2 – Do you speak Chinese?
     (China-language / [announce] / be possible / [question])
3 – No, I can't
     (me / [announce] / not be possible)

ဆာ၈ဝၹ

Notes

① The name of a country followed by the word 語 **go** designates
   the language of the country. 中国   **chūgoku** (*chu-gokoo*),
   China; 中国語 **chūgokugo** (*chu-gokoogo*), *the Chinese
   language*. 日本 **nihon** (*neehon*), *Japan*; 日本語 **nihongo**
   (*neehongo*), *the Japanese language*. The only exception is for
   English, which is 英語 **eigo** (*é-go*), while *England* is イギリ
   ス **igirisu** (*eegeereesoo*).

4 けれども 息子 は よく できます
ke re do mo musu ko wa yo ku de ki ma su
(kérédomo moosooko wah yokoo dékeemahs'

から、つれて行くつもりでした。
ka ra, tsu re te i ku tsu mo ri de shi ta.
kahrah tsoorété eekoo tsoomoree déshtah) ②③

5 しかし 息子 は 都合 が
shi ka shi musu ko wa tsu gō ga
(sheekahshee moosooko wah tsoogo- gah

悪く なりました。
waru ku na ri ma shi ta.
wahrookoo nahreemahshtah)

6 – 中国 へ 何 を し に 行きますか。
chū goku e nani o shi ni i ki ma su ka.
(chu-gokoo é nanee o shee nee eekeemahs' kah)

7 – 仕事 と 観光 です。
shi goto to kan kō de su.
(sheegoto to kanko- dés')

8 – 私 は 中国語 が 少し
watakushi wa chū goku go ga suko shi
(wahtahkooshee wah chu-gokoogo gah s'koshee

できます から、お 供
de ki ma su ka ra, o tomo
dékeemahs' kahrah o tomo

しましょう か。
shi ma shō ka.
sheemahsho- kah)

4   But my son speaks it very well, so I think I'm   **26**
going to bring him
(however / my son / [announce] / well / be possible / because //
bring along / go / intention / it was)

5   However, it turns out he can't go.
(but / my son / [announce] / circumstances / [subject] / be
bad / became)

6 –   What are you going to do in China?
(China / [destination] / what / [object] / do / [goal] / go /
[question])

7 –   I'm going for business and pleasure.
(work / and / tourism / it is)

8 –   I know a little Chinese, shall I go along?
(me / [announce] / China-language / [subject] / a little / be
possible / because // [polite]-accompany-let's do / [question])

හ⳩ɞⳉ

Notes

② Here, 息子 **musuko** (*moosooko*) (cf. Lesson 23, item 1),
because the man is talking about his own son.

③ つれて 行く **tsurete iku** (*tsoorété eekoo*). Note that when
two verbs follow each other directly, the first ends with a final
て **te** (*té*).

9 それ に 来年 の 春 は 暇 です。
so re ni rainen no haru wa hima de su.
(soré nee rainen no hahroo wah heemah dés')

10 – それ は たすかります。 ぜひ
so re wa ta su ka ri ma su. ze hi
(soré wah tahsookahreemahs') (zéhee

おねがい します。
o ne ga i shi ma su.
onégahee sheemahs')

11 今度 の 月曜日 の 晩 一緒
kon do no getsu yō bi no ban is sho
(kondo no gétsooyo-bi no ban ee'sho

に 食事 を しましょう。
ni shoku ji o shi ma shō.
nee shokoojee o sheemahsho-)

12 – はい、そう しましょう。
ha i, sō shi ma shō.
(hai so- sheemahsho-)　　　　□

れん しゅう
練習 renshū

Exercise 1

❶ イギリス人 の 友達 を ピクニック
igirisujin no tomodachi o pikunikku
(eegeereesoojeen no tomodahchee o peekoonee'koo

に 誘う つもり です。
ni sasou tsumori desu.
nee sasou tsoomoree dés')

9 And, I'm free next spring. **26**
(moreover / next·year / [relation] / spring / [announce] / free time / it is)

10 – You're my saviour! Please come!
(that / [announce] / help) (absolutely / please)

11 Let's have dinner together next Monday night.
(next time / [relation] / Monday / [relation] / night / together / [adverbial] / meal / [object] / let's do)

12 – Yes, okay.
(yes / so / let's do)

෨෮෪෨෮

❷ 息子 さん は フランス語
musuko san wa furansugo
(moosooko san wah fooransoogo

が できます か。
ga dekimasu ka.
gah dékeemahs' kah)

❸ 本屋 へ 何 を 買い に
honya e nani o kai ni
(honyah é nanee o kaihee nee

行きます か。
ikimasu ka.
eekeemahs' kah)

❹ 暇 です から、映画 を 見
hima desu kara, eiga o mi
(heemah dés' kahrah é-gah o mee

に 行きましょう。
ni ikimashō.
nee eekeemahsho-)

❺ 郵便局 へ 行きます。子供 を
yūbinkyoku e ikimasu. kodomo o
(yu-beenkyokoo é eekeemahs' kodomo o

つれて 行きます。
tsurete ikimasu.
tsoorété eekeemahs')

***

Exercise 2

...に 言葉 を 入れ なさい

❶ Next year I'll buy a car.

. . . . kaimasu

❷ I speak a little Japanese.

. . . .

❸ I'll go next Saturday.

. . . .

---

27 第二十七課
dai ni jū nana ka *(dai nee ju- nanah kah)*

飛行場 に 着く
hi kō jō ni tsu ku
(heeko-jo- nee tsookoo)

1 – もし もし。 正子 です。
mo shi mo shi. masa ko de su.
(moshee moshee) (mahsahko dés')

Answers to Exercise 1

❶ I'm going to invite some English friends of mine on a picnic.
❷ Can your son speak French? ❸ What are you going to buy at the
bookstore? ❹ Since we're free, let's go to the movies. ❺ I'm going
to the post-office. I'm taking the kids.

✳✳✳

❹ I'll only eat a little bit of bread.
   pan . . . . dake tabemasu
❺ I had a problem.
   tsugō ga . . . . mashita

Answers to Exercise 2

❶ rainen jidōsha o –. ❷ nihongo ga sukoshi dekimasu. ❸ kondo no
doyōbi ni ikimasu. ❹ – wa sukoshi –. ❺ – waruku nari –.

Lesson Twenty-Seven 27

Arriving at the Airport
(airport / [goal] / to arrive)

1 – Hello. This is Masako.
   (hello) (Masako / it is)

2 – 飛行機 は 決まりました か。
hi kō ki wa ki ma ri ma shi ta ka.
(heeko-kee wah keemahreemahshtah kah)

いつ 着きます か。
i tsu tsu ki ma su ka.
(eetsoo tsookeemahs' kah)

3 – 日航 の 四 百 五 十 三
nik kō no yon hyaku go jū san
(nee'ko no yon hyahkoo go ju- san

便 で、しあさって の 午前
bin de, shi a sa t te no go zen
been dé sheeahsah'té no gozen

七 時 十 五 分 に 成田
shichi ji jū go fun ni nari ta
sheechee jee ju- go foon nee nahreeta

空港 に。着きます。①②
kū kō ni tsu ki ma su.
ku-ko- nee tsookeemahs')

4 – 飛行場 まで 迎え に
hi kō jō ma de muka e ni
(heeko-jo- mahdé mookahé nee

行きます から ね。
i ki ma su ka ra ne.
eekeemahs' kahrah né)

2 – Is your flight set yet? When do you arrive? **27**
(airplane / [announce] / be decided / [question]) (when / arrive / [question])

3 – I'll arrive at Narita in two days, at 7:15 in the morning, on Japan Airlines flight 453.
(Japan Airlines / [relation] / four-hundred-five-ten-three - flight-[means] / after-after-tomorrow / [relation] / morning / seven-o'clock-ten-five-minute / [time] / Narita-airport / [goal] / arrive)

4 – I'll meet you at the airport.
(airport / until / go to meet / [goal] / go / because / [agreement])

Notes

① 日航 **nikkō** (*nee'ko-*) is the abbreviation of 日(本)航(空) **nihon kōkū** (*neehon ko-ku-*) (Japan / Airlines), the name of Japan's national airplane company, known best in English as *Japan Airlines*.

② 成田 **narita** (*nahreetah*), the airport servicing Tōkyō.

5 – 朝 早い から、箱崎 の エア・
asa hayai kara, hakozaki no e a
(ahsah hahyahee kahrah hahkozahkee no éah

ターミナル まで リムジン・
tā mi na ru ma de ri mu ji n
tah-meenahroo mahdé reemoojeen

バス で 行きます。そこ で
ba su de i ki ma su. so ko de
bahs' dé eekeemahs') (soko dé

会いましょう。③
a i ma shō.
aheemahsho-)

6 – 大丈夫 です よ。早く 会いたい
dai jō bu de su yo. haya ku a i ta i
(daijo-boo dés' yo) (hahyahkoo aheetai

から 飛行場 まで 行きます。④
ka ra hi kō jō ma de i ki ma su.
kahrah heeko-jo- mahdé eekeemahs')

7 必ず 行きます から、待って
kanara zu i ki ma su ka ra, ma t te
(kanahrahzoo eekeemahs' kahrah mah'té

て ,下さい。
te kuda sa i.
té koodahsai)

8 – そう です か。悪い わ ね。⑤
sō de su ka. waru i wa ne.
(so- dés' kah) (wahrooee wah né)

9 – 荷物 は たくさん あります か。
ni motsu wa ta ku sa n a ri ma su ka.
(neemotsoo wah tahkoosan ahreemahs' kah)

5 – It's early in the morning, so I'll take the bus to Hakozaki terminal. Let's meet there.
(morning / be early / because // Hakozaki / [relation] / terminal / until / bus / [means] / go) (there / [place] / let's meet)

6 – No, that's okay. I can't wait to see you, so I'll go to the airport.
(no problem / it is / [engagement]) (fast / want to meet / because // airport / until / go)

7 I'll be there without fail, so wait for me there.
(without fail / go / because // please wait)

8 – Are you sure? You don't have to.
(so / it is / [question]) (be bad / [softener] / [agreement])

9 – Do you have a lot of baggage?
(baggage / [announce] / a lot / exist / [question])

☙ ☯ ☙ ☯

Notes

③ 箇崎 **hakozaki**, the terminal in the center of Tōkyō. リムジン・バス **rimujin basu** are the so-called *limousine buses* that shuttle from the airport to the terminal in the center of the city, roughly an hour away.

④ The expression 大丈夫 です **daijōbu desu** (*daijo-boo dés'*) is the exact equivalent of our *it's okay*. It affirms that there will be no obstacles in the completion of an action. So it gets used very often!

⑤ After ね **ne** (*né*) and よ **yo**, here is another kind of little word you will find at the end of sentences: わ **wa** (*wah*). But be careful, this one is used **exclusively** by women, and only in situations of familiarity. It is a kind of "softener", usually said following a verb or adjective of the lower degree. Here, we find 悪い **warui** (*wahrooee*) alone. Until now we have always come across expressions like いい です **ii desu** (*ee- dés'*), *it's good* (cf. Lesson 2, item 5; Lesson 9, item 2, etc.). In the accompanying translation we have always explained that いい **ii** (*ee-*) alone means *to be good*. Like the verb, the adjective also has three degrees. いい です **ii desu** (*ee-dés'*) is the middle degree, いい on its own is in low degree. Here, 悪い **warui** (*wahrooee*) is in low degree, as the conversation takes place between two friends. Very often in this kind of exchange, speakers will mix middle and low degrees rather freely.

10 – 小さい バッグ 二つ だけ です。
chii sa i　ba g gu futa tsu da ke　de su.
(chee- sai bah'goo footahtsoo dahké dés')

11 – えっ。それ だけ。おみやげ は？
e.　so re　da ke.　o mi ya ge wa.
(é') (soré dahké) (omeeyahgé wah)

12 – 心配 しないで。いい 物 を
shin pai　shi na i de.　i i　mono o
(sheenpai sheenaidé) (ee- mono o

買って 来ました。
ka t te　ki ma shi ta.
kah'té keemahshtah)

13 – じゃ。兄 と 一緒 に 税関 を
ja.　ani to　is sho ni　zei kan　o
(jah) (anee to ee'sho nee zé-kan o

出た 所 で 待って います。
de ta tokoro de　ma t te　i ma su.
détah tokoro dé mah'té eemahs')

14 – それでは、 よろしく おねがい
so re de wa,　yo ro shi ku　o ne ga i
(sorédéwah yorosheekoo onégahee

します。
shi ma su.
sheemahs')　　　　　□

10 – Only two small bags.
   (be small / bag / two / only / it is)

11 – What? Is that all? What about souvenirs?
   (what!) (that / only) (souvenir / [announce])

12 – Don't worry, I bought some great stuff.
   (worry-do not do) (be good / thing / [object] / buy / came)

13 – Okay. My brother and I will be waiting where
   you get out of customs.
   (then) (older brother / [partnership] / together / [adverbial] / customs / [object] / go out / place / [place] / be waiting)

14 – In that case, thanks in advance!
   (then / well / please)

ॐ

練習　renshū

Exercise 1

❶ 写真 が たくさん あります。
shashin ga takusan arimasu.
(shasheen gah tahkoosan ahreemahs')

❷ 飛行機 が 見えました か。
hikōki ga miemashita ka.
(heeko-kee gah mee'émahshtah kah)

❸ この アパート は 小さい から
kono apāto wa chiisai kara
(kono ahpah-to wah chee-sai kahrah

買いません。
kaimasen.
kaheemahsen)

④ 今日 行く 会社 は ここ から
きょう い かいしゃ

kyō iku kaisha wa koko kara

(kyo- eekoo kaishah wah koko kahrah

近い です。
ちか

chikai desu.

cheekai dés')

⑤ 明日 の 午前 八 時 三 十 五
あした ごぜん はち じ さん じゅう ご

ashita no gozen hachi ji san jū go

(ahshtah no gozen hahchee jee san ju- go

分 に 着く と 思います。
ふん つ おも

fun ni tsuku to omoimasu.

foon nee tsookoo to omoeemahs')

✳✳✳

Exercise 2

... に 言葉 を 入れ なさい
ことば い

❶ I went there by airplane.

・・・・・・ ・・ ・・・・・・・・・

❷ Let's meet up quickly.

・・・・・・ ・・・・・

❸ I got here yesterday morning at 6:12.

kinō .. ・・・・・ ・・・・ ・・ ・・・・ ・・ ... ni tsukimashita

❹ When are you going to China?

・・・・ ・・・・・ ・・ ・・・・・・・ ・・

Answers to Exercise 1

❶ There are many photos. ❷ Did you see the airplanes? ❸ I'm not buying this apartment because it's small. ❹ The company I'm going to today is near here. ❺ I think they arrive tomorrow morning at 8:35.

✳✳✳

❺ I have two large suitcases.

ookii toranku ga . . . . arimasu

❻ You made a beautiful object.

ii . . . . o tsukurimashita ne

Answers to Exercise 2

❶ hikōki de ikimashita. ❷ hayaku aimashō. ❸ – no gozen roku ji jū ni fun –. ❹ itsu chūgoku e ikimasu ka. ❺ –futatsu. ❻ – mono –.

第二十八課

<ruby>第<rt>だい</rt></ruby><ruby>二<rt>に</rt></ruby><ruby>十<rt>じゅう</rt></ruby><ruby>八<rt>はつ</rt></ruby><ruby>課<rt>か</rt></ruby>

dai ni jū hak' ka *(dai nee ju- hah'kah)*

まとめ
matome

Revision and Notes

We have made a big step. But we still have to keep count of what we have learned. And above all, remind yourself, take the time to let it all sink in and be sure you understand everything. We have begun to come across longer sentences and phrases. It is important to note each word, with the help of the transcription and accompanying translation.

By now you have already gotten used to the word order, and soon Japanese sentences will seem completely natural (if it hasn't become so already!).

1. Beginning with the names of the countries you have learned, you can now easily form:

–the word for inhabitants of those countries. All you have to do is add 人 **jin** *(jeen)*, which means *person*:

アメリカ **amerika** *(ahméreekah)*: *America*

アメリカ人 **amerika jin** *(ahméreekahjeen)*: *an American, Americans*

イギリス **igirisu** *(eegeereesoo)*: *England*

イギリス人 **igirisu jin** *(eegeereesoojeen)*: *an English person, the English*

フランス **furansu** *(fooransoo)*: *France*

フランス人 **furansu jin** *(fooransoojeen)*: *a French person, the French*

中国 **chūgoku** (*chu-gokoo*): *China*
中国人 **chūgoku jin** (*chu-gokoojeen*): *a Chinese person, the Chinese*
日本 **nihon** (*neehon*): *Japan*
日本人 **nihon jin** (*neehonjeen*): *a Japanese person, the Japanese*
—the word for the country's language. Simply add the word 語 **go**, which means *language*:
フランス語 **furansu go** (*fooransoogo*): *French*
中国語 **chūgoku go** (*chu-gokoogo*): *Chinese*
日本語 **nihon go** (*neehongo*): *Japanese*
The only exception is English, for which we say:
英語 **eigo** (*é-go*)
—the corresponding adjective. Here you have to add の **no** to indicate the relationship between the country and a noun:
日本 の 映画 **nihon no eiga** (*neehon no é-gah*): *a Japanese movie, Japanese cinema*
フランス の 映画 **furansu no eiga** (*fooransoo no é-gah*): *a French movie, French film*
アメリカ の 映画 **amerika no eiga** (*ahméreekah no é-gah*): *an American movie, American cinema*

2. You are also ready by now to make interrogations. We have now seen just about every way to ask a question:

何 / 何	**nani** or **nan** (*nanee / nan*): *what?* (lessons 2, 5, 8, 16, 24...)
だれ	**dare** (*dahré*): *who?* (lesson 19)
いつ	**itsu** (*eetsoo*): *when?* (lesson 27)
どこ	**doko** (*doko*): *where?* (lessons 1, 4, 5, 15, 20, 22, 23 ...)
いかが	**ikaga** (*eekahgah*): *how?* (lessons 16, 19, 24)

いくら	**ikura** (*eekoorah*):	*how much?* (lesson 17, 22)
いくつ	**ikutsu** (*eekootsoo*):	*how many?* (lesson 15)
どのぐらい	**donogurai** (*donogoorai*):	*about how many?* (lesson 25)
どちら	**dochira** (*docheerah*):	*which one?* (lesson 10)
どんな	**donna** (*do'nah*):	(preceding a noun) *which kind?* (lesson 19, 25)

There are still two or three more question words to complete the list. Some of them we are already familiar with, others not yet, but we have time…

3. But asking questions isn't enough. You have to reply, too, and answer with precision. In the last review chapter (lesson 21, paragraph 2), we saw that an adjective always comes before the noun it modifies. This is a very important principle of Japanese: all words modifying a noun will come before it, no matter what form that modification takes. That could be an adjective (cf. lesson 21, paragraph 2), but also:

–one or more other nouns. In this case, they are linked to the main noun by the relation particle の **no**, and sometimes appear as veritable catalogues (cf. lesson 22, item 4, and exercises 2 and 4; lesson 24, item 6; lesson 25, item 11 and exercise 1).

–a verb, alone (lesson 25, item 4 exercise 4; lesson 26, item 4), or with complements (lesson 26, item 1 and exercise 1; lesson 27, item 13 and exercise 4). Take a good look at these examples, read them over a few times to make sure you have grasped their structure, because it is the only construction possible to Japanese, whereas in English we have many kinds of relative propositions, pronouns, and so on... We will come across this structure again and again, and we will be going into more depth, too!

4. Before diving into the subsequent lessons, let's take another look at the question of degrees. In lesson 21, paragraph 4, we explained it as pertaining to verbs. In fact, it concerns all words with a variable form, which means not only verbs, but adjectives, too (and sometimes even nouns, despite being invariable!). Some examples to reiterate:

Verb:	middle degree	lower degree
do	します **shimasu**	する **suru** (lesson 25, item 4)
become	なります **narimasu**	なる **naru** (lesson 25, item 11)
go	行きます **ikimasu**	行く **iku** (lesson 26, item 1)
exited	出ました **demashita**	出た **deta** (lesson 27, item 13)

Adjectives:
to be bad 悪い です **warui desu**   悪い **warui** (lesson 27, item 8)

So now comes the main question: when do you employ the middle degree, and when the low degree? There are some simple rules:

a. If the word is a verb or an adjective that comes at the **end of a sentence**, the degree used depends on the situation. As with lesson 22, where the conversation takes place between two people who don't know each other very well, such as employee and customer; the middle degree is customary. In lesson 23, the conversation takes place between two people who know each other well, but who want to keep a certain distance: middle degree with a few additions from the higher degree. On the other hand, the conversation in lesson 27 is between two friends: middle degree mixed with a few words from lower degree. Of course, in certain situations, you are sure to find very, very, very polite conversations, entirely in the high degree, or very, very informal conversations completely in the low degree (between classmates in lower or high school, for example), but the boundaries are not always so strict.

This principle also applies to certain verbs and adjectives found at the end of **some** propositions: those that end in が **ga** (cf. lesson 24, item 6) or から **kara** (cf. lesson 22, item 9; lesson 24, item 10; lesson 26, item 4; lesson 27, items 4, 5, 6).

28

b. In all other cases, an adjective or verb **within** a sentence or proposition will be in low degree. We have seen the two main instances of this kind of usage: an adjective or verb used to modify a noun. For adjectives, see the examples given in lesson 21, paragraph 2, and also in lesson 24, item 1: いい アパート **ii apāto** (*ee- ahpah-to*); lesson 27, item 10: 小さい バッグ **chiisai baggu** (*chee-sai ba'goo*).

–For the verbs, see lesson 25, item 4:

出版 する つもり です か。

***shuppan suru* tsumori desu ka.** (*shu'pan sooroo tsoomoree dés' kah*): *do you have the intention of publishing it?*;

–lesson 26, item 1:

来年 の 春 に 中国 へ 行く つもり でした。

***rainen no haru ni chūgoku e iku* tsumori deshita.** (*rainen no hahroo nee chu-gokoo é eekoo tsoomoree déshtah*): *I had the intention of **going to China next Spring**;*

–lesson 27, item 13:

税関 を 出た 所。

***zeikan o deta* tokoro.** (*zé-kan o détah tokoro*): *where you get out of customs*. Here, no matter what the situation, there is no possible choice: this will always be in low degree;

–the same for lesson 25, item 11:

五 百 ページ ぐらい に なる と 思います。

✳✳✳

go hyaku pēji gurai ni naru **to omoimasu**. (*go hyahku pé-jee goorai nee nahroo to omoeemahs'*) *I think that would be about five hundred pages*. Before と 思います **to omoimasu**, (that / to think) *I think that...* you no longer have an option: this will always be in low degree.

At first glance this is sure to look very complicated! But that is only because we don't have the same kind of device in English. So let's say it again: for the moment you don't need to retain everything –that will come in due time. Right now you just have to worry about understanding, noting the differences, and knowing what they correspond to. And, since we will be using these constructions where low degree is required without stop, just be aware and pay attention in the lessons to come. At any rate, don't worry about it –we will talk about it more, and soon!

5. By now you are getting used to the pronunciation. As we have been reminding you from the beginning, it isn't difficult! So we are going to begin the process of detaching ourselves bit by bit from the figurative pronunciation guide. In the next six lessons, we will keep it there for the text of the lesson, but we won't be using it in the notes or in the exercises. You will see, you won't miss it a bit!

***

29 第二十九課
dai ni jū kyū ka (dai nee ju- kyu- kah)

たんじょう び
誕生日
tan jō bi
(tanjo-bee)

こん ど　　　　　　　　か よう び
1 – 今度　の　火曜日　は、あなた
kon do　　　no　　ka yō bi　wa,　　a na ta
(kondo no kahyo-bee wah anahtah

たんじょうび
の　誕生日　だ から、どこか
no　tan jō bi　　da ka ra,　　do ko ka
no tanjo-bee dah kahrah dokokah

しょくじ
で　お　食事　しましょう。①
de　o shoku ji　shi ma　shō.
dé o shokoojee sheemahsho-)

しば い
2 それから　お　芝居　か
so re ka ra　　o　shiba i　ka
(sorékahrah o sheebai kah

おん がっ かい　　　　　　い
音楽会　に　行かない？②
on gak kai　ni　　i ka na i?
onga'kai nee eekanai)

た
3 – てんぷら　が　食べたい　な。③④
te n pu ra　ga　ta be ta i　na.
(tenpoorah gah tahbétai nah)

Birthday
(birthday)

1 – Next Tuesday it's your birthday. Let's go out to dinner somewhere.
(this time / [relation] / Tuesday / [announce] / you / [relation] / birthday / it is / because // somewhere / [place] / [familiarity]-meal-let's do)

2 What if we went to the theatre or to a concert afterwards?
(afterwards / [familiarity]-theatre / or else / concert / [goal] / not go)

3 – I would love to eat tempura!
(tempura / [subject] / be the object of desire of eating / [reflection])

ಲಂಜ಼ಲಂಞ

Notes

① The conversation taking place here is between a woman and her husband. For the most part they use the low degree, particularly when the choice exists between low and middle degrees (at the end of a phrase; before the が **ga** and から **kara**). To begin: だ **da** is the low form of です **desu**: *it is*.

② 行かない **ikanai**, low degree of 行きません **ikimasen**: *not go*. When the tone of conversation is very familiar, there isn't even any need to use か **ka** to indicate the asking of a question, as long as the intonation of the sentence rises towards the end (as we use a higher pitch when asking questions in English). In this case only do we end the sentence with a question mark.

③ てんぷら **tempura**, lightly fried vegetables or fish.

④ な **na**, cf. Lesson 19, note 5.

4 – じゃ　それなら　上原〔うえはら〕　さん　が
ja　　so re na ra　ue hara　sa n　ga
(jah sorénahrah ooéhahrah san gah

教〔おし〕えて　くれた　お　店〔みせ〕　に
oshi e te　ku re ta　o　mise　ni
osheeété kurétah o meesé nee

行〔い〕きましょう。⑤⑥
i ki ma　shō.
eekeemahsho-)

5 – ぴあ　は　どこ。⑦
pi a　wa　do ko?
(peeah wah doko)

6 – そこ　の　ピアノ　の　上〔うえ〕　に
so ko　no　pi a no　no　ue　ni
(soko no peeano no ooé nee

ある　から　取〔と〕って。⑧
a ru　ka ra　to t te.
ahroo kahrah to'té)

7 お　芝居〔しばい〕　は　何〔なん〕　ページ　に
o shiba i　wa　nan　pē ji　ni
(o sheebai wah nan pé-jee nee

出〔で〕て　いる？　音楽会〔おんがっかい〕　は？⑨
de te　i ru?　on gak kai　wa?
dété eeroo) (ongak'kai wah)

4 – In that case, let's go to the restaurant that Mrs. Uehara suggested.
(so / in that case / Uehara-Mrs. / [subject] / teach / have done for me / [familiarity]-store / [goal] / go)

5 – Where is *The Pia*?
(Pia / [announce] / where)

6 – On the piano, pass it to me.
(there / [relation] / piano / [relation] / above / [place] / exist / because // take)

7 What page are the theatres on? And the concerts?
([familiarity]-theatre / [announce] / what-page / [place] / appear) (concert / [announce])

ཨༀༀༀ

Notes

⑤ くれた **kureta**, low degree of くれました **kuremashita**: *having done for me.*

⑥ 店 **mise**, a very general term for all stores, including restaurants.

⑦ ぴあ **pia**, a weekly magazine that lists all shows and spectacles in Tōkyō.

⑧ ある **aru**, the low degree of あります **arimasu**: *exist.*

⑨ 出て いる **dete iru**, low degree for 出て います **dete imasu**: *going out, appearing.*

8 音楽会 なら 今 サモロビッチ
on gak kai na ra ima sa mo ro bi t chi
(onga'kai nahrah eemah sahmorobee'chee

が 日本 に 来て いる から、
ga ni hon ni ki te i ru ka ra,
gah neehon nee keeté eeroo kahrah

聞き に 行きましょう。⑩
ki ki ni i ki ma shō.
keekee nee eekeemahsho-)

9 それとも 歌舞伎 なら 今
so re to mo ka bu ki na ra ima
(sorétomo kahbookee nahrah eemah

五三郎 が「四谷 怪談」を やって
go sabu rō ga yotsu ya kai dan o ya t te
go sahbooro-gah yotsooyah kaidan o yah'té

いる わ よ。⑪⑫⑬
i ru wa yo.
eeroo wah yo)

10 あなた は サモロビッチ と 五三郎
a na ta wa sa mo ro bi t chi to go sabu rō
(ahnahtah wah sahmorobee'chee to gosahbooro-

と どっち が いい の。⑭
to do t chi ga i i no.
to do'chee gah ee- no)

8 If you want to see a concert, Samorovitch is in Japan right now, so let's go see that. **29**
(concert / if it is / now / Samorovitch / [subject] / Japan / [goal] / come / because // listen / [goal] / let's go)

9 Or if you feel like kabuki, Gosaburō is showing *Ghosts of Yotsuya* at the moment.
(otherwise / kabuki / if it is / now / Gosaburō / [subject] / Yotsuya-ghost story / [object] / be doing / [softener] / [engagement])

10 Which do you prefer, Samorovitch or Gosaburō?
(you / [announce] / Samorovitch / and / Gosaburō / and / which one of the two / [subject] / be good / [question])

ഓൽയൽൽ

Notes

⑩ 来て いる **kite iru**, low degree of 来て います **kite imasu**: *coming*.

⑪ 歌舞伎 **kabuki** is one of Japan's national traditional styles of theatre. It is a stylized performance full of special effects, costumes, and lots of color.

⑫ やって いる **yatte iru**, low degree for やって います **yatte imasu**: *doing*
For all forms of て います **te imasu** (middle degree), て いる **te iru** (low degree), cf. Lesson 11, note 2.

⑬ 「四谷怪談」 **yotsuya kaidan**, one of the most famous kabuki plays.

⑭ の **no**, used often, but mostly by women, in place of か **ka** to end an interrogative statement.

29

11 あ、ちょっと 待って。火曜日 は
   a, cho t to ma t te. ka yō bi wa
   (ah cho'to mah'té) (kahyo-bee wah

サモロビッチ の 演奏 は ない
sa mo ro bi t chi no en sō wa na i
sahmorobee'chee no enso- wah nai

わ。歌舞伎 に しましょう。⑮
wa. ka bu ki ni shi ma shō.
(wah) (kahbookee nee sheemahsho-)

12 あたし が 切符 を 買って
   a ta shi ga kip pu o ka t te
   (ahtahshee gah kee'poo o kah'té

おく わ。⑯⑰
o ku wa.
okoo wah)

13 – じゃ たのむ よ。⑱
   ja ta no mu yo.
   (jah tanomoo yo)

14 – あ、これ 先週 の ぴあ よ。
   a, ko re sen shū no pi a yo.
   (ah koré senshu- no peeah yo)

Notes

⑮ ない **nai**, low degree of ありません **arimasen**: *not exist*.

⑯ あたし the pronunciation **atashi** for *me* (from **watashi**) is only used by women.

⑰ おく **oku**, low degree of おきます **okimasu**: *do in advance*.

⑱ たのむ **tanomu**, low degree of たのみます **tanomimasu**: *to ask for*; actually, this corresponds to the familiar conversation use of a formula we have often come across おねがい します ▸

11 Ah, wait a minute. Tuesday there's no **29**
Samorovitch recital. It'll have to be kabuki.
*(ah / a bit / wait) (Tuesday / [emphasis] / Samorovitch /
[relation] / recital / [announce] / not exist / [softener])*
(kabuki / [goal] / let's do)

12 I'll get the tickets.
*(me / [subject] / ticket / [object] / buy / do in advance /
[softener])*

13 – Okay, I'm depending on you.
(good / ask a favor / [engagement])

14 – Ah, this is *The Pia* from last week!
(ah / this / last week / [relation] / Pia / [engagement])

▸ **onegai shimasu** (cf. Lesson 16, item 13; Lesson 19, item 14),
and really means *please*.
So there, that's it. It was a bit tough, but now we're past it. In this
lesson's notes, we have faithfully indicated each time we have used
a low verb form. But we won't do it anymore, promise. That would
be a little too monotonous, wouldn't it? Because for verbs, there
is actually an easy trick to help you recognize low degree forms:
they are just all the forms that don't end with ます **masu**, ません
masen, ました **mashita**, ません でした **masen deshita**, or ま
しょう **mashō** (cf. Lesson 7, paragraph 1). So you are more than
capable of noting low form verbs on your own.

練習 renshū

Exercise 1

❶ 一緒 に 買物 に 行かない？
issho ni kaimono ni ikanai?

❷ 火曜日 に テレビ で 見た 映画 は
kayōbi ni terebi de mita eiga wa

中国 の 映画 でした。
chūgoku no eiga deshita.

❸ また どこか に 忘れました。
mata dokoka ni wasuremashita.

❹ 今 日本 に 来て いる フランス
ima nihon ni kite iru furansu

の 歌手 が 歌って いる 歌 を
no   kashu ga utatte iru uta o

***

Exercise 2

... に 言葉 を 入れ なさい

❶ I think it's Tuesday.

. . . .

❷ I want to eat apples.

ringo .. tabe ... desu

❸ It is on the television.

. . . .

聞きました か。
kikimashita ka.

❺ 音楽会 は 百七 ページ に 出て
ongakkai wa hyaku nana pēji ni dete

います。
imasu.

❻ 先週 から やって いる 「四谷怪談」
senshū kara yatte iru yotsuya kaidan

が ぜひ 見たい です。
ga zehi mitai desu.

Answers to Exercise 1

❶ Won't you go shopping with me? ❷ The movie we saw on television on Tuesday was a Chinese film. ❸ I forgot it somewhere again. ❹ Have you heard the songs by that French singer who is in Japan right now? ❺ The concerts are on page 107. ❻ I absolutely want to see *Ghosts of Yotsuya* that has been showing since last week.

✳✳✳

❹ Which do you prefer, theatre or kabuki?
    shibai .. kabuki .. .. no

❺ I think there isn't any news at this time.
    ima no jikan wa nyūsu wa ... .

Answers to Exercise 2

❶ kayōbi da to omoimasu. ❷ – ga – tai –. ❸ terebi no ue ni arimasu. ❹ – to – to dochi ga ii –. ❺ – nai to omoimasu.

第三十課
<small>だい さん じゅっ か</small>

dai san juk ka *(dai san ju'kah)*

夏 休み
<small>なつ</small> <small>やす</small>

natsu yasu mi
(nahtsoo yahsoomee)

1 – お 久しぶり です ね。 きれい
<small>ひさ</small>
    o hisa shi bu ri   de su ne. ki re i
(o) (heesahsheebooree dés' né) (keeréee

に 小麦 色 に 焼けましたね。①
<small>こ むぎ</small> <small>いろ</small> <small>や</small>
ni ko mugi iro ni ya ke ma shi ta ne.
nee komoogee eero nee yahkémahshtah né)

2 夏 休み は どこ へ 行った
<small>なつ</small> <small>やす</small> <small>い</small>
natsu yasu mi wa do ko e   i t ta
(nahtsoo yahsoomee wah doko é ee'tah

の です か。②
no   de su ka.
no dés' kah)

3 – 大島 へ 行って きました。
<small>おお しま</small> <small>い</small>
oo shima e   i t te ki ma shi ta.
(o-sheemah é ee'té keemahshtah)

Notes

① One of the uses of the particle に **ni** is to allow expressions to do the work of adverbs (cf. Lesson 8, note 2, and Lesson 14, paragraph 3). We have often come across this use in the phrase 一緒に **issho ni**, *together*. Here we see two other examples. ▶
<small>いっしょ</small>

Summer Vacation
(summer-vacation)

1 – It's been a long time since I've seen you! What a beautiful tan, as golden as wheat!
(a long time since / it is / [agreement]) (beautiful / [adverb] / wheat-color / [adverb] / be tan / [agreement])

2 Where were you for vacation?
(summer-vacation / [announce] / where / [destination] / went / it is / [question])

3 – I went to Ōshima.
(Ōshima / [destination] / go / came)

ಙಛಬಳಿಚ

きれい に 小麦色 に 焼けました ね。

▸ ② In Japanese we often find の です **no desu** at the end of a sentence. It adds a slight nuance to an explanation. 行きました **ikimashita**, *I went*; 行った の です **itta no desu**, *it's that I went*. But note: in front of のです **no desu**, you have to use the low degree.

4 瀬戸内海 の 西 に ある 島
se to nai kai　no　nishi　ni　　a ru shima
(sétonaikai no neeshee nee ahroo sheemah

です。そこ の 名物 は みかん
de su.　　so ko　no meibutsu wa　mi ka n
dés') (soko no mé-bootsoo wah meekan)

です。③
de su.
dés')

5 そこ は 太陽 の 光 が
so ko　wa　tai yō　no　hikari　ga
(soko wah taiyo- no heekahree gah

強い です。
tsuyo i　　de su.
tsooyoee dés')

6 ですから、一 日 中 泳ぐ か
de su ka ra,　ichi nichi jū　oyo gu　ka
(dés' kahrah eecheeneecheeju- oyogoo kah

昼寝 しか できません。④
hiru ne　shi ka　de ki ma se n.
heeroo né sheekah dékeemahsen)

7 毎朝 六 時 半 に 起きました。
mai asa roku　ji　han　ni　o ki ma shi ta.
(maheeahsah rokoo jee han nee okeemahshtah)

そして 海 へ 泳ぎ に 行きました。
so shi te　umi　e　oyo gi　ni　i ki ma shi ta.
(soshté oomee é oyogee nee eekeemahshtah)

4   It's an island located in the west Inland Sea of   **30**
Japan. They're famous for tangerines.
*(Inland Sea/ [relation] / west / [place] / exist / island / it
is) (there / [relation] / specialty / [announce] / tangerine /
it is)*

5   The sun is very bright over there.
*(there / [announce] / sun / [relation] / light / [subject] / be
strong / it is)*

6   Because of this, you can do nothing but swim or
sleep all day.
*(because of this / all day / swim / or else / nap / except / not
be possible)*

7   I got up every morning at 6:30. Then I went to
the sea to swim.
*(every morning / six-o'clock-half / [time] / got up) (then /
sea / [destination] / swim / [goal] / went)*

ಬಂಗಿಬಂಗಿ

Notes

③ 瀬戸内海 **setonakai**, *the Inland Sea*. This sea separates the
three large islands that make up Japan. Spotted with islands and
islets of all sizes, it is home to some of the most beautiful scen-
ery in the Japanese archipelago.

④ A grammatical pattern to know well: しか **shika** + verb in the
negative = *only*, or *nothing but*.

8 その 時間 は 海岸 に
so no ji kan wa kai gan ni
(sono jeekan wah kaigan nee

だれも いません。
da re mo i ma se n.
dahrémo eemahsen)

9 朝日 が 水平線 から 出て くる
asa hi ga sui hei sen ka ra de te ku ru
(ahsahhee gah sooeehé-sen kahrah dété kooroo

眺め は すばらしい です。
naga me wa su ba ra shi i de su.
nahgahmé wah soobahrahshee- dés')

10 日中 は とても 暑い です。村
nit chū wa to te mo atsu i de su. mura
(nee'chu- wah totémo ahtsooee dés') (moorah

の 人 は 働いて います が 私
no hito wa hatara i te i ma su ga watakushi
no heeto wah hahtahraheeté eemahs' gah wahtahkooshee

は 昼寝 を して いました。⑤
wa hiru ne o shi te i ma shi ta.
wah heerooné o sheeté eemahshtah)

11 島 で 食べた 魚 や 貝類 は
shima de ta be ta sakana ya kai rui wa
(sheemah dé tabétah sahkanah yah kairooee wah

とても おいしかった です。⑥
to te mo o i shi ka t ta de su.
totémo oeesheekah'tah dés')

8 At that time no one else would be on the beach. **30**
(that / time / [announce] / shore / [place] / no one / wasn't there)

9 The view of the sun rising over the horizon is wonderful.
(sun rise / [subject] / sea horizon / from / exit / come / view / [announce] / be wonderful / it is)

10 The daytime is very hot. The people in the village were at work, but I was napping.
(middle of the day / [announce] / very / be hot / it is) (village / [relation] / person / [announce] / be working / but // I / [announce] / nap / [object] / was doing)

11 The fish and shellfish I ate on the island were delicious.
(island / [place] / ate / fish / and / shellfish / [announce] / very / were good / it is)

೫೦೦೮೮೦೧

Notes

⑤ して いました **shite imashita**. You can guess. It's just the past-tense form of して います **shite imasu**.
して います **shite imasu**, *I (you, he...)* **am/are/is** *doing*
して いました **shite imashita**, *I (you, he...)* **was/were** *doing, I* **did**.

⑥ おいしかった です **oishikatta desu**. おいしかった **oishikatta** is the past-tense form of おいしい **oishii**, *taste good*. おいしい **oishii** on its own means *taste good* (low degree), and おいしかった **oishikatta** alone means *tasted good* (low degree). The following です **desu** indicates that the adjective is actually in the middle degree.

12 その 日 に 釣れた 魚 です
so no hi ni tsu re ta sakana de su
(sono hee nee tsoorétah sahkanah dés'

から、 とても 新鮮 です。
ka ra, to te mo shin sen de su.
kahrah totémo sheensén dés')

13 また 来年 の 夏 も 行く
ma ta rainen no natsu mo i ku
(mahtah rainen no nahtsoo mo eekoo

つもり です。
tsu mo ri de su.
tsoomoree dés')

14 – うらやましい です ね。
u ra ya ma shi i de su ne.
(oorahyahmahshee dés' né)

練習 renshū

Exercise 1

❶ 兄 は 起きて いました が、 私 は
ani wa okite imashita ga, watakushi wa

寝て いました。
nete imashita.

❷ フランス の 西 に ある 村 に 行った
furansu no nishi ni aru mura ni itta

の です。
no desu.

12   Because the fish were caught just that day, they **30**
were very fresh.
*(that / day / [time] / caught / fish / it is / because // very /
fresh / it is)*

13   I'll be going back next summer!
*(again / next year / [relation] / summer / also / go / inten-
tion / it is)*

14 – How I envy you!
(be envious / it is / [agreement])

ಊಬಊಬ

❸ その 島 で 食べた みかん は とても
sono shima de tabeta mikan wa totemo

おいしかった ですが、ビール
oishikatta desu ga, bīru

は とても 高かった です。
wa totemo takakatta desu.

❹ すぐ 行きました が、だれも
sugu ikimashita ga, daremo

いません でした。
imasen deshita.

❺ ここ から は 海 しか 見えません。
koko kara wa umi shika miemasen.

Answers to Exercise 1

❶ My brother was awake, but I was sleeping. ❷ (It's that) I went
to a village in the west of France. ❸ The tangerines I ate on that
island were delicious, but the beer was very expensive. ❹ I went
there right away, but no one was there. ❺ You can't see anything
but sea from here.

...に 言葉 を 入れ なさい

❶ Until eight in the morning there is no one.

gozen .... made ....

❷ I think I'll go at half past eleven.

... ... omoimasu

❸ My son only drinks fruit juice.

.... jūsu ..... nomi .....

❹ There are only books in Japanese or in Chinese.

.... no hon .....
....

---

31 第三十一課

dai san jū ik ka *(dai san ju- ee'kah)*

バーゲン
bā ge n
(bah-gen)

1 – 旅行 に 出る 前 に、小さい
ryo kō ni de ru mae ni, chii sa i
(ryoko- nee déroo mahé nee chee-sai

手提 鞄 と タオル を 三 枚 と
te sage kaban to ta o ru o san mai to
tésahgé kahban to tahoroo o sanmai to

香水 が 買いたい です。①
kō sui ga ka i ta i de su.
ko-sooee gah kaheetai dés')

⑤ That's a road I walk along often.

.... aruku ....

Answers to Exercise 2

❶ – hachi ji – daremo imasen. ❷ jū ichi ji han ni iku to –. ❸ musuko wa – shika – masen. ❹ nihongo ka chūgokugo – shika arimasen. ❺ yoku – michi desu.

Lesson Thirty One   31

On Sale
(bargain)

1 – Before going on vacation, I want to buy a small tote bag, three towels, and perfume.
(travel / [goal] / leave / before / [time] // be small / tote bag / and / towel / [object] / three-sheet / and / perfume / [subject] / be object of desire of purchase / it is)

Notes

① 手提 鞄 **tesagekaban**, a *tote bag* of the sort one might use to go grocery shopping. They're very common in Japan for shopping, and they are sold everywhere in leather, cloth, plastic, and heavy paper.

31

2 – 今　　三越　デパート が バーゲン
ima mitsu koshi de pā to ga bā ge n
(eemah meetsookoshee dépah-to gah bah-gen

を して います から、そこ で
o　shi te　i ma su ka ra,　so ko　de
o sheeté eemahs' kahrah soko dé

買いましょう。②
ka　i ma　shō.
kaheemahsho-)

3　散歩　がてら　東京　駅　から
san po　ga te ra　tō kyō　eki　ka ra
(sanpo gahtérah to-kyo- ékee kahrah

歩いて　行きましょう。③
aru i te　i ki ma　shō.
ahrooeeté eekeemahsho-)

4 – それ は いい 考え です ね。
so re wa i i kanga e　de su　ne.
(soré wah ee- kangahé dés' né)

5 – あ、雨 が 降って きました から、
a,　ame ga fu t te　ki ma shi ta　ka ra,
(ah ahmé gah foo'té keemahshtah kahrah

地下鉄　に　乗りましょう。④
chi ka tetsu　ni　no ri ma　shō.
cheekahtétsoo nee noreemahsho-)

6　タオル は どんな 色 が
ta o ru　wa　do n na　iro　ga
(tahoroo wah do'nah eero gah

いい です か。
i i　de su　ka.
ee- dés' kah)

2 – There's a sale at Mitsukoshi right now, let's go
buy them there!
(now / Mitsukoshi-department store / [subject] / sale /
[object] / be doing / because // there / [place] / let's buy)

3 Why don't we take a walk, then from there step
over to Tōkyō Station!
(walk / while doing / Tōkyō Station / from / walking / let's
go)

4 – That's a great idea!
(that / [announce] / be good / idea / it is / [agreement])

5 – Ah! It's starting to rain, let's take the subway!
(ah / rain / [subject] / fall / came / because // subway /
[goal] / take)

6 What color towels do you want?
(towel / [announce] / what kind / color / [subject] / be good
/ it is / [question])

ೞഏഔഏ

Notes

② 三越 デパート **Mitsukoshi depāto**, the oldest department
store in Tōkyō. The equivalent of Bloomingdale's or Harrods.

③ 東京 駅 **Tōkyō eki**. Tōkyō is teeming with stations, because
urban transportation is mostly taken care of by trains. But 東京
駅 **Tōkyō eki** is *Tōkyō Station*, located in the east part of the
city, which is the principal departure point for all main train
lines.

④ The Japanese use から **kara** very often to link two sentences,
and though から **kara** means *because*, it is used much more
often in Japanese than this word in English.

7 – あそこ に かかって いる 赤い

a so ko ni ka ka t te i ru aka i

(ahsoko nee kahkah'té eeroo ahkai

タオル と 青い タオル を ペア

ta o ru to ao i ta o ru o pe a

tahoroo to ahoee tahoroo o péah

で 買いましょう。

de ka i ma shō.

dé kaheemahsho-)

8 – それ と 三 枚 目 に は その 横

so re to san mai me ni wa so no yoko

(soré to san-mai mé nee wah sono yoko

に ある 白い タオル は いかが。

ni a ru shiro i ta o ru wa i ka ga.

nee ahroo sheeroee tahoroo wah eekahgah)

9 – あ、 この 傘 は 安い です ね。

a, ko no kasa wa yasu i de su ne.

(ah kono kahsah wah yahsooee dés' né)

10 主人 が この 間 姉 から

shu jin ga ko no aida ane ka ra

(shujeen gah kono aidah ané kahrah

もらった 傘 を 電車 に 忘れた

mo ra t ta kasa o den sha ni wasu re ta

morah'tah kahsah o denshah nee wahsoorétah

の です よ。

no de su yo.

no dés' yo)

7 – Why don't we buy the red towel and the blue **31**
towel hanging up over there as a pair.
(over there / [place] / be hanging / be red / towel / and / be blue / towel / [object] / pair / [means] / let's buy)

8 – And for the third towel, how about that white towel just to the side?
(that / and / three-sheet-th / [goal] / [emphasis] / that / side / [place] / exist / be white / towel / [announce] / how)

9 – Ah, this umbrella is pretty cheap!
(ah / this / umbrella / [announce] / be cheap / it is / [agreement])

10 Just the other day, my husband left the umbrella his sister gave him on the train.
(my husband / [subject] / this / time interval / older sister / from / received / umbrella / [object] / train / [place] / forgot / it's that / [engagement])

ဆဌဆဌ

11 あら、この 水色 の 縁 が
   a ra, ko no mizu iro no fuchi ga
(ahrah kono meezoo eero no foochee gah

ついた ガウン も 安い です ね。
tsu i ta ga u n mo yasu i de su ne.
tsooeetah gahoon mo yahsooee dés' né)

一 時間 後
ichi ji kan go
(eechee jeekan go)

12 さあ 帰りましょう。
   sa a kae ri ma shō.
(sah- kahéreemahsho-)

13 帰り に 銀行 に 寄って も
kae ri ni gin kō ni yo t te mo
(kahéree nee geenko- nee yo'té mo

いい です か。⑤
i i de su ka.
ee- dés' kah)

14 お 金 を 全部 使って
   o kane o zen bu tsuka t te
(o kah né o zen boo tsoo kah'té

しまいました ので…⑥⑦
shi ma i ma shi ta no de.
sheemaheemahshtah no dé)

           ☐

***

11   Oh, this robe with the blue edges is pretty
cheap, too!
*(oh / this / water-color / [relation] / edge / [subject] / be
attached / robe / also / be cheap / it is / [agreement])*

One hour later
(one-hour-after)

12   Okay, let's go home!
(well / let's return)

13   Can I stop by the bank on the way?
*(return / [time] / bank / [goal] / stop by / even / be good /
it is / [question])*

14   It's just that I've spent all my money, so…
*([familiarity]-money / [object] / entire / use-have done to
completion / because)*

෨ඤ඀ඥ

Notes

⑤   This is the usual way of asking permission for something.
Literally, "Even if I stop by the bank, is that okay?".

⑥   Contrary to what we are used to, Japanese people almost never
use checks, and only occasionally will they use credit cards. For
most purchases, even large ones, they use cash.

⑦   We have begun to see a number of patterns connecting two verbs
with the 'て' at the end of the first verb, followed by a second. In
this case, the phrase 使って しまいました **tsukatte shimatta**
indicates that she used all of her money, without really intending
to. The Japanese are very fond of this construction, and will use
it for everything from 'I failed my test' to 'I ate all the peanut
butter'.

✳✳✳

<ruby>練習<rt>れん しゅう</rt></ruby> **renshū**

Exercise 1

❶ <ruby>観光<rt>かん こう</rt></ruby> がてら <ruby>仕事<rt>し ごと</rt></ruby> を
kankō gatera shigoto o
するつもり です。
suru tsumori desu.

❷ <ruby>誕生日<rt>たん じょう び</rt></ruby> に <ruby>兄<rt>あに</rt></ruby> から <ruby>鞄<rt>か ばん</rt></ruby>
tanjōbi ni ani kara kaban
をもらいました。
o moraimashita.

❸ <ruby>毎朝<rt>まい あさ</rt></ruby> <ruby>雨<rt>あめ</rt></ruby> が <ruby>降<rt>ふ</rt></ruby>ります。
maiasa ame ga furimasu.

***

Exercise 2

...に <ruby>言葉<rt>こと ば</rt></ruby> を <ruby>入<rt>い</rt></ruby>れ なさい

❶ This teacup is cheap, I'll buy it.
kono chawan wa . . . . , kaimasu

❷ Can I watch the television?
terebi o mite . . . .

❸ Before taking the bus, let's stop by the post office.
. . . . . . noru . . . . . yūbinkyoku . . yorimashō

❹ What color is the car our neighbor bought?
tonari no hito ga katta jidōsha wa . . . .
. . . . . .

❹ ジャズ の コンサート
jazu no konsāto

が 聞^ききたい な。

ga kikitai na.

❺ 夜^{よる} 寝^ねる 前^{まえ} に コーヒー
yoru neru mae ni kōhī

は 飲^のみません。

wa nomimasen.

Answers to Exercise 1

❶ I plan to work while sightseeing. ❷ For my birthday I got a bag from my brother. ❸ It rains every morning. ❹ I would like to hear a jazz concert. ❺ I don't drink coffee before I go to bed at night.

∗∗∗

❺ Is it red, blue, or white?
    akai desu ka . . . .

Answers to Exercise 2

❶ – yasui desu kara –. ❷ – mo ii desu ka. ❸ basu ni – mae ni – ni –.
❹ – donna iro desu ka. ❺ – aoi desu ka shiroi desu ka.

32 第三十二課
だい さん じゅう に か

dai san jū ni ka *(dai san ju- nee kah)*

高速道路
こう そく どう ろ

kō soku dō ro

(ko-sokoodo-ro)

1 – 伯父　が　自動車　を　貸して
おじ　　　じどうしゃ　　　か

o ji　ga　ji dō sha　o　ka shi te

(ojee gah jeedo-shah o kahsheeté

くれた　ので、先週　の　週末、
せんしゅう　　しゅうまつ

ku re ta　no de, sen shū　no　shū matsu,

koorétah nodé senshu- no shu-mahtsoo

会社　の　同僚　と　関西　旅行　を
かい しゃ　　どうりょう　　かんさい　りょこう

kai sha no　dō ryō　to kan sai ryo kō　o

kaishah no do-ryo- to kansai ryoko- o

する　つもり　で　出発　しました。①
しゅっぱつ

su ru tsu mo ri　de shup patsu shi ma shi ta.

sooroo tsoomoree dé shu'pahtsoo sheemahshtah)

2 – いかが　でした　か。

i ka ga　de shi ta　ka.

(eekahgah déshtah kah)

3 – 最初　は　国道　を　走りました　が、
さい しょ　　こく どう　　はし

sai sho wa koku dō　o hashi ri mashi ta　ga,

(saisho wah kokudo- o hasheereemahshtah gah

混んで　いました　ので、高速道路
こ ん　　　　　　　こう そく どう ろ

ko n de　i mashi ta　no de, kō soku dō ro

kondé eemahshtah nodé ko-sokoodo-ro

で　行く　こと　に　しました。
い

de　i ku　ko to　ni　shi ma shi ta.

dé eekoo koto nee sheemahshtah)

The Highway
(highway)

1 – Because my uncle lent me his car, a colleague of mine and I took off last weekend for a little vacation in Kansai.

(my uncle / [subject] / car / [object] / lend / have done for me / because // last week / [relation] / weekend / company / [relation] / colleague / [partnership] / Kansai-trip / [object] / do / intention / [means] / depart-did)

2 – How was it?

(how / it was / [question])

3 – First I took the National Road, but traffic was heavy, so we decided to take the highway.

(first / [emphasis] / national road / [object] / ran / but // was packed / because // highway / [means] / go / fact of / [goal] / did)

෯ඏ෯ඏ

Notes

① 関西 *Kansai*. This term indicates a region in the West part of Japan's main island. It is the region where the former capital Kyōto and the important commercial city of Ōsaka are located.

4
高速道路 で は スピード 制限
kō soku dō ro   de   wa   su pī do   sei gen
(ko-sokoodo-ro dé wah s'peedo sé-gen

が 八 十 キロ な ので、
ga   hachi juk   ki ro   na   no de,
gah hahchee ju'keero nah nodé

早く 進みません でした。
haya ku   susu mi mase n   de shi ta.
hahyahkoo soosoomeemahsen déshtah)

5
それに トラック が たくさん
so re ni   to ra k ku   ga   ta ku sa n
(sorénee torah'koo gah tahkoosan

走って いました。②
hashi t te   i ma shi ta.
hahshee'té eemahshtah)

6
トラック を 追い越す こと
to ra k ku   o   o i ko su   ko to
(torah'koo o oeekosoo koto

は むずかしい です。
wa   mu zu ka shi i   de su.
wah moozookahshee- dés')

7
すぐ スピード 違反 に なります。
su gu   su pī do   i han   ni   na ri ma su.
(soogoo soopeedo eehan nee nahreemahs')

8
ですから 日本 で の 自動車
de su ka ra   ni hon   de   no   ji dō sha
(dés'kahrah neehon dé no jeedo-shah

旅行 は 時間 が かかります。
ryo kō   wa   ji kan   ga   ka ka ri ma su.
ryoko- wah jeekan gah kahkahreemahs')

4 On the highways the speed limit is 80 km/hr, so
I didn't make much progress.
(highway / [place] / [emphasis] / speed-limit / [subject] / eight-ten-kilometer / it is / because // fast / did not advance)

5 Also, there were a lot of trucks.
(furthermore / truck / [subject] / many / was running)

6 It's hard to pass trucks.
(truck / [object] / overtake / fact of / [announce] / be difficult / it is)

7 Before long you're speeding.
(right away / speed-violation / [goal] / become)

8 That's why traveling by car in Japan takes a lot of time.
(for this reason / Japan / [place] / [relation] / car-travel / [announce] / time / [subject] / take)

෨ඐ෪ඏ

Notes

② cf. Lesson 30, note 5.

9 急いで いる 時 は 汽車 か
iso i de i ru toki wa ki sha ka
(eesoeedé eeroo tokee wah keeshah kah

飛行機 で 旅行 した 方 が
hi kō ki de ryokō shi ta hō ga
heeko-kee dé ryoko- sheetah ho- gah

早い です。③
haya i de su.
hahyai dés')

10 それに 高速道路 は いつも
so re ni kō soku dō ro wa i tsu mo
(sorénee ko-sokoodo-ro wah eetsoomo

有料 です から 高く つきます。
yū ryō de su ka ra takaku tsu ki ma su.
yu-ryo- dés' kahrah tahkahkoo tsookeemahs')

11 – 関西 は いかが でした か。
kan sai wa i ka ga de shi ta ka.
(kansai wah eekahgah déshtah kah)

12 – それ が… 静岡 辺り で スピード
so re ga... shizu oka ata ri de su pī do
(soré ga) (sheezoookah ahtahree dé soopeedo

違反 で パトカー に 捉まって
i han de pa to kā ni tsuka ma t te
eehan dé pahtokah- nee tsookahmah'té

しまいました。すごい 罰金 を
shi ma i ma shi ta. su go i bak kin o
sheemaheemahshtah) (soogooee bah'keen o

払う こと に なりました。④⑤
hara u ko to ni na ri ma shi ta.
hahrahoo koto nee nahreemahshtah)

9

When you're in a hurry, it's faster to travel by
train or airplane.

*(hurry / time / [emphasis] // train / or else / airplane /
[means] / travel-did / side / [subject] / be fast / it is)*

10 What's more, because there are tolls on all the
highways, it gets expensive.

*(furthermore / highway / [announce] / always / cost money
/ it is / because // be expensive / arrive)*

11 – And how was Kansai?

(Kansai / [announce] / how / it was / [question])

12 – Oh, that... Around Shizuoka, we were stopped
by a police car for speeding. I had to pay a huge
fine!

*(that / [subject]) (Shizuoka-around / [place] / speed-
violation / [means] / police car / [agent] / was caught /
finish by doing) (be amazing / fine / [object] / pay / fact of /
[goal] / became)*

ಬಿಛಿಉಚ

Notes

③ There are two words that mean *train*: 電車 **densha** means
trains used for urban transportation (as well as for suburban
commutes) and 汽車 **kisha** means long-distance trains.

④ 静岡 *Shizuoka*, an important city located on the coast, roughly
150 km (about 90 miles) South-West of Tōkyō.

⑤ The words we have been seeing in *katakana* (cf. Introduction,
p. XI) have until now been written out fully in their borrow-
ings from English. But very often Japanese will abbreviate
these words as well. We have seen one example: ビル **biru**
(Lesson 24, item 10), abbreviation of ビルヂング **birudingu**
building –but here is another: パトカー **pato kā**, which is an
abbreviation of パトロルカー **patororu kā**, *patrol car*. As you
can see, the result of these abbreviations is sometimes quite a
mystery, or even ambiguous. キロ **kiro** is an abbreviation for
"kilo(meter)", but also for "kilo(gram)"!

13 それで 予算 が 足りなく なった
so re de yosan ga ta ri na ku na t ta
(sorédé yosan gah tahreenahkoo nah'tah

ので、そのまま 東京 に
no de, so no ma ma tō kyō ni
nodé sonomahmah to-kyo- nee

戻りました。
modo ri ma shi ta.
modoreemahshtah)

□

***

練習 renshū

Exercise 1

❶ 姉 はいい店 を 教えて くれました。
ane wa ii mise o oshiete kuremashita.

❷ 汽車 で 行った 方 が 便利 です。
kisha de itta hō ga benri desu.

❸ 雨 が 降って いました から、地下鉄
ame ga futte imashita kara, chikatetsu

で 行く こと に しました。
de iku koto ni shimashita.

***

13 So, since we were over budget already, we went **32**
directly back to Tōkyō.
(so / budget / [subject] / not be enough / became / because //
just like that / Tōkyō / [goal] / returned)

***

❹ 今日 は 日曜日 な ので、銀行
kyō wa nichiyōbi na node, ginkō

は お 休み です。
wa o yasumi desu.

❺ 家賃 が 高く なった の です。
yachin ga takaku natta no desu.

Answers to Exercise 1

❶ My sister told me about an excellent restaurant. ❷ It's more convenient to go by train. ❸ Because it was raining, I decided to go by subway. ❹ It's Sunday, so the banks are closed. ❺ It's that the rent has become expensive.

***

33 Exercise 2

...に 言葉 を 入れ なさい

❶ She became pretty.

utsukushi .. .... mashita

❷ Because it's nice out, I'll wait in front of the bank.

ii tenki .. node, ... matte imasu

❸ Taking the National Road would take too long.

kokudō wa ....

---

33 第三十三課

dai san jū san ka *(dai san ju- san kah)*

ハチ公

ha chi kō
(hahcheeko-)

1 – 渋谷 駅 の 前 に ある 犬
shibu ya eki no mae ni a ru inu
(sheebooyah ékee no mahé nee ahroo eenoo

の 銅像 は 何 です か。
no dō zō wa nan de su ka.
no do-zo- wah nan dés' kah)

2 – これ は ハチ公 と いう 犬
ko re wa ha chi kō to i u inu
(koré wah hahcheeko- to eeu eenoo

の 銅像 です。
no dō zō de su.
no do-zo- dés')

④ I was writing a postcard. **33**
hagaki o kai .. ..

⑤ I decided to get up early.
hayaku okiru ....

⑥ It is hard to stop smoking.
kin.en suru .... desu

Answers to Exercise 2
❶ – ku nari –. ❷ – na – ginkō no mae de. ❸ – jikan ga kakarimasu. ❹
– te imashita. ❺ – koto ni shimashita. ❻ – koto wa musukashii –.

Lesson Thirty-Three   33

Hachikō

1 – What is the bronze statue of a dog in front of
Shibuya station?
*(Shibuya-station / [relation] / before / [place] / exist / dog /
[relation] / bronze statue / [announce] / what / it is / [question])*

2 – That's the statue of a dog named Hachikō.
*(this / [announce] / Hachikō [quotation] / say / dog /
[relation] / bronze statue / it is)*

ೱ ೮ ೫ ೮ ೲ ೮ ೩

3 – なぜ 犬 の 銅像 など を
na ze inu no dō zō na do o
(nahzé eenoo no do-zo- nahdo o

作った の です か。
tsuku t ta no de su ka.
tsookoo'tah no dés' kah)

4 – これ は 話す と 長く
ko re wa hana su to naga ku
(koré wah hahnahsoo to nahgahkoo

なります が…
na ri ma su ga.
nahreemahs' gah)

5 ハチ公 と いう 犬 は とても
ha chi kō to i u inu wa to te mo
(hahcheeko- to eeu eenoo wah totémo

感心 な 犬 でした。①
kan shin na inu deshi ta.
kansheen nah eenoo déshtah)

6 六 十 年 前 の こと です。
roku jū nen mae no ko to de su.
(rokooju- nen mahé no koto dés')

7 上野 英三郎 さん と いう
ue no ei sabu rō sa n to i u
(ooéno é-sahbooro- san to eeu

大学 の 先生 が いました。
dai gaku no sen sei ga i mashi ta.
daigahkoo no sensé- gah eemahshtah)

3 – And why did they build a statue of a dog there? **33**
(why / dog / [relation] / bronze statue-this kind of thing /
[object] / made / it's that / [question])

4 – It's a long story...
(this [announce] / speak / when // be long / become / but)

5 This dog called Hachikō was a very moving dog.
(Hachikō / [quotation] / say / dog / [announce] / very /
wonderful / it is / dog / it was)

6 It was 60 years ago.
(six-ten-years-before / [relation] / thing / it is)

7 There was a university professor named Ueno
Eisaburō.
(Ueno Eisaburō-Mr. / [quotation] / say / university / [rela-
tion] / professor / [subject] / existed)

ဢဢ⋙ဢ

Notes

① 感心 な 犬 **kanshin** *na* **inu**. cf. also Lesson 32, item 4. This
な **na** is the form that takes です **desu**, *it is*, in the position we
call "within a sentence or phrase". We will often find this な **na**,
whenever we have to say *it is*, before ので **node**, *because*.

8 ハチ公 と いう 犬 を
ha chi kō to i u inu o
(hahcheeko- to eeu eenoo o

飼って いました。
ka t te i ma shi ta.
kah'té eemahshtah)

9 毎朝 上野 さん が 大学 へ
mai asa ue no sa n ga dai gaku e
(maiahsah ooéno san gah daigahkoo é

行く 時、ハチ公 は いつも 駅
i ku toki, ha chi kō wa i tsu mo eki
eekoo tokee hahcheeko- wah eetsoomo ékee

まで おくって 行きました。
ma de o ku t te i ki ma shi ta.
mahdé okoo'té eekeemahshtah)

10 夕方 上野 さん が 大学 から
yū gata ue no sa n ga dai gaku ka ra
(yu-gahtah ooéno san gah daigahkoo kahrah

帰って くる 時、ハチ公 は
kae t te ku ru toki, ha chi kō wa
kahé'té kooroo tokee hahcheeko- wah

かならず 迎え に 行きました。
ka na ra zu muka e ni i ki ma shi ta.
kahnahrahzoo mookahé nee eekeemahshtah)

11 – かわいい 犬 です ね。
ka wa i i inu de su ne.
(kahwahee- eenoo dés' né)

（続く）
tsuzu ku
(tsoozookoo) □

8 He had a dog called Hachikō.
(Hachikō / [quotation] say / dog / [object] / was raising)

9 Every morning when Mr. Ueno went to the university, Hachikō would always see him off to the station.
(every morning / Ueno-Mr. / [subject] / university / [destination] / go / time // Hachikō / [announce] / always / station / until / see off / went)

10 And in the evening when Mr. Ueno came back from the university, Hachikō would always meet him there without fail.
(evening / Ueno-Mr. / [subject] / university / from / return / come / time // Hachikō / [announce] / without fail / meet / [goal] / went)

11 – What a great dog!
(be adorable / dog / it is / [agreement])

to be continued

ജ്ഞ്ജ്ഞ

練習 renshū

Exercise 1

❶ 遅くなりましたから、帰りましょう。
osoku narimashita kara, kaerimashō.

❷ 小林 正子 と いう 人 を 知って
kobayashi masako to iu hito o shitte
います か。
imasu ka.

❸ 毎朝 子供 を 幼稚園 に おくって
maiasa kodomo o yōchien ni okutte
いきます。
ikimasu.

✳✳✳

Exercise 2

... に 言葉 を 入れ なさい

❶ This happened two hundred years ago.
.. ..

❷ He's an admirable person.
....

❸ Why don't you go there by highway?
.... kōsokudōro de ....

❹ She's a person named Uehara Michiko.
uehara michiko .. ..

④ タオル は 一 枚 しか 買いません
taoru wa ichi mai shika kaimasen

でした。
deshita.

⑤ 夕方 会社 から 帰る 時、いつも 隣
yūgata kaisha kara kaeru toki, itsumo tonari

の 本屋 さん の 犬 に 会います。
no honya san no inu ni aimasu.

Answers to Exercise 1

❶ It's late, let's go home. ❷ Do you know somebody called Kobayashi Masako? ❸ Every morning I take the children to kindergarten. ❹ I only bought one towel. ❺ When I come back from the office at night, I always meet the dog from the bookstore next door.

✳✳✳

⑤ When I go on a trip, I always take an umbrella.

· · · · · · · · · · · · · · ·, · · · · · · · · · · . motte
ikimasu

Answers to Exercise 2

❶ ni hyaku nen mae no koto desu. ❷ kanshin na hito desu ❸ naze – ikanai no desu ka. ❹ – to iu hito desu. ❺ ryokō ni deru toki, itsumo kasa o –.

第三十四課
だい さん じゅう よん か
dai san jū yon ka *(dai san ju- yon kah)*

不動産屋 さん
ふ どう さん や
fu dō san ya sa n
(foodo-sanyah san)

1 – 青山 辺り に 家 を 捜して
あお やま あた いえ さが
ao yama ata ri ni ie o saga shi te
(ahoyahmah ahtahree nee eeé o sahgahsheeté

いる の です が、 何か
なに
i ru no de su ga, nani ka
eeroo no dés' gah nanee kah

ありません か。①②
a ri ma se n ka.
ahreemahsen kah)

2 – アパート です か、一軒家 です か。
いっ けん や
a pā to de su ka, ik ken ya de su ka.
(ahpah-to dés' kah ee'kenyah dés' kah)

3 – 庭 つき の 一軒家 に
にわ いっ けん や
niwa tsu ki no ik ken ya ni
(neewah tsookee no ee'kenyah nee

住みたい です。
す
su mi ta i de su.
soomeetai dés')

4 庭 は 大きい 方 が いい です。③
にわ おお ほう
niwa wa oo ki i hō ga i i de su.
(neewah wah o-kee- ho- gah ee- dés')

Lesson Thirty-Four 34

At the Real Estate Agent's

(real estate-store-Mr.)

1 – I'm looking for a house around Aoyama, you wouldn't have something like that, would you?
(Aoyama-around / [place] / house / [object] / be looking for / it's that / but // anything / not exist / [question])

2 – Are you looking for an apartment, or for a house?
(apartment / it is / [question] / individual house / it is / [question])

3 – I want to live in a house with a garden.
(garden-attached/ [relation] / individual house / [place] / want to live / it is)

4 I would prefer a large garden.
(garden / [announce] / be big / side / [subject] / be good / it is)

Notes

① 青山(あおやま) *Aoyama*, a part of one of the sections of Tōkyō. One of the most expensive neighborhoods in terms of property, in a city where real estate is already incredibly expensive!

② 何(なに) **nani:** *what*, interrogative. 何(なに)か **nanika**: *something*, or *anything*.

③ 方(ほう) が…です… **hō ga**...**desu**... The usual manner of marking preference in a comparison. Literally, "on the side of… it is…"

庭(にわ) は 大(おお)きい 方(ほう) が いい です
niwa wa ookii hō ga i i desu
literally: "for the garden, the direction of big is good".

5　ダイニング　と　リビング　は
da ni n gu　to　ri bi n gu　wa
(daineengoo to reebeengoo wah

別れて いる 方 が いい です。
waka re te　i ru　hō ga　i i　de su.
wahkahrété eeroo ho- gah ee- dés')

6　妻 が お 茶 と 生け花 を
tsuma ga　o　cha　to　i ke bana o
(tsoomah gah o chah to eekébanah o

します から、八 畳 ぐらい の
shi ma su　ka ra,　hachi jō　gu ra i　no
sheemahs' kahrah hahchee jo- goorai no

和室 も ほしい です。④
wa shitsu mo　ho shi i　de su.
wahsheetsoo mo hoshee- dés')

7　車 が 二台 入る ガレージ
kuruma ga　ni dai　hai ru　ga rē ji
(kooroomah gah needai haheeroo gahré-jee

も 必要 です。⑤
mo　hitsu yō　de su.
mo heetsooyo- dés')

8－台所 は どう します か。
dai dokoro wa　　dō　shi ma su　ka.
(daidokoro wah do- sheemahs' kah)

9－お 客 が 多い ので、便利 に
o kyaku ga　oo i　no de,　ben ri　ni
(o kyahkoo gah o-ee nodé benree nee

使える 台所 が いい です。⑥
tsuka e ru　dai dokoro ga　i i　de su.
tsookahéroo daidokoro gah ee dés')

5   I would prefer the dining room separate from
     the living room.
     (dining room / and / living room / [announce] / be separate /
     [subject] / be good / it is)

6   Because my wife practices tea ceremonies and
     flower arrangement, I also want a traditional-
     style Japanese room, around eight tatami in
     size.
     (my wife / [subject] / [familiarity]-tea / and / flower arrange-
     ment / [object] / do / because // eight-tatami / around /
     [relation] / Japanese room / also / be desirable / it is)

7   I also need a two-car garage.
     (car / [subject] / two-vehicle / enter / garage / also / neces-
     sary / it is)

8 –   And what would you like for the kitchen?
     (kitchen / [announce] / how / do / [question])

9 –   Since we have a lot of guests, we need a kitchen
     that's very easy to use.
     ([polite]-guest / [subject] / be many / because // convenient /
     [adverb] / can use / kitchen / [subject] / be good / it is)

ॐॐॐॐ

Notes

④   The size of a room in a traditional Japanese house is measured by
    the length of tatami that covers the floor. A tatami is a thick mat
    (between 10 and 15 cm, or 4 to 6 inches) and designed for a per-
    son to lie down upon; thus, a tatami is 1.80 meters x 0.90 meters,
    or about 6 feet by 3 feet). In Japan, they speak of a 5 tatami
    room, 6 tatami room, 16 tatami room, etc.

⑤   二台 **ni dai**. 台 is a *measure word* used for counting vehicles
    and machines (cf. Lesson 22, note 3).

⑥   便利 に **benri ni**, cf. Lesson 30, note 1.

34

10 家賃 は どのぐらい に
ya chin wa do no gu ra i ni
(yahcheen wah donogoorai nee

なります か。
na ri ma su ka.
nahreemahs' kah)

11 – 一ヶ月 百 万 円 です。⑦
ik ka getsu hyaku man en de su.
(ee'kahgétsoo hyahkoo man én dés')

12 それに 敷金 と 礼金 は
so re ni shiki kin to rei kin wa
(sorénee sheekeekeen to ré-keen wah

二ヶ月 分 です。
ni ka getsu bun de su.
neekahgétsoo boon dés')

13 だから 入居 する 時 全部
da ka ra nyū kyo su ru toki zen bu
(dahkahrah nyu-kyo sooroo tokee zenboo

で 五 百 万 円 に なります。
de go hyaku man en ni na ri ma su.
dé go hyahkoo man en nee nahreemahs')

14 – そんな に 高い の です か。
so n na ni taka i no de su ka.
(so'nah nee tahkai no dés' kah

私 に は 払う こと が
watakushi ni wa hara u ko to ga
wahtahkooshee nee wah hahrahoo koto gah

できません。あきらめます。
de ki ma se n. a ki ra me ma su.
dékeemahsen) (ahkeerahmémahs') □

10 About how much will the rent be?
(rent / [announce] / about how much / [goal] / become / [question])

11 – One million yen per month.
(one month / hundred-ten thousand-yen / it is)

12 Also, the deposit and fees come to two months' rent.
(furthermore / deposit / and / fee / [announce] / two months-part / it is)

13 So when you move in, you will have to pay five million yen.
(so / move in-do / time // total / [means] / five-hundred-ten thousand-yen / [goal] / become)

14 – It's that expensive? I can't afford it. Never mind!
(this way / [adverbial] / be expensive / it's that [question])
(me / [attribution] / [emphasis] / pay / fact of / [subject] / be impossible) (give up)

৪০৫৪৯৫

Notes

⑦ 一ヶ月 **ikkagetsu**: "duration of one month". Pay special attention here to the writing. Between the two kanji is a small ヶ (**ke** in *katakana*) pronounced **ka**. 二ヶ月 **nikagetsu**, "duration of two months", 三ヶ月 **sankagetsu**, "duration of three months", etc. (Very often this is now written 一か月).

庭 は 大きい 方 が いい です。

練習 renshū
<ruby>練<rt>れん</rt></ruby><ruby>習<rt>しゅう</rt></ruby>

Exercise 1

❶ 何か 見えました か。
nanika miemashita ka.

❷ 早く 出発 した 方 が いい です。
hayaku shuppatsu shita hō ga ii desu.

❸ 子供 が 多い ので、大きい
kodomo ga ooi node, ookii

車 が 必要 です。
kuruma ga hitsuyō desu.

***

Exercise 2

...に 言葉 を 入れ なさい

❶ There are ten cars, total.
...... wa .... ni narimasu

❷ That will be seven million yen.
.... desu

❸ It's easier to take the subway.
.... kantan desu

❹ I also want French perfume.
.... mo ....

④ 今朝 家 を 出た 時、伯父 に
kesa ie o deta toki, oji ni

会いました。
aimashita.

⑤ そんな に 遠い の です か。
sonna ni tooi no desu ka.

Answers to Exercise 1

❶ Did you see something? ❷ It would be better to leave early.
❸ Because I have a lot of children, I need a large car. ❹ When I was
leaving the house this morning, I met my uncle. ❺ Is it that far?

✳✳✳

❺ I looked, but I didn't find anything.

. . . .
. . . .

Answers to Exercise 2

❶ kuruma – zenbu de jū dai –. ❷ nana hyaku man en –. ❸ chikatetsu
de itta hō ga –. ❹ furansu no kōsui – hoshii desu. ❺ sagashimashita
ga nanimo mitsukarimasen deshita.

第<ruby>三<rt>さん</rt></ruby><ruby>十<rt>じゅう</rt></ruby><ruby>五<rt>ご</rt></ruby><ruby>課<rt>か</rt></ruby>

dai san jū go ka *(dai san ju- go kah)*

まとめ
matome
Revision and notes

You have gotten used to the rhythm, and you have been expecting this little break for the seventh lesson. It is true that they are essential in securing our notions and clarifying what we don't understand, so today we are going to take a panoramic look at what we have covered!

1. Let's begin with the particles, the bones of the Japanese sentence. You were warned (cf. Lesson 14, paragraph 3): に **ni** would not cease at finding new uses for itself. The first of these new uses we have already experienced a little bit: it allows us to create an adverbial expression (cf. Lesson 30, note 1). The second, completely new (lesson 32, item 12), shows that に **ni** indicates the agent of an action, which corresponds to the word *by* in English.

Let's take another look back at は **wa** (cf. Lesson 15, note 2). We've spoken of its use as an "emphasis" particle, especially after time adverbs. We will also find that this "emphasis" element holds true when は **wa** follows another particle (cf. Lesson 32, item 4):
<ruby>高速道路<rt>こうそくどうろ</rt></ruby>　で　は **kōsokudōro** *de wa*.

2. In our slew of question words (cf. Lesson 28, paragraph 2), we can now add なぜ **naze**, *why?* (Lesson 33, item 3).

3. Let's take a little tour through the **adjectives** we have studied (cf. Lesson 21, paragraph 2). They have a strange habit of changing form, just like verbs, but after all there are only a few of these forms and we have nearly seen all of them. So now we can seize the moment to look over what we've seen.

おいしい	**oishii**

it's good (low degree)

おいしい です	**oishii desu**

it's good (middle degree)

おいしかった	**oishikatta**

it was good (low degree)

おいしかった です	**oishikatta desu**

it was good (middle degree)

おいしくない	**oishikunai**
or おいしく は ない	**oishiku wa nai**

it's not good (low degree)

おいしく ありません	**oishiku arimasen**
or おいしく は ありません	**oishiku wa arimasen**

it is not good (middle degree).

There is also another form where い **i** is replaced by く **ku** and that's it. This is normal form for certain verbs, particularly with なる **naru**, *become*:

cf. Lesson 26, item 5: 悪く なりました **waruku narimashita**, *became bad* (悪い **warui**, *be bad*);

cf. Lesson 33, item 4: 長く なります **nagaku narimasu**, *to become long* (長い **nagai**, *be long*).

We also find this form with つく **tsuku**, *reach*;

cf. Lesson 32, item 10: 高く つきます **takaku tsukimasu**, *that will become expensive* (高い **takai**, *be expensive*).

This form can also turn an adjective into an adverb: 早い **hayai**, *early* or *fast*, 早く **hayaku**, *early* or *quickly* (cf. Lesson 32, item 4).

Be careful, there is one adjective that might be a bit difficult! Of course, that is the one we use most often! The adjective いい **ii**, *be good,* has a double –よい **yoi** –that means exactly the same thing, except that this twin is used for other forms:

いい	**ii**
it's good (low degree)	
いい です	**ii desu**
it's good (middle degree)	
But: よかった	**yokatta**
it was good (low degree),	
よかった です	**yokatta desu**
it was good (middle degree)	
But: よくない	**yokunai**
it was not good (low degree)	
よく ありません	**yoku arimasen**
it was not good (middle degree).	
And finally, よく なりました	**yoku narimashita**
it became good.	

4. Of course our little tour has to end with **verbs**. We will revisit them many times, but only because there's so much to see here! But look at the distance we've covered since Lesson 7, note 1, where we had already covered most of the forms a verb can take in middle degree. Right now we can set up a similar list for **low degree**:

I [you, s/he . . .] eat[s]		
middle degree:	食べます	**tabemasu**
low degree:	食べる	**taberu**
I [you, s/he...] do[es] not eat		
middle degree:	食べません	**tabemasen**
low degree:	食べない	**tabenai**
I [you, s/he...] ate		
middle degree:	食べました	**tabemashita**
low degree:	食べた	**tabeta**
Let's eat		
middle degree:	食べましょう	**tabemashō**
low degree:	食べよう	**tabeyō**

But don't forget about the other form we know, which implies that we are in the middle of doing something:

I'm [you are, s/he is...] eating

middle degree:	食べて います	**tabete imasu**
low degree:	食べて いる	**tabete iru**

I'm [you are, s/he is...] not eating

middle degree:	食べて いません	**tabete imasen**
low degree:	食べて いない	**tabete inai**

I was [you were, s/he was...] eating

middle degree:	食べて いました	**tabete imashita**
low degree:	食べて いた	**tabete ita**

–And that should set our table pretty well!

But don't forget (cf. Lesson 29, note 15), the low degree form that matches あります **arimasen**, *not located* or *there isn't*, is ない **nai**.

5. Here are a few notes on some of the verbs we have come across:

–don't confuse ある、あります **aru / arimasu** and いる、います **iru / imasu**. The two both can mean *to be located*, and can also mean *there are*, but ある **aru** is used exclusively for things and objects, while いる **iru** can only be used to refer to animate object such as people or animals. We have seen ある **aru** almost perpetually in our lessons, but for いる **iru** see Lesson 15, item 4, and lesson 30, item 8.

–For 帰る **kaeru** and 戻る **modoru**, the two are both translated into English as *to return*, but 帰る **kaeru** specifically means *to return home*, and can also include coming back to the home country, whereas 戻る **modoru** means simply to return back where one was before (cf. lesson 31, items 12 and 13; lesson 33, item 10; lesson 32, item 13).

6. To wrap up our revision lesson, remember what we announced in our last review chapter: from now on we will keep only the "official transcription". By now you are well used to it, and continuing to use the "figurative transcription" would risk overkill. Before we let go, though, here is a reminder for pronunciation:

the delicacy is in the transcription of **ai** and **ei**, which are sometimes pronounced "eye" and "eh", and sometimes "ah-ee" and "eh-ee", depending on the word. So for new words with these sounds, we will keep the figurative transcription. Same thing for **u**, which is

---

36 第三十六課 だい さん じゅう ろっ か dai san jū rok ka

苗字 みょう じ
myō ji

1 – 日本人 の 苗字 は 自然 の 物
ni hon jin no myō ji wa shi zen no mono
を 表す 名前 が 多い です ね。
o arawa su na mae ga oo i de su ne.

2 – そう です ね。それに 同じ
sō de su ne. so re ni ona ji
苗字 を 持って いる 人
myō ji o mo t te i ru hito
が たくさん います。①
ga ta ku sa n i ma su.

3 電話帳 に は 同じ 苗字 が
den wa chō ni wa ona ji myō ji ga
何ページ も 続く こと が
nan pē ji mo tsuzu ku ko to ga
あります。
a ri ma su.

either left unpronounced, as a tightened "oo", or else almost left off
entirely, particularly at the end of words.

At the beginning you might feel like something is missing, but
you'll get used to it quickly.

Lesson Thirty-Six   36

Family Names
(family name)

1 – Many Japanese family names represent things
in nature.
*(Japan-person / [relation] / family name / [announce] /
nature / [relation] / thing / [object] / express / name / [sub-
ject] / be numerous / it is / [agreement])*

2 – Yes. Also, there are many people who have the
same family name.
*(yes) (also / be same / family name / [object] / possess /
person / [subject] / a lot / exist)*

3 In the telephone book the same family name
will continue for pages and pages.
*(telephone book / [place] / [emphasis] / be same / family
name / [subject] / don't know how many pages / continue /
fact of / [subject] / exist)*

ဢ○ဢ

Notes

① いwill **imasu**, cf. Lesson 35, paragraph 5.

4 たとえば、山田 とか 田中 とか
ta to e ba, yama da　to ka　ta naka　to ka

鈴木 など と いう 名前 です。②
suzu ki na do　to　i u　na mae de su.

5 – どうして そんな に 同じ 名前
dō shi te　so n na　ni ona ji　na mae

の 人 が いる の です か。
no hito　ga　i ru　no　de su　ka.

皆 親戚 の 人 です か。③
min na　shin seki　no hito　de su　ka.

6 – いいえ。 必ずしも そう いう
i i e. kanara zu shi mo　sō　i u

わけ で は ありません。
wa ke　de　wa　a ri ma se n.

7 昔 は 公家 と 武家 の 人 しか
mukashi wa ku ge to bu ke no hito shi ka

苗字 が ありません でした。④
myō ji　ga　a ri ma se n　de shi ta.

8 段々 平民 も 苗字 を 持つ
dan dan hei min　mo　myō ji　o　mo tsu

こと に なりました。⑤
ko to　ni　na ri ma shi ta.

9 平民 は 田舎 に 住んで いる
hei min　wa　inaka　ni　su n de　i ru

人 が ほとんど でした。
hito　ga　ho to n do　de shi ta.

4   For example, the names Yamada, Tanaka, or Suzuki.
(for example / Yamada / or / Takana / or / Suzuki / this kind of thing / [quotation] / say / name / it is)

5 – Why are there so many people with the same family name? Are they all related?
(why / this way / [adverb] / be same / name / [relation] / person / [subject] / exist / it's that / [question]) (all / relatives / [relation] / person / it is / [question])

6 – No, not necessarily.
(no) (necessarily / so / say / reason / it isn't)

7   In the past only noble families and warrior families used family names.
(in the past / [emphasis] / court nobles / and / warriors / [relation] / person / other than / family name / [subject] / did not exist)

8   Little by little the common people took family names as well.
(gradually / common people / also / family name / [object] / possess / fact of / [goal] / became)

9   The majority of the common people were people living in the country.
(common people / [announce] / countryside / [place] / reside / person / [subject] / almost totally / it was)

৪০Ⳣৼ৹Ⳣ

Notes

② など **nado**. This little word comes either after a single noun, or else after a list, and is the equivalent of "everything that is like the thing or things I just said." Here, など **nado** is preceded by some of the most widespread family names listed as examples of the different kinds of names. In lists, とか and など **nado** often go together. とか is usually used after everything in the list except that last item, where we would just separate them with commas, and is only used when the list ends with など.

③ の です **no desu**, cf. Lesson 30, note 2.

④ しか…ありません　でした **shika arimasen deshita**, cf. Lesson 30, note 4.

⑤ 段々 **dandan** (cf. Lesson 10, note 3), the sign 々 signifies that the kanji (Chinese character) is repeated. This is the Japanese version of the ditto mark!

10　どう　いう　苗字（みょうじ）を　つけよう　か　と
dō　i u　myō ji　o tsu ke　yō　ka　to

思った　時、自然　に　関係　が
omo t ta　toki,　shi zen　ni　kan kei　ga

ある　苗字（みょうじ）を　作（つく）りました。⑥
a ru　myō ji　o tsu ku ri ma shi ta.

11　たとえば、山（やま）に　田（た）を　持（も）って
ta to e ba,　yama　ni　ta　o　mo t te

いた　人（ひと）は　「山田」　と　いう
i ta　hito　wa　yama da　to　i u

苗字（みょうじ）に　なりました。
myō ji　ni　na ri ma shi ta.

12　「渡辺」　と　いう　名前（なまえ）は　川（かわ）
watana be　to　i u　na mae　wa　kawa

を　渡（わた）る　所（ところ）に　住（す）んで　いた
o　wata ru　tokoro　ni　sun de　i ta

人（ひと）に　つけた　名前（なまえ）です。
hito　ni　tsu ke ta　na mae　de su.

13　「山中」　と　いう　名前（なまえ）は
yama naka　to　i u　na mae　wa

山（やま）の　中（なか）に　住（す）んで　いる
yama　no　naka　ni　sun de　i ru

という　意味（いみ）です。
to　i u　i mi　de su.

10   When it came time to make names for   **36**
          themselves, they often took them from nature.
          (how / say / family name / [object] / let's attach / [question] /
          [quotation] / thought / time // nature / [goal] / connection /
          [subject] / exist / family name / [object] / made)

11   For example, someone who had rice-fields in
          the mountains would take the name Yamada.
          (for example / mountain / [place] / rice-field / [object] / had
          / person / [announce] / Yamada / [quotation] / say / family
          name / [goal] / became)

12   Watanabe is a name given to someone who
          lived near a river-crossing.
          (Watanabe / [quotation] / say / name / [announce] / river /
          [object] / cross / area / [place] / resided / person / [goal] /
          attached / name / it is)

13   The name Yamanaka means "he who lives in
          the mountain".
          (Yamanaka / [quotation] / say / name / [announce] / moun-
          tain / [relation] / inside / [place] / reside / [quotation] / say /
          meaning / it is)

ဆဝ၎ဆဝ၎

Notes

⑥ We have practiced the verb 思う **omou**, *to think*, many times
already. Here it is in the lower degree, past tense: 思った **omotta**
thought. What was thought is found before the verb, linked to it
with the particle と **to**, which is similar to how a comma or colon
introduces quotation marks in English, except that it goes before
the verb. The contents of the thought are expressed directly. Here,
as the contents are a question, we find this question in its entirety
before the と **to**, hence the か **ka**. Literally, it means: "[They]
thought: 'What name shall we be given?'".

36

14 だから 日本人 の 苗字 を
da ka ra　ni honjin　no　myō ji　o

覚える こと は むずかしく
obo e ru　ko to　wa　mu zu ka shi ku

ありません。
a ri ma se n.　　　　　　　　□

✳✳✳

練習　**renshū**

Exercise 1

❶ スミス と いう 名前 は アメリカ人
sumisu to iu namae wa amerikajin

か イギリス人 の 名前 です。
ka igirisujin no namae desu.

❷ 日本人 の 苗字 は 自然 の 物 を
nihonjin no myōji wa shizen no mono o

表す 名前 が ほとんど です。
arawasu namae ga hotondo desu.

❸ 女 の 人 は 皆 香水 が 好き です。
onno no hito wa minna kōsui ga suki desu.

❹ 来年 から 東京 に 住む こと に
rainen kara tōkyō ni sumu koto ni

なります。
narimasu.

14 That's why Japanese family names are so easy **36**
to remember.
(it is why / Japan-person / [relation] / family name / [object] / remember / fact of / [announce] / not be difficult)

✳✳✳

❺ 渡辺 さん で は ない か と
わたなべ
watanabe san de wa nai ka to
思いました。
おも
omoimashita.

Answers to Exercise 1

❶ Smith is an American or English family name. ❷ The majority of Japanese family names represent natural elements. ❸ All women love perfume. ❹ I have to live in Tōkyō beginning next year. ❺ I wondered if it wasn't Mrs. Watanabe.

... に 言葉 を 入れ なさい

❶ All the objects that are here are ancient.
koko ni aru mono .. . .

❷ Sometimes I have to take the bus.
tokidoki .... .. noru ....

❸ We work in the same building.

....

❹ Around the station there are many businesses, such as book-stores and cafés.
.... .. atari .. honya toka kissaten .... ga

....

---

37   第三十七課 **dai san jū nana ka**

ハチ公 (続き)
ha chi kō (tsuzu ki)

1 – ハチ公 は 秋田犬 です から、
ha chi kō wa aki ta ken de su ka ra,

飼い主 に よく 仕えます。①②
ka i nushi ni yo ku tsuka e ma su.

発音 **hatsu. on** *(hahtsoo. on)* – **Pronunciation**
1. kainooshee ... tsookahémahs'

⑤ Only people in the family came.

shinseki no hito ..... ki ....

Answers to Exercise 2

❶ – wa minna furui desu. ❷ – basu ni – koto ga arimasu. ❸ onaji bīru de hataraite imasu. ❹ eki no – ni – nado – takusan arimasu. ❺ – shika – masen deshita.

Lesson Thirty-Seven   37

Hachikō (Part Two)
(Hachikō / continue)

1 –   As an Akita dog, Hachikō was very faithful to his master.
(Hachikō / [announce] / Akita-dog / it is / because // master / [attribution] / good / serve)

Notes

① 秋田犬 **akita ken**, a breed of short-tailed Japanese dogs, very often specially trained. This breed, once close to extinction, is currently enjoying a vogue in Japan and America. The dogs originally come from the province of Akita, the west part of the north point of Honshū island, the largest in the Japanese archipelago.

② 飼い主 **kainushi**, *master*, but only in the sense of being the "master" of an animal.

2 でも その うち に 上野
de mo　so no　u chi　ni　ue no

さん は 亡くなりました 。
sa n　wa　na ku na ri ma shi ta.

3 それでも ハチ公 は 毎日 上野
so re de mo　ha chi kō　wa　mai nichi　ue no

さん を 迎え に 行きました。
sa n　o　muka e　ni　i ki ma shi ta.

4 毎日 何 時間 も 待ちました
mai nichi　nan　ji kan　mo　ma chi ma shi ta

が、上野 さん は 帰って きません
ga,　ue no　sa n　wa　kae t te　ki ma se n

でした。
de shi ta.

5 何 年 間 も の 間、ハチ公 は
nan　nen　kan　mo　no　aida,　ha chi kō　wa

毎日 上野 さん を 迎え
mai nichi　ue no　sa n　o　muka e

に 行きました。
ni　i ki ma shi ta.

6 ある 日、ハチ公 も 死にました。
a ru　hi,　ha chi kō　mo　shi ni ma shi ta.

---

2. sono oochee ... nakoonahreemahshtah 3. maineechee
6. ahroohee yu-mé- ... neehonju-

2 But shortly after, Mr. Ueno passed away.
(but / soon / [adverbial] / Ueno-Mr. / [announce] / passed away)

3 However, each day Hachikō would still go to greet Mr. Ueno.
(despite this / Hachikō / [announce] / every day / Ueno-Mr. / [object] / greet / [goal] / went)

4 Every day he would wait for hours, but Mr. Ueno never came.
(every day / don't know how many hours / waited / but // Ueno-Mr. / [announce] / return / didn't come)

5 Hachikō went every day to meet Mr. Ueno for years.
(don't know how many years / [relation] / time interval / Hachikō / [announce] / every day / Ueno-Mr. / [object] / greet / [goal] / went)

6 Then one day, Hachikō died.
(certain / day / Hachikō / also / died)

സ‍ാൽ‍ോൽ‍ാ

7 渋谷 の 人々 は ハチ公 に
shibu ya no hito bito wa ha chi kō ni

感心 した ので、駅 の 前 に
kan shin shi ta no de, eki no mae ni

ハチ公 の 銅像 を 建てる
ha chi kō no dō zō o ta te ru

こと に しました。③
ko to ni shi ma shi ta.

8 今 では ハチ公 の 銅像 は
ima de wa ha chi kō no dō zō wa

有名 です。日本中 の 人 が
yū mei de su. ni hon jū no hito ga

皆 その 話 を 知って います。
minna so no hanashi o shi t te i masu.

9 渋谷駅 の 前 で 人 と 会う
shibu ya eki no mae de hito to a u

約束 を する 時、人々 は 必ず
yaku soku o su ru toki, hito bito wa kanara zu

「ハチ公 の 銅像 の 前 で
ha chi kō no dō zō no mae de

会いましょう」と 言います。④
a i ma shō to i i ma su.

9. *ahoo*

7   Because the people of Shibuya admired
      Hachikō, they decided to erect a statue for him
      in front of the station.
      *(Shibuya / [relation] / people / [announce] / Hachikō /
      [attribution] / admiration-did / because // station / [rela-
      tion] / front / [place] / Hachikō / [relation] / bronze statue /
      [object] / build / fact of / [goal] / did)*

8   Now the statue of Hachikō is famous. All
      people throughout Japan know the story.
      *(now / [time] / [emphasis] / Hachikō / [relation] / bronze
      statue / [announce] / famous / it is) (throughout Japan /
      [relation] / person / [subject] / all / this / story / [object] /
      know)*

9   When they make a date to meet in front of
      Shibuya station, people always say, "Let's meet
      in front of Hachikō's statue!"
      *(Shibuya-station / [relation] / front / [place] / person /
      [partnership] / meet / date / [object] / do / time // people /
      [announce] / without fail / Hachikō / [relation] / bronze
      statue / [relation] / in front / [place] / let's meet / [quotation] /
      say)*

৯০৩৪৩০৫

Notes

③ 人々 **hitobito** (cf. Lesson 36, note 5): 人 **hito** plus yet another
人 **hito**. But the initial **h** becomes **b**, hence 人々 **hitobito**. The
repetition is a simple way of expressing plurality. It is a method
that is used only for certain words, in a very limited number.

④ cf. Lesson 36, note 6. With the verb 言う **iu**, *to say*, what precedes the particle と **to** is the quotation itself.

10 今晩　渋谷　の　辺り　で、一杯
kon ban shibu ya no ata ri de, ip pai

いかが　です　か。⑤
i ka ga de su ka.

11 – じゃ、ハチ公　の　前　で
ja, ha chi kō no mae de

会いましょう。
a i ma shō.　□

---

10. *ee'pai*

***

練習　**renshū**

Exercise 1

❶ 三越　デパート　で　働いて　いた
mitsukoshi depāto de hataraite ita

時、渋谷　に　住んで　いました。
toki, shibuya ni sunde imashita.

❷ 田中　さん　を　迎え　に　行く
tanaka san o mukae ni iku

こと　に　しました。
koto ni shimashita.

❸ 伯父　は　六　年　間　ぐらい
oji wa roku nen kan gurai

10   What would you say to a drink tonight around   **37**
          Shibuya?
          *(tonight / Shibuya / [relation] / around / [place] / one-glass
          / how / it is / [question])*
11 – So, let's meet in front of Hachikō!
          (so / Hachikō / [relation] / front / [place] / let's meet)

ഇൻരുഇൻരു

Notes

⑤ 杯 **hai** (cf. Lesson 22, note 3). This word is used when counting
   (full) cups or glasses. 一杯 **ippai**, literally, "one glass", can also
   mean *a drink*.

✳✳✳

中国 に いました。
chūgoku ni imashita.

❹ 兄 は 車 を 二 台 持って います。
ani wa kuruma o ni dai motte imasu.

❺ 朝 早く 人 と 会う 時、「おはよう
asa hayaku hito to au toki, "o hayō

ございます」 と 言います。
gozaimasu" to iimasu.

Answers to Exercise 1

❶ When I worked at the Mitsukoshi department store, I lived in
Shibuya. ❷ I decided to go meet Mr. Tanaka. ❸ My uncle stayed
in China for about six years. ❹ My older brother has two cars.
❺ When we meet someone in the morning, we say "o hayō
gozaimasu [hello]".

...に 言葉 を 入れ なさい
ことば　　　い

❶ I get up every day at eight thirty.

. . . .　. . . . . .　. .　. . . . .

❷ Do you know the story of Hachikō?
hachikō . .　. . . . . . .　. . . . . .

❸ Suzuki's car is also red.
. . . . . .　. . . . . .　. . kuruma . .　. . . . . .

❹ I worked in that airport for ten years.
kono hikōjō de . .　. . . . .　. . . hataraite imashita

38　第三十八課 dai san jū hak ka
だい さん じゅう はっ か

書類
しょ るい
sho rui

1 – この　　書類　　は　　わからない
　　 ko no　shorui　　wa　　wa ka ra na i
しょ るい

　　 ところ　　が　　たくさん　あります
　　 to ko ro　　ga　　ta ku sa n　a ri ma su

　　 から、説明　　して　　下さい。
　　 ka ra, setsu mei　shi te　kuda sa i.
せつ めい　　　　　　　くだ

発音　**hatsu. on** *(hahtsoo. on)* – **Pronunciation**
はつ おん
1. shorooee … wahkahranai … sétsoomé-

⑤ All the trucks in my company are blue.   **38**

.... kaisha .. .. wa .....

... .

Answers to Exercise 2

① mainichi hachi ji han ni okimasu. ② – no hanashi o shitte imasu
ka. ③ suzuki san no – mo akai desu. ④ – jū nen kan –. ⑤ watakushi
no – no torakku – minna aoi desu.

Lesson Thirty-Eight 38

The Form
(form)

1 – There are a lot of things I don't understand on
this form, can you explain it to me?
*(this / form / [announce] / not be understandable / area /
[subject] / a lot / exist / because // explain-do please)*

職業 と は どう いう 意味 です か。

2 名前と 苗字 の 意味 は
na mae to myō ji no i mi wa

わかります が、国籍 と は
wa ka ri ma su ga, koku seki to wa

何 です か。
nan de su ka.

3 – 国籍 と いう の は あなた
koku seki to i u no wa a na ta

は どこ の 国 の 人 です
wa do ko no kuni no hito de su

か と いう こと です。①②
ka to i u ko to de su.

4 必 ずしも 生まれた 国 で
kanara zu shi mo u ma re ta kuni de

は ありません。
wa a ri ma se n.

5 たとえば 由美 さん は
ta to e ba yu mi sa n wa

オーストラリア で 生まれました
ō su to ra ri a de u ma re ma shi ta

が、国籍 は 「日本」 です。
ga, koku seki wa ni hon de su.

6 あなた の 国籍 は 「スペイン」
a na ta no koku seki wa su pe i n

です。
de su.

2   I understand the meaning of "namae (given   **38**
name)" and of "myōji (family name)", but what
is "kokuseki (nationality)"?
(given name / and / family name / [relation] / meaning /
[announce] / be understandable / but // nationality / [quo-
tation] / [announce] / what / it is / [question])

3 –   With "kokuseki (nationality)", that means the
country you're from.
(nationality / [quotation] / say / [replacement] / [announce]
/ you / [announce] / where / [relation] / country / [relation]
/ person / it is / [question] / [quotation] / say / fact of / it is)

4   It's not necessarily the country where you were
born.
(necessarily / be born / country / it is not)

5   For example, Yumi was born in Australia, but
her nationality is "Japanese".
(for example / Yumi-Miss / [announce] / Australia / [place]
/ be born / but // nationality / [announce] / Japan / it is)

6   Your nationality, that would be "Spanish".
(you / [relation] / nationality / [announce] / Spain / it is)

৪০ 귿৪০ 귿

2. kokoosékee 3. koonee 4. oomahrétah 5. yumee … osoo-
torahreeah

Notes

① 国籍 と いう の は **kokuseki to iu *no* wa**. This の **no** that
we have here is another の **no**. Up till now we have learned the の
no of relation, which comes between two nouns. This here in item 3
is placed between a verb and a particle. It is used to replace either a
noun already spoken early, or else a noun that is made obvious from
the context. Here, the antecedent noun is 言葉 **kotoba**, *word* (cf. the
title of Exercise 2 in each lesson). Literally, "**that** (the word) which
says 'kokuseki'". In the word-for-word translation, we express the
function of this の **no** with a "[replacement]".

② cf. Lesson 37, note 4. Literally, "That's a thing that says: from
which country are you?"

38

7 – 住所 は わかります。住んで
jūsho wa wakarimasu. sunde

いる 所 です ね。
iru tokoro desu ne.

8 職業 と は どう いう
shokugyō to wa dō iu

意味 です か。
imi desu ka.

9 – あなた が して いる 仕事
anata ga shite iru shigoto

の こと です。
no koto desu.

10 この 書類 は 何 の ため
kono shorui wa nan no tame

の 物 です か。
no mono desu ka.

11 滞在 許可証 の ため です か。
taizai kyokashō no tame desu ka.

12 大学 に 入学 する ため
daigaku ni nyūgaku suru tame

です か。
desu ka.

13 – いいえ。テニス・クラブ に
iie. tenisu kurabu ni

入る ため です。
hairu tame desu. □

7 – "jūsho (address)" I understand. That's the place   **38**
where you live!
(address / [announce] / be understandable) (live in / place / it is / [agreement])

8 What does "shokugyō (profession)" mean?
(profession / [quotation] / [announce] / how / say / meaning / it is / [question])

9 – That's the work that you do.
(you / [subject] / be doing / work / [relation] / thing / it is)

10 What's this form for?
(this / form / [announce] / what / [relation] / goal / [relation] / thing / it is / [question])

11 Is it for your residence license?
(residence-license / [relation] / goal / it is / [question])

12 Is it to enter a university?
(university / [goal] / enter university-do / goal / it is / [question])

13 – No. It's to enter a tennis club.
(no) (tennis-club / [goal] / enter / intention / it is)

ജ⟩ᏻᎥᏻᏄ

練習　renshū

Exercise 1

❶ 意味 が わからない 言葉 が
imi ga wakaranai kotoba ga

たくさん あります。
takusan arimasu.

❷ 住所 とは 住んで いる ところ です。
jūsho to wa sunde iru tokoro desu.

❸ 書類 とは どう いう 意味 ですか。
shorui to wa dō iu imi desu ka.

✳✳✳

Exercise 2

... に 言葉 を 入れ なさい

❶ What does "kippu (ticket)" mean?
kippu .. .. dō ....

❷ That's for my trip next week.
....

❸ I understand "kuni (country)", but I don't understand "kokuseki (nationality)".
kuni .. .. kokuseki ..
....

❹ What country does he come from?
....

❹ 仕事 の ため です。
しごと
shigoto no tame desu.

❺ この 道 は 犬 を 散歩 させる
みち　　　　いぬ　　　　さんぽ
kono michi wa inu o sanpo saseru

ため の 道 です。
みち
tame no michi desu.

Answers to Exercise 1

❶ There are many words that I do not understand. ❷ Address, that's the place where you live. ❸ What does "shorui" mean? ❹ That's for my work. ❺ This road is made for walking dogs.

***

❺ I was born in China, but I am Japanese.

watakushi wa ....

....

Answers to Exercise 2

❶ – to wa – iu imi desu ka. ❷ raishū no ryokō no tame desu. ❸ – wa wakarimasu ga – wa wakarimasen. ❹ doko no kuni no hito desu ka. ❺ – chūgoku de umaremashita ga kokuseki wa nihon desu.

第三十九課 dai san jū kyū ka

両親 へ の 手紙
ryō shin　e no　tegami

1 おととい の 木曜日 は お祖父さん
o to to i no mokuyōbi wa　o jii sa n

と お祖母さん と 上野 の 動物園
to　o baa sa n　to ue no　no dōbutsu en

へ 行って きました。①②
e　i tte　ki ma shi ta.

2 私達　は 初 めて 動物園 へ
watashi tachi wa haji me te　dō butsu en　e

行った ので、大喜び でした。
i tta　no de, oo yoroko bi　de shi ta.

3 一 時間 以上 並びました。
ichi　ji kan　i jō　nara bi ma shi ta.

4 「どうして こんな に 皆 並ぶ
dō shi te　ko n na　ni minna narabu

の です か」と お祖父さん
no　de su　ka to　o jii sa n

に 聞きました。
ni　ki ki ma shi ta.

Letter to the Parents
(mother and father / [destination] / [relation] / letter)

1   The day before yesterday, Thursday, we went to the Ueno zoo with Grandpa and Grandma.
(day before yesterday / [apposition] / Thursday / [emphasis] / grandpa / and / grandma / [partnership] / Ueno / [relation] / zoo / [destination] / go / came)

2   Because it was the first time for us to go to the zoo, we were very happy.
(we / [announce] / for the first time / zoo / [destination] / went / because // big joy / it was)

3   We waited in line for over an hour
(one-hour-over / wait in line)

4   I asked Grandpa, "Why are there so many people waiting in line?"
(why / this way / [adverbial] / all / wait in line / it's that / [question] / [quotation] / grandpa / [attribution] / asked)

෨○෪෨○෪

発音　はつ　おん　**hatsu. on** *(hahtsoo. on)* – **Pronunciation**
1. ototoee … mokooyo-bee … do-bootsooen

Notes

① This passage is in the voice of a child. We have seen that when speaking of members of your own family, an adult will never follow a familial term with さん **san** (cf. Lesson 26, note 2), though it is used for familial terms when speaking of the families of others (cf. Lesson 15, notes 1 and 3; Lesson 23, note 1). But part of the language of children is to use さん **san** after the terms for members of their own families.

② 上野 うえ の *Ueno*, area in the north section of Tōkyō. In addition to a zoo, Japan's largest national art museum is also in this part of town.

5 「春 は 子供 が 生まれる 季節
haru wa ko domo ga u ma re ru ki setsu

なので、皆 見 に くる の です」
na no de, minna mi ni ku ru no de su

と お祖父さん が 答えました。③
to o jii sa n ga kota e ma shi ta.

6 先ず 首 が 長い きりん を
ma zu kubi ga naga i ki ri n o

見ました。それから しわ だらけ
mi ma shi ta. so re ka ra shi wa da ra ke

の 三 頭 の 象 を 見ました。④
no san tō no zō o mi ma shi ta.

7 一 頭 は 耳 が 小さい アフリカ
it tō wa mimi ga chii sa i a fu ri ka

象 でした。もう 二頭 は 耳
zō de shi ta. mō ni tō wa mimi

が 大きい インド 象 でした。
ga oo ki i i n do zō de shi ta.

8 愛嬌 が いい 熊 は ピーナッツ
ai kyō ga i i kuma wa pī na t tsu

を むしゃむしゃ 食べて いました。⑤
o mu sha mu sha ta be te i ma shi ta.

5. keesetsoo **6.** nagai **8.** aikyoo

5   "Because Spring is the season where little ones are born, everyone is coming to see," Grandpa replied.
(Spring / [announce] / child / [subject] / born / season / it is / because // all / watch / [goal] / come /it's that/ [quotation] / grandpa / [subject] / responded)

6   First we saw a giraffe with its long neck. Then we saw three wrinkly elephants.
(first / neck / [subject] / be long / giraffe / [object] / watched)
(following / wrinkle-covered / [relation] / three-big animal / [relation] / elephant / [object] / watched)

7   One was an **African** elephant with small ears. The other two were **Indian** elephants with large ears.
(one-big animal / [announce] / ear / [subject] / be small / Africa-elephant/it was) (more/two-big animal/[announce]/ ear / [subject] / be big / India-elephant / it was)

8   A funny bear was eating peanuts with fervor.
(charms / [subject] / be good / bear / [announce] / peanuts / [object] / yummy / was eating)

ᲜᲝᲚᲤᲒᲝᲚᲥ

Notes

③ な　ので **na node**, cf. Lesson 33, note 1.

④ 頭 <ruby>とう</ruby> **tō**, used whenever counting large animals. Literally, it means "head".

⑤ むしゃむしゃ　**musha musha**, one of the many words of Japanese, which while both numerous and amusing, are nearly always untranslatable. They represent noises, impressions of gestures, of light, etc. Here, it is the way of chewing. Not quite onomatopoeia, they are sonic depictions of the character of the action itself.

9 川崎 先生 に よく 似た
kawa saki sen sei ni yoku ni ta

猿 が 木 の 枝 から枝 へ
saru ga ki no eda ka ra eda e

飛び移って いました。
to bi utsu t te i ma shi ta.

10 眠そう な 目 を した らくだ
nemu sō na me o shi ta ra ku da

が ゆっくり 歩いて いました。⑥
ga yu k ku ri aru i te i ma shi ta.

11 ライオン が 檻 の 中 で 吠えた
ra i o n ga ori no naka de ho e ta

時 に は、妹 の かおる
toki ni wa, imōto no ka o ru

ちゃん が 驚いて 泣きました。
cha n ga odoro i te na ki ma shi ta.

きっと こわかった の でしょう。⑦
ki t to ko wa ka t ta no de shō.

12 パンダ の 檻 の 前 は たくさん
pa n da no ori no mae wa ta ku sa n

の 人 が 並んで いた ので 見る
no hito ga nara n de i ta no de mi ru

こと が できません でした。
ko to ga de ki mase n de shi ta.

9 A monkey that looked a lot like my teacher, Mr. **39** Kawasaki, was leaping from branch to branch.
(Kawasaki-teacher / [attribution] / quite / resemble / monkey / [subject] / tree / [relation] / branch / from / branch / [destination] / was jumping side to side)

10 A camel with sleepy eyes was walking slowly.
(appear asleep / it is / eye / [object] / did / camel / [subject] / slowly / was walking)

11 When the lion roared in his cage, my little sister Kaoru was so surprised she started to cry. She sure was scared.
(lion / [subject] / cage / [relation] / inside / [place] / roared / time / [time] / [emphasis] // little sister / [apposition] / Kaoru / [subject] / surprised / cried) (certainly / ceased with fear / I believe it is)

12 Because there was a long line in front of the panda cage, we couldn't see it.
(panda / [relation] / cage / [relation] / before / [announce] / many / [relation] / person / [subject] / was waiting in line / because // watch / fact of / [subject] / was not possible)

හ෬ෂ෮ඥ

9. *tobeeootsoo'té* **10.** *némooso- … yoo'kooree* **11.** *odoroeeté*

Notes

⑥ 眠そう **nemusō**, cf. Lesson 25, note 1.

⑦ かおる ちゃん **kaoru chan**. ちゃん **chan**, a derivation of さん **san**, is often used with the name of a small child, especially the name of a little girl.

13 その 代<small>か</small>わり、お祖父<small>じい</small>さん が
    so no ka wa ri, o jii sa n ga

パンダ の 絵葉書<small>えはがき</small> を 一枚<small>いちまい</small>
pa n da no e ha gaki o ichi mai

ずつ 買って くれました。
zu tsu ka t te ku re ma shi ta.

14 とても 楽<small>たの</small>しい 一日<small>いちにち</small> でした。 □
    to te mo tano shi i ichi nichi de shi ta.

***

練習<small>れんしゅう</small> **renshū**

Exercise 1

❶ 先週<small>せんしゅう</small> の 木曜日<small>もくようび</small> 初<small>はじ</small>めて インド
senshū no mokuyōbi hajimete indo

料理<small>りょうり</small> を 食<small>た</small>べました。
ryōri o tabemashita.

❷ 東京<small>とうきょう</small> から 静岡<small>しずおか</small> まで は 百<small>ひゃく</small>
tōkyō kara shizuoka made wa hyaku

五<small>ご</small> 十<small>じゅっ</small> キロ 以上<small>いじょう</small> あります。
go juk kiro ijō arimasu.

❸ 「なぜ 泣<small>な</small>く の」と 妹<small>いもうと</small> に
naze naku no to imōto ni

13 Instead, Grandpa bought us each a postcard of a panda. **39**
(of this / replace / grandpa / [subject] / panda / [relation] / postcard / [object] / one-sheet / each / buy / did for us)

14 This was a marvelous day.
(very / be joyous / day / it was)

***

聞<ruby>き<rt>き</rt></ruby>ました。
kikimashita.

❹ 飼い主 に 似た 犬 です。
kainushi ni nita inu desu.

❺ 向こう の 店 に おいしそうな
mukō no mise ni oishisō na

お菓子 が あります。
o kashi ga arimasu.

Answers to Exercise 1

❶ I ate Indian cuisine for the first time last Thursday. ❷ It is more than 150 kilometers from Tōkyō to Shizuoka. ❸ I asked my little sister why she was crying. ❹ It's a dog that resembles its master. ❺ In the store opposite there are cakes that seem delicious.

...に 言葉 を 入れ なさい

❶ I went to do the shopping with Yumi and Kaoru.

. . . . kaimono ni

. . . .

❷ Because it was Sunday the bank was closed.

. . . . datta node, ... yasumi

. . . .

❸ My son replied to me that he had seen giraffes, elephants, and lions.

. . . .

. . . .

---

40 第四十課 dai yon juk ka

工場　見学
kō jō　ken gaku

1 – よう こそ いらっしゃいました。①
　　 yō　ko so　i ra s sha　i ma shi ta.

2 これから　　私共　の　工場
　 ko re ka ra watakushi domo no　kō jō

を ご 案内 しましょう。②③
o　go　an nai　shi ma shō.

Notes

① The way to say *welcome* in Japanese is just like the construction of
the English word, which is literally "very **well** / to have **come**". ▶

④ We waited in front of the bear cage.

. . . .

⑤ Give me tangerines and apples, two of each, please.

. . . . *futatsu* . . . .

Answers to Exercise 2

❶ yumi san to kaoru san to – ikimashita. ❷ nichiyōbi – ginkō wa – deshita. ❸ kirin to zō to raion o mimashita to musuko ga kotae- mashita. ❹ kuma no ori no mae de machimashita. ❺ mikan to ringo o – zutsu kudasai.

Lesson Forty   40

Visit to the Factory
(factory-visit)

1 – Welcome!

2   We shall now begin the visit to our factory.
(from now / we / [relation] / factory / [object] / [polite]- guide-let's do)

> はつ おん
> 発音 **hatsu. on** *(hahtsoo. on)* – **Pronunciation**
> *1. eerahshshaeemahshtah 2. annai*

▶ ② 私共 **watakushidomo**, *we / us*, used exclusively for an offi- cial "we". Here, the "we" represents a company.

③ ご案内 **go annai**. 案内 **annai** on its own indicates the act of guiding someone. With an added ご **go** it places the noun in high degree. This is also the use of お **o**, cf. Lesson 34, item 9.

40

3 ここ で は 電気 製品 を
ko ko de wa den ki seihin o

主 に 作って います。
omo ni tsuku t te i ma su.

4 どうぞ、こちら へ。足元 に
dō zo, ko chi ra e. ashi moto ni

気 を つけて 下さい。
ki o tsu ke te kuda sa i.

5 ここ は できあがった 電気 製品
ko ko wa de ki a ga t ta den ki sei hin

の 倉庫 です。できた 年代 ごと
no sō ko de su. de ki ta nen dai go to

に 置いて あります。
ni o i te a ri ma su.

6 右 の 建物 は 事務所 です。左
migi no tate mono wa ji mu sho de su. hidari

の 建物 は 製造 工場 です。
no tate mono wa sei zō kō jō de su.

7 – すみません が、ちょっと 質問
su mi ma se n ga, cho t to shitsu mon

が ある の です けれども…。
ga a ru no de su ke re do mo.

8 – どうぞ。何 です か。
dō zo. nan de su ka.

3   Here we mainly make electronics equipment.   **40**
(here / [place] / [emphasis] / electric-manufacture goods /
[object] / main / [adverbial] / be making)

4   This way, please. Watch your step.
(please / this side / [destination]) (step / [goal] / your atten-
tion / [object] / attach)

5   Here is the warehouse for our completed
products. They are classified based on the
chronological order of when they were made.
(here / [announce] / be finished / electric-manufacture
goods / [relation] / warehouse / it is) (be finished / chrono-
logical order / [adverbial] / be placed)

6   In the building on the right, there are offices.
Those on the left are buildings for manufacturing.
(right / [relation] / building / [announce] / office / it is) (left /
[relation] / building / [announce] / manufacting-factory /
it is)

7 –   Excuse me, but I would like to ask a question.
(excuse me / but // a little / question / [subject] / exist / it's
that / even though...)

8 –   Go ahead. What would you like to know?
(go ahead) (what / it is / [question])

꧁꧂

3. sé-heen 5. nendai 6. sé-zo- 7. sheetsoomon

40

9 – 工員 が 全然 見えません が、
kō in ga zenzen mi e ma se n ga,
どこ に いる の です か。
do ko ni i ru no de su ka.

10 – 前 は 工員 が して いた
mae wa kō in ga shi te i ta
仕事 を 今 は ロボット が
shi goto o ima wa ro bo t to ga
全部 して います。
zen bu shi te i ma su.

11 コンピュータ が ロボット を
ko n pyū ta ga ro bo t to o
動かして います。
ugo ka shi te i ma su.

12 – 失業 者 は 出なかった の
shitsu gyō sha wa de naka t ta no
です か。④
de su ka.

13 – 工員 は 私達 が 持って
kō in wa watakushi tachi ga mo t te
いる ロボット を 作る 工場 と
i ru ro bo t to o tsuku ru kō jō to
コンピュータ を 組み立てる
ko n pyū ta o ku mi ta te ru
工場 で 働いて います。 □
kō jō de hatara i te i ma su.

9 – I don't see any workers. Where are they? **40**
(worker / [subject] / not at all / not be visible / but // where / [place] / exist / it's that / [question])

10 – What was done in the past by workers is now entirely done by robots.
(before / [emphasis] / worker / [subject] / was doing / work / [object] / now / [emphasis] / robot / [subject] / entirely / be doing)

11 And the computers command the robots.
(computer / [subject] / robot / [object] / make move)

12 – Isn't there unemployment?
(unemployed / [announce] / not appeared / it's that / [question])

13 – The workers work in a factory that make robots and in a factory that make computers, factories that belong to us.
(worker / [announce] / we / [subject] / possess / robot / [object] / make / factory / and / computer / [object] / assemble / factory / [place] / be working)

ಬಲಚಿಲಚ

---

11. konpyu-tah … oogokahsheeté 13. koomeetahtéroo

Notes

④ 出なかった **denakatta**, low degree form of 出ません　でした **demasen deshita**, *not to appear (or come out)*.

40 練習 renshū

Exercise 1

❶ すみません、郵便局 は どこ に
sumimasen, yūbinkyoku wa doko ni
あります か。
arimasu ka.

❷ この 駅 から は 主 に 西 の 方
kono eki kara wa omo ni nishi no hō
へ 行く 汽車 が 出発 します。
e iku kisha ga shuppatsu shimasu.

❸ 私共 は 自動車 を 組み立てる
watakushidomo wa jidōsha o kumitateru
工場 と 電話 を 作る 工場 を
kōjō to denwa o tsukuru kōjō o
持って います。
motte imasu.

✳✳✳

Exercise 2

...に 言葉 を 入れ なさい

❶ Watch out for cars.
jidōsha .. ..

❷ The company where I worked made electronics equipment.
watashi ga .. .. wa .. ..
. .. .

④ 皆 入院 した ので、家 に
みんな にゅういん いえ
minna nyū.in shita node, ie ni

だれも いません。
daremo imasen.

⑤ 鞄 を 作る ロボット を 動かす
かばん つく うご
kaban o tsukuru robotto o ugokasu

コンピュータ を 作る 工場 です。
つく こうじょう
konpyūta o tsukuru kōjō desu.

Answers to Exercise 1

❶ Excuse me, where is the post office? ❷ From this station leave primarily trains going west. ❸ Our company owns a factory for constructing automobiles and a factory for constructing telephones. ❹ Because they are all in the hospital, there is no one at home. ❺ This is a factory that makes computers that control robots that make bags.

✳✳✳

❸ The robots do all the work but there is no unemployment.
. . . .
. . . . demasen . . . .

❹ I don't understand at all.
. . . .

❺ Right now we are constructing buildings.
. . . . tate . . . .

Answers to Exercise 2

❶ – ni ki o tsukete kudasai. ❷ – hataraite ita kaisha – denki seihin o tsukutte imashita. ❸ robotto ga shigoto o zenbu shite imasu ga shitsugyōsha wa – deshita. ❹ zenzen wakarimasen. ❺ ima jimusho o – te imasu.

変わった 人
か　　　　　ひと
ka wa t ta　　hito

1 – 私 の 友達 の マノリータ
わたし　　　とも だち
watashi no tomo dachi no　ma no　rī　ta

に 会った こと が あります か。
あ
ni　a t ta　ko to　ga　a ri ma su ka.

2 – 会った こと が ありません。
あ
a t ta　ko to　ga　a ri ma se n.

3 – とても おもしろい アルゼンチン人
じん
to te mo　o mo shi ro　i　a ru ze n chi n jin

です。 ①
de su.

4 – 職業 は？
しょくぎょう
shoku gyō wa ?

5 – 作曲家 です。
さっきょく か
sak kyoku ka de su.

6 – 女 の 作曲家 です か。
おんな　　　　　さっきょく か
onna　no　sak kyoku ka　de su　ka.

めずらしい です ね。
me zu ra shi i　　de su　　ne.

Someone Eccentric
(changed / person)

1 –   Did you meet my friend Manolita?
*(me / [relation] / friend / [apposition] / Manolita / [goal] /
met / fact of / [subject] / exist / [question])*

2 –   No.
(met / fact of / [subject] / not exist)

3 –   She's a very interesting person from Argentina.
(very / be amusing / Argentine-person / it is)

4 –   What does she do?
(profession / [announce])

5 –   She's a composer.
(composer / it is)

6 –   A female composer? That's rare!
*(woman / [apposition] / composer / it is / [question]) (be
rare / it is / [agreement])*

೬೦೦೩೮೦೦೩

発音 はつ おん **hatsu. on** *(hahtsoo. on)* – **Pronunciation**
6. *mézoorahshee-*

Notes

① アルゼンチン人 じん **aruzenchinjin**, cf. Lesson 28, paragraph 1.

41

7 – そう です ね。でも マノリータ
sō　desu　ne.　demo　manorīta

は　変わった　人　です。
wa　kawatta　hito　desu.

8 今　オペラ　を　作曲　して
ima　opera　o　sakkyoku　shite

いる　そう　です。
iru　sō　desu.

9 とても　いそがしい　と　言って
totemo　isogashii　to　itte

います。他　の　約束　は
imasu.　hoka　no　yakusoku　wa

断る　のに、マージャン　に
kotowaru　noni,　mājan　ni

誘う　と　必ず　来ます。②
sasou　to　kanarazu　kimasu.

10 この　間　も、アルゼンチン　料理
kono　aida　mo,　aruzenchin　ryōri

を　ごちそう　して　くれる　と　いった
o　gochisō　shite　kureru　to　itta

ので、楽しみ　に　して　いました。
node,　tanoshimi　ni　shite　imashita.

11 三　時間　前　に　電話　が
san　jikan　mae　ni　denwa　ga

かかって　きました。
kakatte　kimashita.

7 – Yes. But Manolita is quite an eccentric!
(yes) (but / Manolita / [announce] / changed / person / it is)

8 At the moment she says she's writing an opera.
(now / opera / [object] / composition-be doing / have heard)

9 She says she's very busy. Even though she's
been refusing all her other dates, whenever we
invite her for Mah-jong she always shows up.
*(very / be busy / [quotation] / say) (other / [relation] / date
/ [announce] / refuse / even though // mah-jong / [goal] /
invite / when // without fail / come)*

10 The other day she had said she would make us
an Argentinian diner and so we rejoiced.
*(this / time interval / also / Argentina-cuisine / [object] /
delight-do / do for us / [quotation] / have said / because //
rejoice / [goal] / was doing)*

11 Three hours earlier, the telephone rang.
*(three-hour-before / [time] / telephone / [subject] / function
/ came)*

ဆဝ၁၈ဝ၈

---

*8. sah'kyokoo **9.** kotowahroo … sahso/oo*

Notes

② マージャン **Mah-jong** is a game originally from China,
played with four people, with rules similar to Rummy. It was
very popular in America and Europe in the 1920s and is today
a semi-obligatory part of all Japanese employees. In Japan it is
played with large sums of money, and very often large sections
of a paycheck will be won or lost. It has also been experiencing
a resurgence in popularity in the west in the past several years.

41

12 前 の 日 から 病気 だった そう
   mae no hi ka ra byō ki da t ta　sō

です。ですから お 料理 は
de su. de su ka ra　o ryō ri　wa

作れなく なった そう です。でも
tsuku re na ku na t ta　sō　de su. de mo

食後 に する マージャン は
shoku go ni　su ru　mā ja n　wa

大丈夫 だ と 言う の です。③
dai jō bu　da to　i u　no de su.

13 マノリータ は いつも この 調子
   ma no rī ta　wa　i tsu mo　ko no chō shi

です が、とても 温かい 人 な
de su　ga,　to te mo　atata ka i　hito na

ので、友達 が たくさん います。
no de, tomo dachi ga　ta ku sa n　i ma su

14 今度 紹介 します。
   kon do　shō kai　shi ma su.　　　　□

---

12. tsookoorénahku … chokoogo 13. ahtahtahkai 14. cho-kai

Notes

③ だった **datta**, low degree equivalent for でした **deshita**, *it was*.

12 Apparently, she had been sick since the day **41**
before. And so she couldn't make dinner. But
she said mah-jong after dinner was always all
right.
*(before/ [relation] / day / from / sickness / it was / have
heard) (for this reason / [familiarity]-cuisine / [announce] /
could not make / became / have heard) (however / dinner-
after / [time] / do / mah-jong / [announce] / without problem / it is / [quotation] / say / it's that)*

13 With her it's always like that, but because she's
a very warm person, she has many friends.
*(Manolita / [announce] / always / this / manner / it is / but //
very / be warm / person / it is / because // friend / [subject] /
many / exist)*

14 I'll introduce you next time.
(next time / introduce-do)

ဆာ‌ဂ္ဇ‌ဆာ‌ဂ္ဇ

41

<ruby>練<rt>れん</rt></ruby><ruby>習<rt>しゅう</rt></ruby> **renshū**

Exercise 1

❶ <ruby>二<rt>に</rt></ruby> <ruby>階<rt>かい</rt></ruby> だて の イギリス の バス
ni kai date no igirisu no basu

に <ruby>乗<rt>の</rt></ruby>った こと が あります か。
ni notta koto ga arimasu ka.

❷ この <ruby>建<rt>たて</rt></ruby><ruby>物<rt>もの</rt></ruby> だけ <ruby>倉<rt>そう</rt></ruby><ruby>庫<rt>こ</rt></ruby> です。<ruby>他<rt>ほか</rt></ruby>
kono tatemono dake sōko desu. hoka

の <ruby>建<rt>たて</rt></ruby><ruby>物<rt>もの</rt></ruby> は <ruby>皆<rt>みんな</rt></ruby> <ruby>事<rt>じ</rt></ruby><ruby>務<rt>む</rt></ruby><ruby>所<rt>しょ</rt></ruby> です。
no tatemono wa minna jimusho desu.

✳✳✳

Exercise 2

... に <ruby>言<rt>こと</rt></ruby><ruby>葉<rt>ば</rt></ruby> を <ruby>入<rt>い</rt></ruby>れ なさい

❶ Have you already eaten Japanese food?

. . . .

❷ Yesterday I met your American friend.
kinō anata no . . . .
. . aimashita

❸ There are two children.
. . . . . . ga . . . .

❸ 仕事 が いそがしい のに 山
しごと　　　　　　　　　　　　　　やま
shigoto ga isogashii noni yama

へ 行く の です か。
　　い
e iku no desu ka.

❹ 簡単 な ので すぐ できました。
かんたん
kantan na node sugu dekimashita.

❺ 雨 が 降って いる そう です。
あめ　　ふ
ame ga futte iru sō desu.

Answers to Exercise 1

❶ Have you already been on an English double-decker bus? ❷ Only this building is a warehouse. All the others are offices. ❸ Will you go to the mountain even if you are so busy? ❹ Oh, it's so easy, I got it right away. ❺ I have heard it's raining.

✳✳✳

❹ I have heard there are bears in the mountains.

. . . .　. .　. . . . .　. .　. . . .　. . . .

❺ Because I love it, I bought it all.

. . . .　. .　. . . . ,　. . . . .　. . . . .

Answers to Exercise 2

❶ nihon ryōri o tabeta koto ga arimasu ka. ❷ – amerikajin no tomo-dachi ni –. ❸ kodomo – futari imasu. ❹ yama ni kuma ga iru sō desu. ❺ daisuki na node, zenbu kaimashita.

まとめ
matome
Revision and Notes

1. So it is working out all right with just the official transliteration? It is not that difficult, is it? So now we are going to take another step further. You have certainly noticed that in the vast majority of cases, the **u** in the official transcription is closer to our "oo". So we won't bother with notifying you, unless it is pronounced differently. That is, either it's pronounced as a more closed in "ü", or else it is left unpronounced completely.

2. It has been a long time since we have said anything about the **writing**. There is something particular about kanji. You have already seen that each kanji character can correspond to one, two, and sometimes three syllables. And when it is in a compound word, we can usually tell which syllable(s) corresponds to which character.

For example: in 建物 **tatemono**, *building*, 建 is pronounced **tate** (*construct*) and 物 is pronounced **mono** (*thing*). But (there's always a but) in some compounds two kanji will correspond to one or more syllables and we cannot tell which syllable goes with which character. Take three very common words: *today* (cf. Lesson 11, item 6, and Lesson 12, item 1): 今日 where the two characters together are pronounced **kyō**. And *yesterday* (cf. Lesson 8, item 1; Lesson 12, item 13) 昨日 where the two characters are pronounced **kinō** and cannot be separated. The same is true of *tomorrow*, (cf. Lesson 2, ietm 7) 明日, a two-character compound pronounced **ashita**, also without possible separation. The same phenomenon shows up again in a number of familial terms: 伯父 **oji**, *my uncle* (Lesson 32, item 1), お祖父さん **ojiisan**, *grandfather*, お祖母さん **obaasan**, *grandmother* (Lesson 39, item 1).

3. In every language there exist a number of decisive words. In Japanese, one of these words is こと **koto**. Its meaning is difficult to define in English, but it's something like "thing, event, fact, element...". At any event, this **koto** is used in many common and necessary constructions, following the form: verb + こと **koto** + particle + another verb. We have seen the most important instances of this pattern.

It's time to take another look:

…こと に します (する) **koto ni shimasu (suru)** (literally: "fact of / [goal] / to do"), *to decide to* (cf. Lesson 32, item 3; Lesson 37, item 7).

…こと に なります (なる) **koto ni narimasu (naru)** (literally: "fact of / [goal] / become"), *turn out that* (cf. Lesson 32, item 12; Lesson 36, item 8).

…こと が できます （できる） **koto ga dekimasu (dekiru)** (literally: "doing / [subject] / possible"), *can*, plus its corresponding negation (cf. Lesson 34, item 14; Lesson 39, item 12).

Verb in low degree ending in **u** + こと が あります （ある） **koto ga arimasu (aru)** (literally: "fact of / [subject] / fact of"), *it happens that*, plus its corresponding negative form (cf. Lesson 36, item 3). Not confused with: verb in low degree ending in **ta** + こと が あります （ある）, *to have already had the occasion of* (cf. Lesson 41, items 1 and 2).

Another construction: …こと は **koto wa** + adjective, *it is... to* (cf. Lesson 32, item 6; Lesson 36, item 14). We can also look at Lesson 38, item 3: …と いう こと です **to iu koto desu**, or Lesson 38, item 9: …の こと です **no koto desu**, to explain the concept further.

4. We will finish our revision chapter with a bit of a tour –or perhaps a grand tour –through the **verbs** we have covered recently. You have noticed already that these verbs don't have much by way of conjugation! All the same, it is important to know how to construct each form for each verb. That is what we are going to tackle right now.

An enormous quantity of verbs are formed from a noun of Chinese origin, usually two kanji, plus the Japanese verb します **shimasu** (middle degree) or する **suru** (low degree), which means *to do*. We have already come across them often, but here we will lay them all out in the low degree of the present-future tense.

Lesson 15, item 3, and Lesson 25, item 8: 結婚する **kekkon suru** ("marriage-do"), *to get married*. Lesson 15, item 9: 再婚する **saikon suru** ("remarriage-do"), *to remarry*. Lesson 20, item 12, 禁煙する **kin.en suru** ("no smoking-do"), *to quit smoking*. Lesson 23, item 2: 卒業する **sotsugyō suru** ("diploma-do"), *to graduate*; item 9: 入院する **nyū.in suru** ("enter hospital-do"), *to go to the hospital*; item 13: 退院する **tai.in suru** ("leave hospital-do"), *to get out of the hospital*; item 14: 安心する **anshin suru** ("tranquility-do"), *calm*. Lesson 25, item 4: 出版する **shuppan suru** ("publication-do"), *to publish*. Lesson 27, item 12: 心配する **shinpai suru** ("worry-do"), *to worry*. Lesson 32, item 1: 出発する **shuppatsu suru** ("depart-do"), *to leave*; item 9: 旅行する **ryokō suru** ("travel-do"), *to travel*. Lesson 34, item 13: 入居する **nyūkyo suru** ("enter the house-do"), *to settle in a house*. Lesson 38, item 1: 説明する **setsumei suru** ("explanation-do"), *to explain*; item 12: 入学する **nyūgaku suru** ("enter school-do"), *to enter school or university*. Lesson 40, item 2: 案内する **annai suru** ("guide-do"), *to guide*. Lesson 41, item 8: 作曲する **sakkyoku suru** ("composition-do"), *to compose*; item 10: ごちそうする **gochisō suru** ("delight-do"), *to delight*; *to prepare a meal*; item 14: 紹介する **shōkai suru** ("introduction-do"), *to introduce*.

That is quite a long list, but there are hundreds more like that. A great advantage is that each of those nouns can be used as a noun no matter what the sentence; and all you need is to know one verb –する

suru –able to speak hundreds of verbs in this format. So する **suru** 42
is simple: aside from the low degree する **suru**, all other forms
are built on the base of し **shi**. Therefore: *I (you...) do:* する **suru**
(low degree), します **shimasu** (middle degree); *I don't do:* しない
shinai (low degree), しません **shimasen** (middle degree); *I (you...)
did:* した **shita** (low degree), しました **shimashita** (middle degree);
I didn't do: しなかった **shinakatta** (low degree), しません
でした **shimasen deshita** (middle degree).

And for the series of verbs indicating that one is in the middle of
doing something: *I'm doing:* して いる **shite iru** (low degree),
して います **shite imasu** (middle degree); *I am not doing:*
して いない **shite inai** (low degree), して いません **shite
imasen** (middle degree); *I was doing:* して いた **shite ita** (low
degree), して いました **shite imashita** (middle degree). These are
all forms you are just about fully familiar with by now. And what
happens in the end? There is a base し **shi**, and the change of forms
consists of nothing more than adding different suffixes to the same
base. It is a principle worth noting, because it is how we proceed in
changing the forms for all verbs, and **for all verbs the suffixes are
the same**. The only small difficulty is that at times the same verb
will be used with more than one base for the suffixes. But let's not
get ahead of ourselves. We will see that in our next revision chapter.
Nothing to worry about, though, just keep an eye on how the verbs
work in the next few lessons!

5. Some final notes on a few verbs here: the verb 聞く **kiku** means
either *to listen* (cf. Lesson 29, item 8), or *to ask* (cf. Lesson 39, item 4).
The verb できる **dekiru** also has two different definitions. The first
is *be possible* (cf. Lesson 13, item 9; Lesson 18, item 12; Lesson 26,
items 2, 3, 4; Lesson 30, item 6; Lesson 34, item 14). The second is *to
be produced, to be made* (cf. Lesson 40, items 5 and 12).

ಬಂಣಬಣ

S. F.
esu efu

1 – あさって 映画 を 見 に いきます。
a sat te ei ga o mi ni i kima su.

2 – どんな 映画 を 見る の です か。
don na ei ga o mi ru no de su ka.

3 – 僕 は S. F. が 大好き です。
boku wa esu efu ga dai su ki de su.

4 あさって 見 に 行こう と
a sat te mi ni i kō to

思って いる 映画 は 「宇宙
omot te i ru ei ga wa u chū

冒険」 と いいます。①
bō ken to i i ma su.

5 – 僕 は もう 見ました。おもしろい
boku wa mō mi ma shi ta. o moshi ro i

です よ。
de su yo.

6 それ は 二千 五百 六 年
so re wa ni sen go hyaku roku nen

に 起こる 物語 です。
ni o ko ru mono gatari de su.

Lesson Forty-Three   43

Science Fiction
(science fiction)

1 – I'm going to the movies the day after tomorrow.
   (day after tomorrow / movies / [object] / watch / [goal] / go)

2 – What kind of movie are you going to see?
   (what kind / movie / [object] / watch / it's that / [question])

3 – I love science fiction.
   (me / [announce] / science fiction / [subject] / be loved / it is)

4   The film I'm thinking about going to see the day after tomorrow is called *Space Adventure*.
   (day after tomorrow / watch / [goal] / let's go / [quotation] / think / movie / [announce] / space-adventure / [quotation] / say)

5 – I've seen it. It's good!
   (me / [announce] / already / have watched) (interesting / it is / [engagement]

6   It's a story that takes place in the year 2506.
   (that / [announce] / two thousand-five hundred-six-year / [time] / take place / story / it is)

ॐ○ஃ৪০৫

Notes

① 行こう **ikō**, *let's go*, low degree form for 行きましょう **ikimashō**. Before the phrase と 思って いる *to omotte iru* (cf. Lesson 28, paragraph 4), the low degree is mandatory.

7 地球 の ロケット の 出発点
chi kyū no ro ke t to no shup patsu ten

は 月 です。
wa tsuki de su.

8 そして 他 の 星 と 惑星 へ
so shi te hoka no hoshi to waku sei e

そこ から 飛び立つ の です。
so ko ka ra to bi ta tsu no de su.

9 でも 宇宙 の 果て から 地球
de mo u chū no ha te ka ra chi kyū

を 侵略 する 悪者 が 出て
o shin ryaku su ru waru mono ga de te

きます。
ki ma su.

10 ヒーロー は 地球 の 安全 を
hī rō wa chi kyū no an zen o

守る ため に、宇宙 の 彼方
mamo ru ta me ni, u chū no kanata

まで 冒険 に 行く の です。
ma de bō ken ni i ku no de su.

11 そして 敵国 の 悪者 の 妹
so shi te teki koku no waru mono no imōto

に 恋 を する の です。
ni koi o su ru no de su.

最後 は ハッピ・エンド です。
sai go wa ha p pi e n do de su.

7 The earth's rockets depart from the moon.
(earth / [relation] / rocket / [relation] / departure point / [announce] / moon / it is)

8 That's where they take off from towards other stars and planets.
(then / other / [relation] / star / and / planet / [destination] / there / from / take off / it's that)

9 But from the far reaches of the universe, a bad guy appears to invade the earth.
(but / universe / [relation] / end / from / earth / [object] / invasion-do / bad guy / [subject] / appear / come)

10 To save the planet, the hero leaves on an adventure to the other side of the universe.
(hero / [announce] / earth / [relation] / security / [object] / protect / in order to // universe / [relation] / far side / until / adventure / [goal] / go / it's that)

11 Then he falls in love with the younger sister of the bad guy from the enemy country. It has a happy ending.
(then / enemy country / [relation] / bad guy / [relation] / younger sister / [goal] / love / [object] / do / it's that) (end / [announce] happy ending / it is)

ഔൽ

43

12 – それなら 宇宙 冒険 で は
so re na ra　u chū　bō ken　de　wa

ありません ね。恋 の 冒険
a ri ma se n　ne. koi　no　bō ken

です ね。
de su　ne.

13 話 の 内容 を 全部 聞いて
hanashi no　nai yō　o　zen bu　ki i te

しまった ので もう 見 に 行く
shi ma t ta　no de　mō　mi　ni　i ku

気 が しません。僕 に は、恋 の
ki　ga shima se n. boku ni　wa, koi　no

冒険 なんて 興味 が ありません。
bō ken　na n te　kyō mi　ga　a ri ma se n. □

***

練習　renshū
れん しゅう

Exercise 1

❶ 来年 の 春 アパート を 買おう
rainen no haru apāto o kaō

と 思って います。
to omotte imasu.

❷ このごろ は とても いそがしい
konogoro wa totemo isogashii

です から もう 旅行 に 行く
desu kara mō ryokō ni iku

12 – Then it isn't an adventure in space, it's an adventure in love!
(if so / space-adventure / it's not / [agreement]) (love / [relation] / adventure / it is / [agreement])

13   Now that I've heard the whole story, I don't want to go see it anymore. I'm not interested in adventures in love!
(story / [relation] / contents / [object] / entire / hear / do to completion / because // anymore / watch / [goal] / go / spirit / [subject] / not do) (me / [attribution] / [emphasis] / love / [relation] / adventure / so-called / interest / [subject] / don't exist)

✳✳✳

気 が　しません。
ki ga shimasen.

❸ 自動車　を　作る　ため　に
jidōsha o tsukuru tame ni
工場　を　建てます。
kōjō o tatemasu.

❹ パン　を　作る　ため　に　小麦
pan o tsukuru tame ni komugi
を　使います。
o tsukaimasu.

43

⑤ それなら 先生 も S. F. に
sorenara sensei mo esu efu ni

興味 が ある でしょう。
kyōmi ga aru deshō.

✳✳✳

Exercise 2

... に 言葉 を 入れ なさい

❶ What kind of song do you like?

..... uta .. ..

❷ I bought a book that seems interesting.

.... hon . ...

❸ It is entitled, *Depart for the Stars*.

....

❹ There are 1,298 pages.

... . pēji ....

৵৹ড়৵৹ড়

Answers to Exercise 1

43

❶ I'm thinking about buying an apartment in the spring of next year. **❷** Because I am very busy this time, I don't want to travel anymore. **❸** To make cars, we build factories. **❹** To make bread, we use wheat. **❺** Under those conditions, you too, Professor, are interested in science fiction.

***

❺ Are you interested in tennis?

. . . .

❻ I've already seen it.

. .   . .

Answers to Exercise 2

❶ donna – ga suki desu ka. **❷** omoshirosō na – o kaimashita. **❸** hoshi e no shuppatsu to iimasu. **❹** sen ni hyaku kyū jū hachi – ari-masu. **❺** tenisu ni kyōmi ga arimasu ka. **❻** mō mimashita.

ഓ൫ൌ൮

44 第四十四課 dai yon jū yon ka
だい よん じゅう よん か

ホテル
ho te ru

1 – おはよう　ございます。プリンス・
o ha yō　go za i ma su.　pu ri n su
ホテル　で　ございます。①
ho te ru　de　go za i ma su.

2 – 部屋　の　予約　を　おねがい
he ya　no　yoyaku　o　o ne ga i
したい　の　です　けれども…②
shi ta i　no　de su　ke re do mo…

3 – お　一人　さま　です　か。③
o　hito ri　sa ma　de su　ka.

4 – いいえ、家内　と　子供　が
i i e,　ka nai　to　ko domo　ga
二人　います。
futa ri　i ma su.

5 – 大人　二人、子供　二人　全部
otona　futa ri,　ko domo　futa ri　zenbu
で　四名　さま　です　ね。ご
de　yon mei　sa ma　de su　ne.　go
滞在　は　いつ　まで　です　か。
tai zai　wa　i tsu　ma de　de su　ka.

Lesson Forty-Four 44

The Hotel
(hotel)

1 – Good Morning. This is the Prince Hotel.
(good morning) (prince hotel / it is)

2 – I would like to reserve a room...
(room / [relation] / reservation / [object] / request-want to do / it's that / even though)

3 – For one person?
([polite]-one person-Mr / it is / [question])

4 – No, there are also my wife and two children.
(no / my wife / and / child / [subject] / two person / exist)

5 – Two adults and two children, in total four people. How long will you be staying?
(adult / two person / child / two person / total / [means] / four person Mr / it is / [agreement]) ([polite]-stay / [announce] / when / until / it is / [question])

৩০৩৪৩০৪

Notes

① で　ございます **de gozaimasu**. Step back a bit and take another look at Lesson 21, paragraph 4. Here is a special example of a verb in high degree. For the most common verbs, high degree is not a different form of the same verb, but actually a different verb altogether. This is the case for the most common adjective in Japanese, いい **ii** (cf. Lesson 23, note 5).
で　ございます **de gozaimasu** is the high degree form of です **desu**, *it is*, if you are speaking of yourself or of those close to you.

② けれども　**keredomo**, at the end of a preposition, means *even though*, but it is also used, as in the current example, as a softener, where we might say "Excuse me, but...". It is very common to end a sentence this way when being noncommittal. (cf. also Lesson 40, item 7)

③ お　一人　さま **o hitori sama**. *One single person* is 一人 **hitori**. The お **o** and さま **sama** are there to indicate politeness (cf. also item 5).

6 – 来月 の 十二日 から 十五日
rai getsu no　jū ni nichi ka ra　jū go nichi
まで おねがい したい の です が…
ma de　o ne ga i　shi ta i　no　de su ga…

7 – 来月 は 大変 混んで おります
rai getsu wa　tai hen　ko n de　o ri ma su
ので、ちょっと 離れた 二部屋
no de,　cho t to hana re ta　futa he ya
です が、よろしい でしょう か。④⑤
de su　ga,　yo ro shi i　de shō　ka.

8 – 同じ 階 です か。
ona ji　kai　de su　ka.

9 – はい、そう で ございます。⑥
ha i　sō　de　go za i ma su.

10 – よろしく おねがい します。
yo ro shi ku　o ne ga i　shi ma su.

11 – チェック・イン の 時間 は
che k ku　i n　no　ji kan　wa
正午 から で ございます。①
shō go　ka ra　de　go za i ma su.

12 – (妻 に) 部屋 の 予約 を したよ。
(tsuma ni)　he ya　no yoyaku o　shi ta yo.
ちょっと 離れて いる 部屋 だ
cho t to hana re te　i ru　he ya　da
けど 同じ フロア だって。⑦⑧
ke do　ona ji　fu ro a　da t te.

6 – I would like to make the reservation for next month, from the 12th to the 15th.
(next month / [relation] / ten-two-day / from / ten-five-day / until / request-want to do / it's that / even though)

7 – We're very busy next month, would it be alright to have two rooms not next to each other?
(next month / [emphasis] / terribly / be congested / because // a bit / be distant / two-room / it is / but // be good / you think that / [question])

8 – Are they on the same floor?
(be same / floor / it is / [question])

9 – Yes.
(yes / so / it is)

10 – That'll do.
(well / please)

11 – You can check in any time after noon.
(check in / [relation] / time / [announce] / noon / from / it is)

12 – (to his wife) I made the reservations. The rooms are a little apart, but she said they're both on the same floor.
(his wife / [attribute]) (room / [relation] / reservation / [object] / did / [engagement]) (a little / distant / room / it is / even though // be same / floor / she said that)

ഇാരുന്നു

Notes

④ おります **orimasu**, the high degree version of います **imasu**, if you are speaking of yourself and those close to you.

⑤ よろしい **yoroshii**, cf. Lesson 23, note 5.

⑥ そう で ございます **sō de gozaimasu**, cf. note 1. High degree version of そう です **sō desu**, *it is, yes*, when speaking of yourself.

⑦ けど **kedo**, abbreviated form of けれども **keredomo**, *although*, in familiar language.

⑧ だって **datte**. In casual and familiar language, this is used to report what someone else has said.

13 – それじゃ、仕方 が ない わ ね。
so re ja, shi kata ga na i wa ne.

まあ、いい わ。
ma a, i i wa. □

✳✳✳

練習 renshū

Exercise 1

❶ もしもし 上原 で ございます。
moshimoshi uehara de gozaimasu.

❷ 小さい バッグ しか ありません
chiisai baggu shika arimasen

が、よろしい でしょう か。
ga, yoroshii deshō ka.

❸ 二十二日 から 三十日 まで
ni jū ichi nichi kara san jū nichi made

プリンス・ホテル に います。
purinsu-hoteru ni imasu.

❹ 正午 に ホテル の 前 で
shōgo ni hoteru no mae de

会いましょう。
aimashō.

✳✳✳

13 – Well, nothing to be done. I suppose that's fine!   **44**
*(so / way to do / [subject] / doesn't exist / [softener] /
[agreement]) (well / be good / [softener])*

❺ 切符 を 三 枚 おねがい したい
きっ ぷ   さん まい
kippu o san mai o negai shitai

の です けれども…
no desu keredomo...

Answers to Exercise 1

❶ Hello, this is Mr. Uehara. ❷ We only have small bags, would that
be alright? ❸ From the 21st to the 30th, I'll be at the Prince Hotel.
❹ Let's meet at noon in front of the hotel. ❺ I would like three
tickets, please.

***

...に 言葉 を 入れ なさい
<small>こと ば</small> <small>い</small>

❶ The vacation is from the 23rd to the 26th.

. . . . kara .. ..

. . . . . made desu

❷ There are two of us.

. . . .

❸ We can't do anything about it.

. . . . desu ne

❹ Starting next month, I only work in the afternoon.

. . . . wa . . . .

---

45 第四十五課 **dai yon jū go ka**
<small>だい よん じゅう ご か</small>

銀行
<small>ぎん こう</small>

gin kō

1 – 度々 日本 に 来る から、口座
<small>たびたび</small> <small>に ほん</small> <small>く</small> <small>こう ざ</small>

tabi tabi ni hon ni kuru kara, kō za

を 開きたい の です が…
<small>ひら</small>

o hira ki ta i no de su ga...

2 口座 は 簡単 に 開く こと
<small>こう ざ</small> <small>かん たん</small> <small>ひら</small>

kō za wa kan tan ni hira ku ko to

が できます か。①

ga de ki ma su ka.

⑤ Because we made reservations in the same hotel, let's leave together! **45**

.... ni ...., ...
ikimashō

Answers to Exercise 2

❶ yasumi wa ni jū san nichi – ni jū roku nichi –. **❷** futari desu.
❸ shikata ga nai –. **❹** raigetsu kara – gogo shika hatarakimasen.
❺ onaji hoteru – yoyaku shita node issho ni – .

Lesson Forty-Five   45

The Bank
(bank)

1 – Because I often come to Japan, I would like to open an account.
(often / Japan / [place] / come / because // bank account / [object] / want to open / it's that / but)

2 Is it possible to open an account easily?
(bank account / [announce] / easy / [adverb] / open / fact of / [subject] / be possible / [question])

ഇൗ൩ൠൡ

Notes

① cf. Lesson 42, paragraph 3.

3 – はい。普通 口座 なら、外国人
ha i. fu tsū kō za na ra, gai koku jin

でも 開く こと が できます。
de mo hira ku ko to ga de ki ma su.

4 – それでは、 私 も 口座 を
so re de wa, watakushi mo kō za o

開きましょう。
hira ki ma shō.

5 後 二日 で カナダ へ 帰ります。
ato futsu ka de ka na da e kae ri ma su.

6 帰国 の 前 に、残った 日本
ki koku no mae ni, noko t ta ni hon

円 を 預けて いく こと に
en o azu ke te i ku ko to ni

します。②
shi ma su.

7 – 普通 口座 でも 利子 が
fu tsū kō za de mo ri shi ga

つきます から、来年 の 冬 また
tsu ki ma su ka ra, rai nen no fuyu ma ta

日本 に 遊び に 来る 時、
ni hon ni aso bi ni ku ru toki,

お 金 が 増えて います。③
o kane ga fu e te i ma su.

3 – Yes. If it is a standard account, even a foreigner **45**
can open one.
*(yes) (standard-account / if it is / foreigner / even / open /
fact of / [subject] / be possible)*

4 – So then I'll open one.
(so / me / too / account / [object] / let's open)

5 In two days I return to Canada.
(after-two days / [time] / Canada / [destination] / return)

6 Before I go back, I want to deposit the yen I
have left over.
*(return to country / [relation] / before / [time] / remain /
Japan-yen / [object] / deposit / go / fact of / [object] / do)*

7 – There is interest even on a standard account, so
when you come back to Japan for vacation next
winter, your money will have increased.
*(standard-account / even / interest / [subject] / be attached /
because // next year / [relation] / winter / again / Japan /
[place] / enjoy / [goal] / come / time // [familiarity]-money /
[subject] / be increased)*

೮೦ಐ೮೦ಐ

Notes

② cf. Lesson 42, paragraph 3.

③ 遊ぶ **asobu**. This verb is the opposite of 働く **hataraku**, *to
work*. It can therefore indicate anything that is not work.

45

8 じゃ、明日 一時半 に 銀行
ja, ashita ichi ji han ni ginkō
の 前 で 会いましょう。
no mae de a i ma shō.

翌日、銀行 の 前 で
yoku jitsu, ginkō no mae de

9 – 予定外 の 買物 を した ので、
yo tei gai no kai mono o shi ta no de,
お 財布 が 空っぽ に なって
o sai fu ga kara p po ni na t te
しまいました。
shi ma i ma shi ta.

10 だから 口座 を 開く こと
da ka ra kō za o hira ku ko to
が できなく なりました。
ga de ki na ku na ri ma shi ta.

11 それに 空港 まで の バス代
so re ni kū kō ma de no ba su dai
も なく なって しまいました。
mo na ku na t te shi ma i ma shi ta.

12 空港 で は 飛行場 使用料
kū kō de wa hi kō jō shi yō ryō
も 払わなければ なりません。
mo hara wa na ke re ba na ri ma se n.

Good, so we'll meet tomorrow at 1:30 in front **45**
of the bank.
(good / tomorrow / one-o'clock-half / [time] / bank / [relation] / front / [place] / let's meet)

The next day, in front of the bank
(next day / bank / [relation] / front / [place])

9 – I bought more than I planned, so my wallet is
completely empty!
(unplanned / [relation] / purchase / [object] / did / because // [familiarity]-wallet / [subject] / completely empty / [goal] / become / do to completion)

10 So I can't open the account.
(so / account / [object] / open / fact of / [subject] / not be possible / became)

11 I don't even have enough to pay for the bus to
the airport!
(also / airport / until / [relation] / bus ticket cost / also / not exist / became / do to completion)

12 And I have to pay the airport tax there!
(airport / [place] / [emphasis] / airport tax / also / must pay)

ഇയങ്കൾ

後二日で カナダ へ 帰ります。

13 こんな おねがいで 悪<ruby>わる</ruby>い けれど、
ko n na　o ne ga i de waru i　ke re do,

一万円<ruby>いちまんえん</ruby> 貸<ruby>か</ruby>して くれません か。④
ichi man en　ka shi te　ku re ma se n　ka.　□

***

練習<ruby>れんしゅう</ruby>　renshū

Exercise 1

❶ 一緒<ruby>いっしょ</ruby> に 行<ruby>い</ruby>った 方<ruby>ほう</ruby> が いい です。
issho ni itta hō ga ii desu.

❷ カナダ人<ruby>じん</ruby> の 友達<ruby>ともだち</ruby> から もらった お
kanadajin no tomodachi kara moratta o

酒<ruby>さけ</ruby> は 全部<ruby>ぜんぶ</ruby> 飲<ruby>の</ruby>んで しまいました。
sake wa zenbu nonde shimaimashita.

❸ 山口<ruby>やまぐち</ruby> さん の ところ へ 度々<ruby>たびたび</ruby>
yamaguchi san no tokoro e tabitabi

遊<ruby>あそ</ruby>び に 行<ruby>い</ruby>きます。
asobi ni ikimasu.

***

13   I feel terrible, but you couldn't let me 10,000   **45**
yen, could you?
(this sort / request / [means] / be bad / although // one-
10,000-yen / lend / not do for me / [question])

ඞൠൠ

Notes

④ けれど **keredo**. Yet another abbreviation for けれども **keredomo**, *although*, in casual language (cf. Lesson 44, note 7).

***

❹ そんな に 簡単 な 料理 なら
sonna ni kantan na ryōri nara

子供 でも できます。
kodomo demo dekimasu.

❺ 遠い です けれども、ぜひ 行きたい
tooi desu keredomo, zehi ikitai

と 思います。
to omoimasu.

Answers to Exercise 1

❶ It would be better if I went with you. ❷ I drank all the alcohol my Canadian friend gave me. ❸ I often go to Yamaguchi's place. ❹ A recipe so easy, even children can do it! ❺ Although it's far, I absolutely want to go.

***

...に 言葉 を 入れ なさい

❶ Come see us one of these days!

zehi .... kite kudasai

❷ I decide to open an account.

....

❸ Even though he's still a child, he's interested in the opera.

mada ...., ...

.. ..

---

46 第四十六課 **dai yon jū rok ka**

医者
i sha

1 – あなた が 胃 が 痛い と
    a na ta   ga   i   ga ita i   to

言って いました ので、 私
i t te   i ma shi ta   no de, watashi

が 知って いる お 医者 さま
ga shi t te i ru o i sha sa ma

に 予約 を 取りました。①
ni   yo yaku o   to ri ma shi ta.

④ I still want to think about it a little. **46**
mō chotto shirabe . . . . . omoimasu

⑤ When you come back next winter, I will introduce you.
mata . . . . kuru . . . . , ...
. . . .

Answers to Exercise 2
❶ – asobi ni –. ❷ kōza o hiraku koto ni shimasu. ❸ – kodomo desu
keredomo, opera ni kyōmi ga arimasu. ❹ – tai to –. ❺ – rainen no
fuyu – toki, shōkai shimasu.

Lesson Forty-Six 46

At the Doctor's
(doctor)

1 – Since you told me you had a stomach ache, I
made you an appointment with a doctor I know.
*(you / [subject] / stomach / [subject] / be hurt / [quotation]
/ was saying / because // I / [subject] / know / [polite]-doc-
tor-Mr. / [place] / appointment / [object] / took)*

൸ඣൺ൶

Notes
① お 医者 さま **o isha sama**, cf. Lesson 44, note 3.

2 – ありがとう ございます。胃潰瘍
a ri ga tō　　go za i ma su.　i kai yō

では ない か と 心配 して
de wa na i　ka　to　shinpai　shi te

います。②
i ma su.

3 – それ は 早く お 医者 さん へ
so re wa hayaku　o　i sha sa n　e

行った 方 が いい です ね。
i tta　hō ga　i i　de su　ne.

4　このごろ は 胃潰瘍 でも 早く
ko no go ro　wa　i kai yō　de mo haya ku

治療 する と、問題 なく
chi ryō　su ru　to, mon dai　na ku

直る そう です から。
nao ru　sō　de su　ka ra.

5 – それで 予約 は いつ です か。
so re de　yo yaku wa　i tsu　de su　ka.

6 – 再来週 の 水曜日 の 午後
sa rai shū　no　sui yō bi　no　go go

四時 十五分 前 です。③
yo ji　jū go fun　mae　de su.

✂∽ℭℬ∽ℛ

2 – Thank you very much. I'm worried it might be an ulcer. **46**

(thank you very much) (stomach-ulcer / it's not / [question] / [quotation] / worry-be doing)

3 – Then you should go see a doctor quickly.

(that / [announce] / quickly / [polite]-doctor-Mr. / [destination] / went / direction / [subject] / be good / it is / [agreement])

4 I hear that these days even an ulcer will heal without problems if you treat it quickly.

(these days / [emphasis] / stomach-ulcer / even / fast / treatment-do / when // problem / not exist / heal / have heard that / because)

5 – And what time is the appointment at?

(and / appointment / [announce] / when / it is / [question])

6 – Wednesday of the week after next, at quarter to four in the afternoon.

(week after next / [relation] / Wednesday / [relation] / after-noon / four-o'clock-fifteen minutes-before / it is)

ഇൗ൝൙഻

Notes

② cf. Lesson 36, note 6. 心配 する **shinpai suru**, *worry,* is considered to be an act of thought. So the object of this worry is followed by and linked to it by と **to**.

③ 四時 **yo ji**. Oh, yes, when you tell time, *four* is pronounced よ **yo** instead of よん **yon** (take a quick glance at the number of this lesson!)

びょういん
病院
byō in

7 – お　かけ　下さい。どう
　　　o　ka ke kuda sa i.　　dō

なさいました　か。④
na sa i ma shi ta　　ka.

8 – 食後　一時間　ぐらい　経つ　と、胃
　　　shoku goi chi ji kan　gu ra i　ta tsu to,　i

が　じんと　痛く　なります。胃潰瘍
ga　ji n to　ita ku　na ri ma su.　i kai yō

で　は　ない　でしょう　か。⑤
de　wa　na i　de shō　ka.

9 – ちょっと　見て　みましょう。舌
　　　cho t to　mi te　mi ma shō.　shita

を　出して　下さい。その　ベッド
o　da shi te kuda sa i.　so no　be d do

に　横　に　なって　下さい。
ni　yoko　ni　na t te　kuda sa i.

10 ここ　を　押す　と、痛い　です
　　　ko ko　o　o su　to,　ita i　de su

か。　―いいえ。
ka.　　　–i i e.

11 – ここ　は？　―いいえ。　―ここ
　　　ko ko　wa?　　―i i e.　　　―ko ko

は？　―いいえ。
wa?　　―i i e.

(hospital)

7 – Please be seated. What seems to be the problem?
   (sit down) (how / did / [question])

8 – About an hour after I eat, a deep pain hits my
   stomach. You don't think it's an ulcer, do you?
   *(after meal / one-hour-around / pass / when // stomach /
   [subject] / sharply / be hurt / become) (ulcer / it isn't / one
   could think / [question])*

9 – Let's take a look. Stick out your tongue. Lie
   down on the bed over there.
   *(a bit / look / let's see) (tongue / [object] / put out) (that /
   bed / [place] / side / [goal] / become)*

10 When I press here, does it hurt? –No.
   (here / [object] / press / when // be hurt / it is / [question]) (no)

11 – Here? –No. –Here? –No.

ᏚᎤᏣᏚᎤᏣ

Notes

④ なさいました **nasaimashita**. The high degree equivalent of
   しました **shimashita**, when speaking of the other person:
   "**You** did…".

⑤ じんと **jin to**. Another word that's almost impossible to
   translate (cf. Lesson 39, note 5), implying all sorts of sensory
   impressions. Here, the manner in which pain is produced. It
   feels as if it's coming from very far, and then all of a sudden it's
   quite strong. Go translate that in one word!

12 – 大丈夫 です。わかりました。
daijōbu desu. wakarimashita.

何でも ありません。ただ の
nandemo arimasen. tada no

食べすぎ です。
tabesugi desu.

13 一週間 ぐらい 胃 を
isshūkan gurai i o

休ませる ため に、少し
yasumaseru tame ni, sukoshi

食物 を 控えて 下さい。
tabemono o hikaete kudasai.

14 – でも 今晩、昇進 祝い に
demo konban, shōshin iwai ni

フランス・レストラン に 行く こと
furansu resutoran ni iku koto

に なって います が…⑥
ni natte imasu ga… □

***

練習 **renshū**

Exercise 1

❶ 事故 に 会った の で は ない
jiko ni atta no de wa nai

12 – It's fine. I see. It's nothing. You just overate.
(fine / it is) (have understood) (anything / it's not) (simple / [relation] / overeating / it is)

13 Cut down a bit on your food for a week to give your stomach a rest.
(one-week / about / stomach / [object] / make rest / for // a bit / food / [object] / please reduce)

14 – But tonight I'm going to a French restaurant to celebrate my promotion…
(but / tonight / promotion-celebration / [goal] / France-restaurant / [place] / go / fact of / [goal] become / although)

ജ്ഞൠ

Notes

⑥ こと に なって います **koto ni natte imasu**. cf. Lesson 42, paragraph 3.

✳✳✳

か と 心配 して います。
ka to shinpai shite imasu.

❷ 足 が 痛い。
ashi ga itai.

❸ 三時 二十五分 前 に 工場
san ji ni jū go fun mae ni kōjō

を 出 ました。
o demashita.

❹ お 誕生日 祝い に 芝居 を
o tanjōbi iwai ni shibai o

見 に 行きましょう。
mi ni ikimashō.

46

⑤ 医者 の ところ へ 行く と、
isha no tokoro e iku to,

いつも 何か こわい です。
itsumo nanika kowai desu.

＊＊＊

Exercise 2

... に 言葉 を 入れ なさい

❶ He says his ear hurts.

. . . .

❷ Thank you.

. . . .

❸ We will arrive at a quarter to four.

. . .. tsukimasu

❹ It would be best to buy the tickets quickly.

. . . . katta .. . .

ಐഡ‍ඎ‍

307 • san byaku shichi (nana)

❶ I'm worried they might have had an accident. ❷ My foot hurts.
❸ I left the factory at twenty-five to three. ❹ To celebrate your birthday, let's go to the theatre. ❺ When I go to the doctor, I'm always afraid.

✳✳✳

❺ It so happens that I am also going to the doctor's this afternoon.

watakushi .. kyō no .... o ....
. iku .... .. natte imasu

Answers to Exercise 2

❶ mimi ga itai to itte imasu. ❷ arigatō gozaimasu. ❸ yo ji jū go fun mae ni –. ❹ kippu o hayaku – hō ga ii desu. ❺ – mo – gogo – isha san no tokoro e – koto ni –.

だい よん じゅう なな か

音楽
おん がく
on gaku

カクテル・パーテイー で。
ka ku te ru pā tī de.

1 – 何か お 飲み に なります か。
なに   の
nani ka o no mi ni na ri ma su ka.

シャンペン は お 好き です か。①
す
sha n pe n wa o su ki de su ka.

2 加藤 さん から 音楽 が お 好き
か とう   おん がく   す
ka tō sa n ka ra ongaku ga o su ki

だ と うかがいました が…②
da to u ka ga i ma shi ta ga…

3 – はい。特 に クラシック 音楽
とく   おん がく
ha i. toku ni ku ra shi k ku on gaku

が 好き です。
す
ga su ki de su.

4 – 何か 楽器 を なさいます か。
なに がっ き
nani ka gak ki o na sa i ma su ka.

5 – はい。オーボエ を 趣味 で
しゅ み
ha i. ō bo e o shu mi de

やって います。
ya t te i ma su.

Lesson Forty-Seven 47

Music

(music)

At a cocktail party.
(cocktail / [place])

1 – Are you drinking anything? Do you like champagne?
(something / [polite]-drink /[goal] / become / [question]) (champagne / [announce] / [polite]-be liked / it is / [question])

2 I learned from Mr. Katō that you like music.
(Katō-Mr. / from / music /[subject] / [polite]-be liked / it is / [quotation] / have heard / but)

3 – Yes. Especially classical music.
(yes) (principally / [adverbial] / classical-music / [subject] / be liked / it is)

4 – Do you play an instrument?
(something / musical instrument / [object] / do / [question])

5 -- Yes. I play the oboe as a hobby.
(yes) (oboe / [object] / pastime / [means] / be doing)

Notes

① お 飲(の)み に なります **o nomi ni narimasu**. In note 1 of Lesson 44, concerning the high degree, we said that for certain very common verbs, the high form was actually a different verb altogether. But in other cases, the high degree is formed from the verb in its "normal" state. Here it is the verb 飲(の)む **nomu**, *to drink* surrounded by the elements お **o** and に なります **ni narimasu**. The two elements are indeed the mark of high degree verbs, when speak of the other person: ***you** drink*. Also in high degree is the お **o** before 好き **suki**: ***you** like*.

② うかがいました **ukagaimashita**, high degree form for 聞(き)きました **kikimashita**, when the subject is the speaker: ***I** heard*.

6 – もう　どのぐらい　なさって
mō　do no gu ra i　na sa t te

いる　の　です　か。③
i ru　no　de su　ka.

7 – 五　六　年　です。高等学校　の
go roku nen　de su.　kō tō gakkō　no

時　クラブ　活動　で　始めた
toki　ku ra bu　katsu dō　de　haji me ta

の　が　きっかけ　です。④
no　ga　ki k ka ke　de su.

8　卒業　して　から　なかなか
sotsu gyō　shi te　ka ra　na ka na ka

吹く　機会　が　ありません。
fu ku　ki kai　ga　a ri ma se n.

9　ですから　最近　は　自分　で　吹く
de su ka ra　sai kin　wa　ji bun　de　fu ku

より、もっぱら　レコード　や　カセット
yo ri,　mō p pa ra　re kō do　ya　ka se t to

や　ラジオ　を　聞いて　います。
ya　ra ji o　o　ki i te　i ma su.

10　家　に　いる　時　は　ラジオ
ie　ni　i ru　toki　wa　ra ji o

を　つけっぱなし　です。
o　tsu ke p pa na shi　de su.

6 – How long have you been playing?
(already / about how much / be doing / it's that / [question])

7 – Five or six years. I started it in a club in high school.
(five-six-year / it is) (high school / [relation] / time / club-activity / [means] / have started / fact of / [subject] / chance / it is)

8 Since I graduated, I haven't had many chances to play.
(graduate-do / since / quite / blow / opportunity / [subject] / not exist)

9 So these days, rather than playing my own music, I listen to records, tapes, and the radio.
(so / recently / [emphasis] / oneself / [means] / blow / more than / especially / record / and / tape / and / radio / [object] / listen)

10 When I'm at home, the radio is always on.
(house / [place] / be / time / [emphasis] // radio / [object] / left on / it is)

☙ဢ☙ဢ

Notes

③ なさって　いる **nasatte iru**, cf. Lesson 46, note 4: *you do*.

④ 始めた　の　が **hajimeta no ga**. We know こと **koto**, meaning "fact of + verb", in the expressions we reviewed in Lesson 42, paragraph 3. In addition to these phrases, where it's mandatory to use こと **koto**, we can also substitute の **no**, meaning *fact of*. Here, literally: "the fact of having begun as a club activity was the origin".

一人　で　練習　する　より　楽しい　です。

11 – 僕の 家に 音楽 好き の 仲間 が
boku no ie ni on gaku zu ki no naka ma ga

十二 人 ぐらい 日曜日 に 隔週
jū ni nin gu ra i nichi yō bi ni kaku shū

で 集まります。 よろしかったら、
de atsu ma ri ma su. yo ro shi ka t ta ra,

いらっしゃいません か。 ⑤⑥
i ra s sha i ma se n ka.

12 – ぜひ 仲間 に 入れて 下さい。
ze hi naka ma ni i re te kuda sa i.

その 方 が 一人 で 練習
so no hō ga hito ri de ren shū

する より 楽しい です。 □
su ru yo ri tano shi i de su.

*** *** ***

練習 renshū

Exercise 1

❶ このごろ は 映画 を 見 に 行く より
konogoro wa eiga o mi ni iku yori

もっぱら テレビ で 見る の です。
moppara terebi de miru no desu.

11 – Every other Sunday, 12 music-loving friends of mine meet at my house. If you're interested, why not come along?
(me / [relation] / house / [place] / music-loved / [apposition] / friend / [subject] / ten-two-person / about / Sunday / [time] / every other week / [means] / meet up) (if it's good / not come / [question])

12 – Count me in! That's much more fun than practicing alone!
(absolutely / friend / [place] / please allow in) (that / direction / [subject] / alone / practice-do / more than / be pleasant / it is)

ഗ്രൗഃഈ

Notes

⑤ In counting people, *one person* is 一人 **hitori** (cf. Lesson 44, item 3) and **two people** is 二人 **futari** (cf. Lesson 44, item 4). But from three onwards it's just the number, plus 人 **nin** in familiar situations and the number plus 名 **mei** in official situations (cf. Lesson 44, item 5).

⑥ いらっしゃいません **irasshaimasen**, the high degree equivalent to 来ません **kimasen**, when speaking of the other person: *you do not come.*

✳✳✳

❷ 日本 へ 両親 を つれて 行った
nihon e ryōshin o tsurete itta
の が きっかけ です。
no ga kikkake desu.

❸ 生け花 を 趣味 で やって います。
ikebana o shumi de yatte imasu.

❹ ざんねん です が、日本語 で 話す
zannen desu ga, nihongo de hanasu
機会 が なかなか ありません。
kikai ga nakanaka arimasen.

❺ 伯父 さん から 歌舞伎 が
oji san kara kabuki ga

お好き だ と 聞きました。
o suki da to kikimashita.

✳✳✳

Exercise 2

...に 言葉 を 入れ なさい

❶ There were two hundred people at the cocktail party last night.
. . . . kakuteru-pātī ni hito ga .. . .
. . . .

❷ How long have you been speaking English?
. . . . nasaimashita ka

❸ Every other Saturday I go to a concert.
. . . . ongakkai .. . .

❹ I love to listen to jazz.
jazu o kiku .. ga suki desu

🙖🙔🙖🙔

Answers to Exercise 1

❶ These days, rather than going to the movies, it's mostly on television that I watch movies. ❷ The occasion was a trip to Japan with my parents. ❸ I do flower arrangements as a hobby. ❹ It's too bad, but I have almost no chance to speak Japanese. ❺ I heard your uncle say that you love kabuki.

✳✳✳

❺ It's more pleasant to play than to listen.

kiku .... fuku .. ..

Answers to Exercise 2

❶ kinō no – ni hyaku nin imashita. ❷ eigo wa donogurai –. ❸ doyōbi ni kakushū de – ni ikimasu. ❹ – no –. ❺ – yori – hō ga tanoshii desu.

৩৫৮০৫৪

秋 の 日 の…
aki no hi no…

1 – もう　そろそろ　夏　が
　　　mō　　　so ro so ro　natsu　ga

終わります　ね。
o wa ri ma su　ne.

2　秋　の　足音　が　聞こえる
　　aki　no　ashi oto　ga　ki ko e ru

みたい　です　ね。
mi ta i　de su　ne.

3　いわし雲　が　浮かんで　いる　空
　　i wa shi gumo ga　u ka n de　i ru　sora

や　夕焼け　を　見る　と、この
ya　yū ya ke　o　mi ru　to,　ko no

世　が　空しく　なります。①
yo　ga　muna shi ku　na ri ma su.

4　枯葉　が　落ちる　の　を　見て
　　kare ha　ga　o chi ru　no　o　mi te

いる　と　悲しく　なります。②
i ru　to　kana shi ku　na ri ma su.

Lesson Forty-Eight   48

Autumn Days...
(autumn / [relation] / day / [relation])

1 –   The summer will soon be gone.
(already / softly / summer / [subject] / finish / [agreement])

2   It's as if one can hear the footsteps of autumn.
(autumn / [relation] / foot-noise / [subject] / be audible / as if / it is / [agreement])

3   When I look at the sky and see the floating autumn clouds, and the setting of the sun, the world appears so empty.
(cirrus cloud / [subject] / be floating / sky / and / twilight / [object] / look / when // this / world / [subject] / be empty / become)

4   When I see the falling dead leaves, I become sad.
(deadleaf / [subject] / fall / fact of / [object] / be looking / when // be sad / become)

હ્ય૦ભ૮૪૦૦૪

Notes

① いわし雲 **iwashigumo**. These are the great wisps of clouds that lay out in the sky so thinly, resembling little waves, and form little clusters in the sky. The technical term for them is "cirrus clouds", but where is the poetry in that? So in Japanese we have いわし雲 **iwashigumo** (literally: "sardine cloud"!), which is inseparable from the poetic sensation of autumn.

② の **no**, cf. Lesson 47, note 4. Item 4 is literally, "when I see **the fact of** dead leaves falling", and item 6: "when I see **the fact of** rays of the sun shining"

5 全く「秋の日の ビオロン
mattaku aki no hi no bioron

の 溜息…」の 詩の よう
no tame iki... no shi no yō

です な。③
de su na.

6 夏の 終わりの 日暮れの 太陽
natsuno owari no higure no taiyō

の 光が 庭の 柿の 木の 葉
no hikari ga niwa no kaki no ki no ha

に 輝いて いるのを 見ると、
ni kagayai te iru no o miru to,

もう 秋に なって しまった
mō aki ni natte shimatta

のかと 思います。④
no ka to omoimasu.

7 時が あまりにも 早く 過ぎる
toki ga amari nimo hayaku sugiru

ので、寂しい 気持に なります。
node, sabishii kimochi ni narimasu.

8 人の 命 なんて はかない
hito no inochi nante hakanai

もの です ね。
mono desu ne.

5   It's exactly as in the poem: "The long sobs of
      autumn's violins…"
      *(exactly / autumn / [relation] / day / [relation] / violin /
      [relation] / sigh / [relation] / poem / [relation] / appear-
      ance / it is / [reflection])*

6   When I see the rays of the evening sun of late
      summer, shining on the leaves of the kaki tree
      in the garden, I see that fall is indeed here.
      *(summer / [relation] / end / [relation] / sundown / [rela-
      tion] / sun / [relation] / ray / [subject] / garden / [relation] /
      kaki / [relation] / tree / [relation] / leaf / [place] / be shining /
      fact of / [object] / look / when // already / autumn / [goal] /
      become / do to completion / it's that / [question] / [quota-
      tion] / think)*

7   Time passes too quickly, and this makes me sad.
      *(time / [subject] / too / fast / pass / because // be sad / feel-
      ing / [goal] / become)*

8   Human life is but a transient thing!
      *(person / [relation] / life / so-called / be transient / thing /
      it is / [agreement])*

ഉറ‍ുശ‍ുഝ‍ുറ‍ു

Notes

③ 秋 の 日 の ビオロン の 溜息… **aki no hi no
bioron no tameiki…** These are the first famous words of a
translation by an equally famous Japanese poet (Ueda Bin 1874
– 1916) of the most famous line of Verlaine: "The long sobs of
autumn's violins…". In the entire world, Japan has translated,
and continues to translate, the most literature from other languages and countries.

④ 柿 **kaki**, an autumn fruit, bright orange in color.

9 – あら、あなた の ご 主人 は
a ra, a na ta no go shujin wa

ロマンチック な 方 です ね。⑤
ro ma n ti k ku na kata de su ne.

10 いつも こんな 風 です か。
i tsu mo ko n na fū de su ka.

11 – いいえ。酔っ払った 時 だけ
i i e. yo ppara t ta toki da ke

です。お 酒 を 飲んで いない
de su. o sake o no n de i na i

時 は 現実的 な 人 です よ。
toki wa gen jitsu teki na hito de su yo.

12 そう で なければ、どうやって
sō de na ke re ba, do ya t te

冷凍 食品 を 売る 商売
rei tō shoku hin o u ru shō bai

が できます か。
ga de ki ma su ka.

□

&CI%&CI%

9 – Wow, your husband is such a romantic person! **48**
(ah / you / [relation] / [polite]-husband / [announce] / romantic / it is / person / it is / [agreement])

10 Is he always like that?
(always / that way / manner / it is / [question])

11 – No. Only when he's drunk. When he's sober he's much more of a realist.
(no) (be drunk / time / only / it is) ([familiarity]-alcohol / [object] / not be drinking / time / [emphasis] // realist / it is / person / it is / [engagement])

12 Otherwise, how could he do his job of selling frozen foods?
(so / if it is not / how / frozen-food / [object] / sell / business / [subject] / be possible / [question])

∞⌘∞⌘

Notes

⑤ 方 **kata**, even though this is a noun, we can consider it as the high degree version of 人 **hito**, *person, human being*.

<ruby>練<rt>れん</rt></ruby><ruby>習<rt>しゅう</rt></ruby> **renshū**

Exercise 1

❶ そう で なければ、 どう やって この
sō de nakereba, dō yatte kono

<ruby>工場<rt>こうじょう</rt></ruby> で <ruby>働<rt>はたら</rt></ruby>く こと が できます か。
kōjō de hataraku koto ga dekimasu ka.

❷ <ruby>水族館<rt>すいぞくかん</rt></ruby> の <ruby>中<rt>なか</rt></ruby> に <ruby>入<rt>はい</rt></ruby>る みたい です。
suizokukan no naka ni hairu mitai desu.

❸ <ruby>銀行<rt>ぎんこう</rt></ruby> に <ruby>入<rt>はい</rt></ruby>る と、 すぐ <ruby>右<rt>みぎ</rt></ruby>
ginkō ni hairu to, sugu migi

に あります。
ni arimasu.

***

Exercise 2

... に <ruby>言葉<rt>ことば</rt></ruby> を <ruby>入<rt>い</rt></ruby>れ なさい

❶ When I see the moon rise, I get sad.
. . . . deru . . . . , ...
. . . .

❷ Your husband is a realistic person.
go shujin . . . .

❸ It's only when he's eaten a lot.
takusan . . . .

❹ It's difficult to make something good.
. . mono . . . .

❹ 一人 で 散歩 する の が

ひとり　　　　さんぽ

hitori de sanpo suru no ga

大好き です。

だい　す

daisuki desu.

❺ 海 の よう です。

うみ

umi no yō desu.

Answers to Exercise 1

❶ Otherwise, how could he work in this factory? ❷ We think we are entering an aquarium. ❸ It's just on the right when you enter the bank. ❹ I love taking a walk alone. ❺ It looks like the sea.

✳✳✳

❺ I watch the rain fall.

. . . . . futte iru . . . mi . . . .

Answers to Exercise 2

❶ tsuki ga – no o miru to, kanashiku narimasu. ❷ – wa genjitsuteki na kata desu ne. ❸ – tabeta toki dake desu. ❹ ii – o tsukuru no wa muzukashii desu. ❺ ame ga – no o – te imasu.

まとめ
matome

Revision and Notes

Excellent! You have reached the end of the first volume of *Japanese with Ease*! After this revision chapter, you will be finished with the passive phase, during which you have been inseminated with the Japanese language. Now you are ready to move on and enter the active phase, where you will productively use what you have been storing up, all while acquiring new elements!

The active phase begins with Lesson 50 in the Volume 2. No doubt you are already eager to jump in, but first, we still need to take a slight pause to make sure we really know what we know, before we can truly gain from the active phase.

1. First, we will take another look at –you guessed it –**verbs**. We have to "dismantle" them a bit so you can be sure to understand them and use them in all forms and degrees without difficulty. Remember what we said in Lesson 42 at the end of paragraph 4. The principle is simple (and not very unique, because it is what happens in most languages, even English!): the basic verb is a root appended with suffixes. And we now know nearly all the suffixes. For **middle degree**, we have been running over them now for such a long time they should seem second nature: it is the series of ます **masu** and its derivatives. We won't go through that one again here. But if you think you have got a gap in your memory, or a little question you would like to look over, you can go back to Lesson 7, paragraph 1, where we outlined the whole series, and to Lesson 35, paragraph 4.

For the the suffixes of **low degree**, we may be a bit less familiar, but we have also gone through just about everything that する **suru**, *to do*, has to offer in Lesson 42, paragraph 4. These are:

– ない **nai**, used to negate a verb (cf. Lesson 29, item 2: 行かない **ika*nai***, *not to go*; Lesson 38, item 1: わからない **wakara*nai***, *not to be understandable*; Lesson 41, item 12: 作れない **tsukure*nai***, *not to be able to make*; Lesson 48, item 11: 飲んで　いない **nonde i*nai***, *not to be drinking*).

– なかった **nakatta**, used to negate a verb in the past tense (cf. Lesson 40, item 12: 出 なかった **de*nakatta***, *not to have appeared*)

– たい **tai**, used to say "I **want** to do such and such" (cf. Lesson 27, item 6: 会いたい **ai*tai***, *I want to meet*; Lesson 31, item 1: 買いたい **kai*tai***, *I want to buy*; Lesson 34, item 3: 住みたい **sumi*tai***, *I want to live in*; Lesson 45, item 1: 開きたい **hiraki*tai***, *I want to open*).

Now look what happens. Take any of the verbs we have just listed, in low degree form, the form you will find in dictionaries, the most stripped-down form. *To go*, 行く **iku**, which we covered in Lesson 43, item 13, and Lesson 46, item 14. *To appear*, *to go out*, 出る **deru**, we saw in Lesson 31, item 1. This form, as you probably noticed long ago, always ends in **u**. And this is, in fact, true of all verbs. For example, *to drink* is 飲む **nom*u***, *to be understandable* is わかる **wakar*u***.

But let's take another look at *to go*, 行く **iku**, and *to appear*, *to go out*, 出る **deru**. This is where you get to prove how insightful you are. So take these verbs in middle degree, that is, with the suffix ます **masu**.

出る **deru**	行く **iku**
出ます **demasu**	行きます **ikimasu**

Take a look. The suffix ます **masu** is indeed the same in both cases, but you should be able to discover a difference in how it switches

49

from one form to another. Come on… Take a good look… Almost there… Got it? That's right: for 出る **de**ru the ます **masu** replaces the る **ru**: 出る **de**ru, 出ます **de**masu. And look at some other forms: 出ない **de**nai, *not to go out*, 出なかった **de**nakatta, *not to have gone out*, 出たい **de**tai, *I want to go out*, and even 出た **de**ta, *went out* (cf. Lesson 27, item 13, low degree with the suffix た **ta**, for the past tense, which we will speak about in more detail later). So you understand that for this verb, there is one base, 出 **de**, and all suffixes add on to this root. Not too tough, is it? So there are, then, a group of verbs that work this way, whose most stripped-down form, the form found in dictionaries, necessarily ends in **iru** or **eru**. And for the suffixes to come, る **ru** must go (but be careful, because not all verbs that end in **eru** or **iru** necessarily work this way).

Let's try another verb that "works" this way: *to eat* 食べる **taberu**: the **ru** goes away and leaves the **tabe**; *to eat* (middle degree): 食べます *tabe*masu; *not to eat* (low degree) 食べない *tabe*nai, *to have eaten* (low degree) 食べた *tabe*ta, *I want to eat* 食べたい *tabe*tai.
Or try again with *to look*, 見る **miru**: the **ru** goes away and leaves the **mi**; *to look* (middle degree), 見ます *mi*masu; *not to look* (low degree) 見ない *mi*nai; *to have looked* 見た *mi*ta.

It is pretty clear for these verbs, isn't it? No problem. But it is only a bit more complicated with other verbs. Let's go back to *to go*, 行く **iku**: 行く **iku** 行きます **ikimasu**. Here, nothing goes away, but there is a vowel that changes: **ik**u, **ik**imasu. The **ik** stays, but between it and the suffixes, there is always a vowel, which changes depending on the suffix. Let's take the forms we know already: *to go* (middle degree), 行きます **ik**imasu; *I want to go,* 行きたい **ik**itai, but *not to go* is 行かない **ik**anai. So that is not too bad, is it? Before the ます **masu** series, and before たい **tai**, it is **i**, but before ない **nai** it is **a**. Sometimes we have to use **o** and **e**, but we don't want to get ahead of ourselves. We decided at the beginning to pace ourselves! Just keep these two here in mind for the moment. And be observent about the forms we know already. Of course, there are minor exceptions from time to time, but we will talk about those in due time. For example, there are some issues that arise when the suffix you add is the past-tense た **ta** or the て **te**, but we still have 50 more lessons to go! So don't panic!

2. Let's talk a bit about the **high degree**, because we will be using it more and more in the chapters to come. There are two things you should know about the high degree, about how it diverges from the other two degrees. The first we have already mentioned (cf. Lesson 47, note 1): for some of the most common verbs, such as *to go*, *to come*, *to be located*, or *it is*, the high degree is not a form of the verb, but rather a completely different verb altogether.

We have already seen some of this: Lesson 44, items 1 and 9: で ございます **de gozaimasu**, *it is*; Lesson 46, item 7 and Lesson 47, item 4: the forms of なさる **nasaru**, which are equivalent to する **suru**, *to do*; Lesson 47, item 2: one form of うかがう **ukagau**, the high degree version of *heard say*; Lesson 47 again, item 11, one of the forms of いらっしゃる **irassharu**, the high form equivalent of 来る **kuru**, *to come*. For the less common verbs, there are a few different ways of forming the high degree, one of which we met in Lesson 47, item 1, note 1.

The second point worth noting is all new, and quite foreign to our English-speaking ears. The middle degree forms do not change based on whether the subject is an "I" or a "you" to whom the "I" is speaking. Look at Lesson 3: question: 食べます　か **tabemasu ka**, *do you eat...?*; answer: 食べます **tabemasu**, *I eat*: The same form 食べます **tabemasu** can mean both *I eat* and *you eat*. But this is impossible with the high degree forms. There is one form used with "I", and another form used with "you".

Take a look at Lesson 47. A young man meets a woman at a cocktail party. To tell the truth, he is kind of hitting on her! But with great etiquette, as he would have to in such a situation. To ask if she likes something, he must say: ...お 好き です か *o* **suki desu ka** (cf.

49 item 2) (literally, it is "… to be loved of you?"). She replies (item 3): … 好き です **suki desu**, which is the only possible answer: *I like…* For verbs in the high degree, it is the same thing. A form such as お 飲み に なります **o nomi ni narimasu** (lesson 47, item 1, note 1) can only be used with "**you**": *you drink*. We found this most in the questions. For the most common verbs, where the high degree uses a different verb, there are specializations, which are in fact two different high degrees, one for "I" and the other for "you". So なさる **nasaru**, *to do* is specialized for "you" (cf. Lesson 46, item 7; Lesson 47, item 4), いらっしゃる **irassharu**, *to come* is specialized for "you" (cf. Lesson 47, item 11).

ഹഗ൫ൽ

On the other hand, で ございます **de gozaimasu** (cf. Lesson 44, items 1 and 9), means *it is*, but specialized for "I", which is to say: "(as it concerns **me**) it is". At any rate, we will always indicate use of the high degree, and we will also note, directly in the word-for-word translation, use of the "specialized" forms for "I" and "you".

So congratulations! It may have seemed long, but the first volume and passive phase of Japanese with Ease *is now done, giving you all the tools you need to tackle the second, active phase, which you can now move on to without delay!*

ဆဝ3ဆဝ3

Appendix I

The following pages contain charts of the two syllabic alphabets (kana) in the Japanese language: *Hiragana* and *Katakana*. The official transcription is included with each syllable as a pronunciation guide.

These charts are here to help you, in case you'd like to read the lessons in this volume without consulting the accompanying transcriptions or pronunciation.

But please don't try to write them yet. That will come soon enough, during the active phase (Volume II). You will have all the explanation and guidance you'll need to memorize and write these characters the way the Japanese do.

For now, get your eye used to looking at the kana. **Look at the syllables, learn how to read them**. That's the first step, which is absolutely essential before you can learn to write them.

(Note that the charts are to be read, like all "normal" Japanese texts, from top to bottom and from right to left–nearly exactly the opposite of how we read in English–and following the Japanese "alphabetical" order A, I, U, E, O, KA, KI, KU, KE, KO, etc.).

平仮名
ひらがな
HIRAGANA

a あ	i い	u う	e え	o お
ka か	ki き	ku く	ke け	ko こ
ga が	gi ぎ	gu ぐ	ge げ	go ご
sa さ	shi し	su す	se せ	so そ
za ざ	ji じ	zu ず	ze ぜ	zo ぞ
ta た	chi ち	tsu つ	te て	to と
da だ			de で	do ど
na な	ni に	nu ぬ	ne ね	no の
ha は	hi ひ	fu ふ	he へ	ho ほ
ba ば	bi び	bu ぶ	be べ	bo ぼ
pa ぱ	pi ぴ	pu ぷ	pe ぺ	po ぽ
ma ま	mi み	mu む	me め	mo も
ya や		yu ゆ		yo よ
ra ら	ri り	ru る	re れ	ro ろ
wa わ				o を
				n ん

片仮名
かたかな
KATAKANA

a ア	i イ	u ウ	e エ	o オ
ka カ	ki キ	ku ク	ke ケ	ko コ
ga ガ	gi ギ	gu グ	ge ゲ	go ゴ
sa サ	shi シ	su ス	se セ	so ソ
za ザ	ji ジ	zu ズ	ze ゼ	zo ゾ
ta タ	chi チ	tsu ツ	te テ	to ト
da ダ			de デ	do ド
na ナ	ni ニ	nu ヌ	ne ネ	no ノ
ha ハ	hi ヒ	fu フ	he ヘ	ho ホ
ba バ	bi ビ	bu ブ	be ベ	bo ボ
pa パ	pi ピ	pu プ	pe ペ	po ポ
ma マ	mi ミ	mu ム	me メ	mo モ
ya ヤ		yu ユ		yo ヨ
ra ラ	ri リ	ru ル	re レ	ro ロ
wa ワ				o ヲ
				n ン

Appendix II

Index

In the following pages you will find an index where all the words we have studied in this volume are listed with pronunciation and translation. **For each word, a number refers to the first lesson where the word was used. When there is more than one number listed, the supplementary number(s) will indicate any lesson where the word was accompanied by a note.** In this respect, it's like any other index you might find!

But… **you will no doubt be surprised by the order of the index…** at least if you haven't studied the order of the tables in Appendix I. We are of course used to the Latin alphabetical order, A, B, C, D, and so on, which seems only natural (if not universal). **But since we are studying Japanese, let's do what they do!** As you already know, in Japanese there is a different writing system, and a different order of classification to go with it. **The Japanese version of "alphabetical order" is what we find in the kana tables of Appendix I.** The syllables, read from top to bottom and right to left, are put in the order A, I, U, E, O, KA, KI, KU, KE, KO, SA, SHI, SU, SE, SO, etc. This order is used in Japan under all circumstances, whether for dictionaries (which you'll get to later), telephone books, all sorts of index, and any list of words or names. So we should get used to it as soon as possible. However, the order used here is slightly different from the normal Japanese order, as we've tried to make things a bit simpler for you. But we'll take care of that when we go over how to write the kana on our own. That is, in not very much time at all.

aikyō	愛嬌	charm	39
aida	間	interval	37
au	会う	to meet	23
aoi	青い	to be blue *(or green)*	31
aoyama	青山	AOYAMA *(place name)*	34
akai	赤い	to be red	31
aki	秋	autumn	48
akita	秋田	AKITA *(place name)*	37
akirameru	あきらめる	to give up	34
asa	朝	morning	11
asatte	あさって	the day after tomorrow	43
asahi	朝日	sunrise	30
ashi	足	foot, leg	40
ashioto	足音	sound of footsteps	48
ashita	明日	tomorrow	2
asoko	あそこ	over there	1
asobu	遊ぶ	to play	45
azukeru	預ける	to deposit, entrust	45
atashi	あたし	me, I *(female speaker)*	29
atatakai	温かい	to be warm	41
atari	辺り	surroundings	32
atsui	暑い	to be very hot	1
atsumaru	集まる	to gather	47
ato	後	after	45
anata	あなた	you	29
ani	兄	my older brother	27
ane	姉	my older sister	31
afurika	アフリカ	AFRICA	39
apāto	アパート	apartment	24
amarinimo	あまりにも	too (much)	48
ame	雨	rain	31
amerika	アメリカ	America, U.S.A.	8
arawasu	表す	to express	36
arigatō (gozaimasu)	ありがとう （ございます）	Thank you!	9, 18
aru	ある	to exist *(for inanimate beings)*	4, 35
aru (+ noun)	ある	a certain	37
aruku	歩く	to walk	6
aruzenchin	アルゼンチン	ARGENTINA	41
anshin	安心	peace of mind	23

koi	恋	love	43
kōin	工員	worker, employee	40
kokuseki	国籍	nationality	38
kokudō	国道	national highway	32
kōkūbin	航空便	airmail	22
koko	ここ	here	5
kōsui	香水	perfume	31
kōsokudōro	高速道路	freeway	32
kōza	口座	bank account	45
kōjō	工場	factory	40
kotaeru	答える	to answer	39
kochira	こちら	this way (this direction)	40
kōtsū	交通	traffic	23
koto	こと	fact, event	32, 42
kōtōgakkō	高等学校	high school	47
kotoshi	今年	this year	23
kotoba	言葉	word	1
kotowaru	断る	to refuse	41
kodomo	子供	child	15
kono	この	this (+ *noun*)	18
kono aida	この間	recently	31
konogoro	このごろ	nowadays	46
kōhī	コーヒー	coffee	3
komaru	こまる	to be in trouble	13
komu	混む	to be crowded	32
komugi	小麦	wheat	30
kore	これ	this	17
korekara	これから	from now on	40
kowai	こわい	to be scared/scary	39
konsāto	コンサート	concert	19
kondo	今度	this time	19
konna	こんな	of this kind	45
konna ni	こんなに	so, like this	39
konnichi wa	こんにちは	Hello!	12
konban	今晩	tonight	9
konpyūta	コンピュータ	computer	40

ga *(after noun)*	が	[subject]	4, 7
ga *(after verb)*	が	but	19

sake	酒	alcohol, sake	4
sagasu	捜す	to look for	34
sasou	誘う	to invite	16
sabishii	寂しい	to be lonely	48
...sama	…さま	*after someone's name (high degree)*	44
saraishū	再来週	the week after next	46
saru	猿	monkey	39
san	三	three	11
...san	…さん	*after someone's name*	12, 16, 19
sandouitchi	サンドウイッチ	sandwich	16
sanpo	散歩	walk	31

SHI

shi	詩	poem	48
shiasatte	しあさって	two days after tomorrow	27
shīzun	シーズン	season	10
shika *(+ neg.)*	しか	only	30
shikashi	しかし	but, however	26
shikata ga nai	仕方がない	can do nothing about it	44
shikikin	敷金	(security) deposit	34
shigatsu	四月	April	23
shigoto	仕事	work	23
shizuoka	静岡	SHIZUOKA *(place name)*	32
shizen	自然	nature	36
shita	舌	tongue	46
shichi	七	seven	27
shitsugyōsha	失業者	the unemployed	40
shitsumon	質問	question	40
shinu	死ぬ	to die	37
shibai	芝居	theatre, play	29
shibuya	渋谷	SHIBUYA *(place name)*	6
shima	島	island	30
shimau	しまう	to finish, to complete	31
shashin	写真	photograph	19
shanpen	シャンペン	champagne	47
shūkan	週間	week	46
shujin	主人	my husband	31
shujinkō	主人公	hero *(of a novel)*	25
shuppatsu	出発	departure	32
shuppan	出版	publication	25
shūmatsu	週末	weekend	32

ZA

zannen	ざんねん	too bad .19

JI

…ji	…時	*(number +)* o'clock. 11
jikan	時間	hour. 13
jiko	事故	accident, incident 23
jitsu wa	実は	really/actually 15
jidai	時代	age, period 17
jidōsha	自動車	automobile, car. 23
jibun	自分	oneself. 18
jimusho	事務所	office. .40
jazu	ジャズ	jazz 19
jū	十	ten. 11
jūsho	住所	address 38
jūsu	ジュース	juice 16
…jō	…畳	*measure word for tatamis* 34
joyū	女優	actress. 19
…jin *(after country name)*	…人	*… national of this country* . .13, 28
jinto	じんと	strong and deep *(pain)* 46

ZU

zuibun	随分	very, extremely 13
…zutsu	…ずつ	each. 39

ZE

zeikan	税関	customs. 4
zehi	是非	absolutely, without fail 19
zenzen *(+ neg.)*	全然	not at all, absolutely not 24
zenbu	全部	entirely, wholly. 31

ZO

zō	像	elephant. 39

TA

ta	田	rice field 36
taiin (suru)	退院(する)	to leave hospital 23
taizai	滞在	stay 38
taihen	大変	very/greatly. 11
taiyō	太陽	sun. 30

taoru	タオル	towel 31
takai	高い	to be high, to be expensive 5
takusan	たくさん	many 6
tasukaru	たすかる	to be saved 20
tatsu	経つ	to pass, to go by *(time)* 46
tatsu	立つ	to stand 24
tatemono	建物	building. 40
tateru	建てる	to build, to construct. 37
tatoeba	たとえば	for example. 36
tada	ただ	ordinary, common. 46
tanoshii	楽しい	to be pleasant 39
tanoshimi ni suru	楽しみにする	to be delighted 41
tanomu	頼む	to request 29
tabako	タバコ	cigarette 20
tabakoya	タバコ屋	tobacco dealer's 20
tabitabi	度々	often 45
tabesugi	食べすぎ	overeat 46
tabemono	食べ物	food. 46
taberu	食べる	to eat 3
tamago	卵	egg 3
tame *(after noun)*	ため	for, on account of 16
tame *(after verb)*	ため	to, in order to 38
tameiki	溜息	sigh 48
tariru	足りる	to be enough, to suffice 32
tawā	タワー	tower. 6
tanjōbi	誕生日	birthday. 29

CHI

chiisai	小さい	to be small. 27
chekku.in	チェック・イン	
		check-in 44
chikai	近い	to be near/close. 6
chikatetsu	地下鉄	subway 31
chikyū	地球	the Earth 43
cha	茶	tea 34
chawan	茶碗	teacup .17
…chan	…ちゃん	*after someone's name (very informal)* 39
chūkaryōri	中華料理	Chinese food. 9
chūgoku	中国	CHINA 29

DO

NA

natsu	夏	summer .30
…nado *(after noun)*	…など	that kind of object 33, 36
namae	名前	someone's name 36
nara *(after noun)*	なら	if it is 29
narabu	並ぶ	to line, to queue 39
narita	成田	NARITA *(place name)* 27
naru	なる	to become 22
nan/nani	何	what? 2
nanika	何か	something 34
nanimo (+ *neg.*)	何も	nothing .24
nante	なんて	so-called 43

NI

ni	に	[place], [goal], [adverbial] . . .4, 14
ni	に	[addition] 16
ni	に	[agent] 35
ni	二	two 24
niku	肉	meat 9
nikkō	日航	Japan Air Lines 27
nishi	西	west 30
nitchū	日中	daytime/day 30
nichiyōbi	日曜日	Sunday .16
nihon	日本	JAPAN .18
nimotsu	荷物	baggage, luggage 27
nyūin (suru)	入院（する）	to be in hospital 23
nyūgaku (suru)	入学（する）	to enter school 38
nyūkyo (suru)	入居（する）	to move in (*to a new house*) 34
nyūsu	ニュース	news 10
niru	似る	to resemble, to look like 39
niwa	庭	garden, yard 34
…nin	…人	*measure word for people* 47

NE

ne	ね	[agreement] 1
negai	願い	request 45
nemui	眠い	to be sleepy 39
neru	寝る	to go to bed 11
…nen	…年	year 15
…nenkan	…年間	year (*duration*) 37
nendai	年代	period, era 40

NO

HA

HI

hi	日	sun, day	30
hikaeru	控える	to hold back	46
hikari	光	light	30
hikōki	飛行機	plane	27
hikōjō	飛行場	airport	27
higure	日暮れ	sunset	48
hitsuyō	必要	necessary	34
hito	人	person	19
hitobito	人々	people	37
hitori	一人	one person	44
hitori de	一人で	alone, by oneself	47
hidari	左	left	17
hima	暇	free time	26
hyaku	百	hundred	22
hiraku	開く	to open	45
hirune	昼寝	nap	30
hīrō	ヒーロー	hero	43

FU

fū	風	style, manner	48
fasshon.moderu	ファッション・モデル		
		fashion model	25
fueru	増える	to increase	45
fōku	フォーク	fork	9
fuku	吹く	to blow	47
futatsu	二つ	two (*objects*)	27
futari	二人	two persons	15
fuchi	縁	edge	31
futsū	普通	usual	45
futsuka	二日	two days	45
fudōsanya	不動産屋	real estate agency	34
fuyu	冬	winter	45
furansu	フランス	FRANCE	13
furu	降る	to fall (*rain, snow...*)	31
furui	古い	to be old	17
furoa	フロア	floor, storey	44
fun	分	minute	24

HE

heimin	平民	the people, the common people .36
heiwa	平和	peace 18
heya	部屋	room 44
hen	辺	surroundings 20

HO

hō	方	direction, way 32
hoeru	吠える	to bark 39
hoka	他	other 41
hoshi	星	star .43
hoshii	ほしい	to be wanted 34
hoteru	ホテル	hotel 44
hotondo	ほとんど	almost all 36
hōmu.dorama	ホーム・ドラマ	
		"home drama" television series .10
hon	本	book .4
hontō	本当	true, real 19
honya	本屋	bookstore 18

BA

bā	バー	bar 11
bakkin	罰金	fine, penalty 32
bāgen	バーゲン	sale .31
baggu	バッグ	bag .27
basu	バス	bus 6
ban	晩	evening 26

BI

bioron	ビオロン	violin *(old)* 48
byōin	病院	hospital 46
byōki	病気	illness, disease 41
biru	ビル	building 24, 32
bīru	ビール	beer .3
…bin	…便	*flight number* 27
(after number)		

BU

buke	武家	warrior 36
bun	分	part .34

BE

beddo	ベッド	bed 46
benri	便利	convenient. 24

BO

boku	僕	me, I (*male speaker*). 20
bōken	冒険	adventure 43

PA

pato.kā	パトカー	patrol car. 32
pan	パン	bread. 3
panda	パンダ	panda. .39

PI

piano	ピアノ	piano. 29
pikunikku	ピクニック	picnic .16
pīnattsu	ピーナッツ	peanuts 39

PE

pea	ペア	pair 31
pēji	ページ	page. 25

MA

...mai	…枚	*measure word for flat objects* . . .22
maiasa	毎朝	every morning. 30
maido	毎度	(thank you) for each time 18
(arigatō	(ありがとう	
gozaimasu)	ございます)	
mainichi	毎日	every day 37
mae	前	before, in front 13, 15
magaru	曲がる	to turn .20
mājan	マージャン	mahjong (*Chinese game*) 41
massugu	まっすぐ	straight ahead 20
mazu	先ず	firstly. 6
mata	また	or, again 9
mattaku	全く	completely, quite. 48
matsu	待つ	to wait. 13
mada (+ *neg.*)	まだ	not yet 2
made	まで	until. .6, 7
mamoru	守る	to guard, to keep 43
man	万	ten thousand 17

MI

mieru	見える	to be visible. 8
mikka	三日	three days 20
mikan	みかん	tangerine, mandarin 16
migi	右	right. .17
mise	店	store, shop. 6, 19
miseru	見せる	to show 17
mizu	水	cold water 31
…mitai	…みたい	seems, looks like. 48
michi	道	road, street, way 20
mitsukaru	みつかる	to be found 24
mitsukoshi	三越	MITSUKOSHI 31
		(*Japanese department store*)
mina/minna	皆	all 36
mimi	耳	ear. 39
miyage	みやげ	gift, souvenir. 6
myōji	苗字	family name 36
miru	見る	to look, to see 2

MU

mukai	向かい	opposite, across. 24
mukaeru	迎える	to meet, to welcome 27
mukashi	昔	a long time ago 36
mukō	向こう	on the other side, opposite 39
mushamusha	むしゃむしゃ	munching (*sound*). 39
musuko	息子	my son 26
musuko san	息子さん	your son 23
muzukashii	むずかしい	to be difficult. 32
munashii	空しい	to be vain 48
mura	村	village 30
muri	無理	unreasonable, excessive 19

ME

…me	…目	…th, …nd. 31
me	目	eye. 39
…mei	…名	*measure word for persons (official)* 44
meibutsu	名物	specialty 30
megane	眼鏡	eyeglasses 8
meguro	目黒	MEGURO (*place name*). 6
mezurashii	めずらしい	to be rare 41

MO

YA

YU

YO

ഗ്രൂഗ്രൂ

ryōri	料理	cooking, food 9
ringo	りんご	apple 3

RU

rusu	留守	absence .18

RE

reikin	礼金	reward. .34
reitō	冷凍	freezing. 48
rekōdo	レコード	record 47
resutoran	レストラン	restaurant 46
renshū	練習	practice, exercise 1, 47

RO

roku	六	six 30
roketto	ロケット	rocket 43
robotto	ロボット	robot 40
romantikku	ロマンチック	romantic 48

WA

wa	は	[emphasis]. 11
wa	は	[announce] 15
wa	わ	[softener]. 27
wakaru	わかる	to be understandable, to be known .1
wakareru	別かれる	to be separated 34
wakusei	惑星	planet 43
wake	わけ	reason, cause. 36
washitsu	和室	Japanese-style room 34
wasureru	忘れる	to forget. 8
watakushi, watashi	私	me, I .9, 12
watakushidomo	私共	us, we (*official*). 40
watashitachi	私達	us, we 39
wataru	渡る	to cross .36
warui	悪い	to be bad 19
warumono	悪者	bad guy .43

ഇൻഗ്രൂഗ